RUSSIA'S REVOLUTIONARY EXPERIENCE, 1905–1917

STUDIES OF THE HARRIMAN INSTITUTE OF COLUMBIA UNIVERSITY

RUSSIA'S REVOLUTIONARY EXPERIENCE, 1905–1917

TWO ESSAYS

LEOPOLD H. HAIMSON
with an Introduction by David McDonald

COLUMBIA UNIVERSITY PRESS   NEW YORK

Columbia University Press
Publishers Since 1893
New York   Chichester, West Sussex

Copyright © 2005 Columbia University Press
All rights reserved
Publication of this book was made possible in part with
a grant from the Harriman Institute of Columbia University.

Library of Congress Cataloging-in-Publication Data
Haimson, Leopold H.
Russia's revolutionary experience, 1905–1917 : two essays /
Leopold H. Haimson ; with an introduction by David McDonald.
p.   cm.
Includes bibliographical references and index.
Contents: Lenin, Martov and the issue of power—
The worker's movement after Lena :
the dynamics of labor unrest in the wake of
the Lena goldfields massacre (April 1912–July 1914).
ISBN 0–231–13282–4 (cloth : alk. paper)
1. Russia—Politics and government—1894–1917.
2. Working class—Russia—Political activity—History—20th century.
3. Socialism—Russia—History—20th century. I. Title.

DK262.H25 2005

320.947'09'041—dc22

2004056134

TO THE MEMORY OF VALENTIN SEMENOVICH DIAKIN

CONTENTS

INTRODUCTION

David McDonald

If you can look into the seeds of time,
and say which grain will grow and which will not . . .

A half-century ago, Leopold Haimson chose these lines from *Macbeth* to introduce his classic study, *The Russian Marxists and the Origins of Bolshevism.*[1] The story Haimson told in that book traced the interplay among deep-seated continuities in the intelligentsia tradition, the social transformations stemming from Russia's industrialization, and the contingencies of personality and politics that led Russian Marxism to split along the two branches of Bolshevism and Menshevism.

Consciously or not, Haimson's choice of this metaphor from the Scottish play echoed a venerable motif in intelligentsia rhetoric, which hopefully likened the historical process to organic growth in its law-governed nature [*zakonomernost'*]. In this view, just as the acorn contained within itself the future oak, so too did the slumbering *narod* harbor the capacity to become a self-conscious historical actor as nation or hegemonic class, through a process guided or abetted by those members of the intelligentsia who had already attained self-consciousness. When the moment of self-awareness and self-determination arrived, this new actor would unbind itself from an autocracy that had denied it its human destiny for so long. Whatever else their differences, generations of Russian dissidents—Hegelians, *shestidesiatniki, narodniki,* and Marxists alike—would have subscribed to the basic dictates of this law-governed process. Indeed, they staked their lives and their resistance to autocracy on its promise for Russia's future and their own.

---

1.   Leopold H. Haimson, *The Russian Marxists and the Origins of Bolshevism* (Cambridge: Harvard University Press, 1955).

Yet, by choosing Shakespeare's rendering of this image, with its emphasis on the contingent, complex and unpredictable in the realization of the plant from the seed, Haimson also indicated his differences with this deterministic optimism, a set of distinctions that have defined his *oeuvre* both as a historian of late imperial Russia and as a trainer of several generations of scholars in that field. To that extent, and in the context of the organic metaphor, Haimson's invocation of Macbeth recalls nobody so much as Aleksandr Herzen, a one-time student of embryology himself, who sought a scientifically grounded historical view that could accommodate human freedom. Yet, in his examination of the processes that gave rise to two decades and more of revolutionary upheaval in early twentieth-century Russia, Haimson places power, its getting and its making, much more squarely at the center of his attention than Herzen often did. Haimson's emphasis on power and change suggests yet another reason for his epigraphic allusion to Macbeth.

The two essays in this volume examine the "issue of power" in late imperial Russia. At first blush, they appear to address very different concerns. One follows the social and political aftermath of the notorious repression of labor unrest in the Lena goldfields during the spring of 1912. The other looks at Iulii Martov and Vladimir Lenin during the critical months spanning April and October 1917. Yet, together the two essays form the complementary links in a chain whose contours Haimson's students and readers will recognize from his previous work on the intelligentsia, the transformation of the Russian countryside and, most of all, the problem of social stability in urban Russia, first broached in bold and hypothetical form as a pair of essays that appeared in *Slavic Review* forty years ago.[2]

Each study depicts a pivotal moment in the lives of the two social groups that played decisive roles in the destruction of the imperial regime and its replacement by the Soviet order. The story of the post-Lena labor movement portrays the crystallization of the St. Petersburg working-class population into a self-aware and politically engaged agent in pursuit of its own interests. In the other essay, we witness how ideology and personal proclivities framed the actions taken by Lenin and Martov as the revolutionary tide mounted

---

2.   Ibid.; L. H. Haimson, ed., *The Politics of Rural Russia* (Bloomington: Indiana University Press, 1979), introduction and conclusions; L. H. Haimson, "The Problem of Social Stability in Urban Russia, 1905–1917," part 1, *Slavic Review* 23, no. 4 (Dec. 1964): 619–642, part 2, *Slavic Review*. 24, no. 1 (March 1965): 1–22.

from April into the fall of 1917. Each essay—and both taken together—permits an appreciation of the uniqueness and consistency of a vision that has shaped our field since the 1950's.

Haimson's study of the reaction to the Lena massacre revisits in greater detail a set of events he first identified as an important juncture in his landmark articles from *Slavic Review* in 1964 and 1965 on "the problem of social stability in urban Russia." In the article presented in this volume, Haimson provides a close examination of the inner, psychological *cum* behavioral, side of a process that saw a sustained and powerful mobilization of worker discontent in the two years spanning the Lena incident and the outbreak of the Great War in the summer of 1914. In this way, the article stands as a companion-piece to the considerable quantitative research on the movement that Haimson and several collaborators have published over the last twenty years.[3]

Reemphasizing the importance of literacy, occupational qualifications and enterprise size as crucial factors associated with the upsurge in labor activity, Haimson brings to bear new perspectives and new sorts of evidence to underscore the novelty and importance of the post-Lena period as a formative moment in an identifiable, politically conceived sense of working-class identity. Thus, he stresses more than previously the importance of the influx of dispossessed male peasants into the ranks of urban workers, alongside the existence of a social milieu that could absorb and socialize them much more quickly than had been the case even ten years previously. Drawing on his long-time interests in anthropology and psychology, Haimson also points to a new confidence and self-assertiveness among militant workers and describes the social practices they deployed to forge a newfound solidarity. Of particular interest in this connection is his analysis of the use of shaming as a device for shaping a sense of class-consciousness among industrial workers.

Equally important, however, Haimson depicts this growth in the labor movement against the background of the multifaceted crisis that now beset the imperial social and political orders. Building on a broad literature dealing

---

3.   For good examples of this vein in his research, see: Leopold Haimson, with Eric Brian, "Changements démographiques et grèves ouvrières à Saint-Pétersbourg, 1905–1914," *Annales: Économies, Sociétés, Civilisations* 40, no. 4 (1985): 781–804; and his collaborative contributions, with Eric Brian and Ron Petrusha, in Leopold H. Haimson and Charles Tilly, eds., *Strikes, Wars, and Revolutions: Strike Waves in the Late Nineteenth and Early Twentieth Centuries* (New York: Cambridge University Press, 1989).

with the "crisis of autocracy" in the early twentieth century,[4] Haimson's account demonstrates the disarray that had overtaken the imperial government as well as the oppositional political groups represented in the State Duma. Disputes dogged the government and local authorities at every level, from disagreements over how to deal with the Lena goldfields strike and the ensuing massacre that occurred there to the unraveling of the system of "united government" that provided a front against criticism from the ranks of conservative and liberal politicians alike. For its part, "society" [obshchestvo] proved equally unable to re-create the appearance of cohesion that had fuelled the "all-nation struggle" against autocracy in 1905. As W. B. Yeats wrote about a related crisis on the other end of Europe, the center would not hold.

The appearance of a bold and assertive workers' movement formed simply the most dynamic part of a process in which all of imperial society was becoming more corpuscular as various social groups, as well as the state bureaucracy, seemed to break down into ever smaller constituents, each defining itself in the particularistic language long associated with soslovnost'. This fracture in Russia's body politic figures prominently in many of Haimson's works, from his underappreciated article on political parties in the late empire through his reflections on rural politics to his most recent articles on the problem of social identity in early-twentieth-century Russia.[5] More than ever, the

4.   In his references on this topic, Haimson frequently acknowledges his debt to historians long associated with the Leningrad/St. Petersburg branch of the Russian Academy of Sciences Institute of History. Particularly V. S. Diakin, R. Sh. Ganelin, and B. V. Anan'ich, who collaborated as editors on the most comprehensive Russian-language treatment of this problem, *Krizis samoderzhaviia v Rossii, 1894–1917* (Leningrad: Nauka, 1984). Many of Haimson's own students have also gravitated to this theme over the years. Several contributed to *Politics of Rural Russia*, op. cit. Others include: F. W. Wcislo, *Reforming Rural Russia: State, Local Society, and National Politics, 1855–1914* (Princeton: Princeton University Press, 1990); Andrew Verner, *The Crisis of Russian Autocracy: Nicholas II and the Revolution of 1905* (Princeton: Princeton University Press, 1990); R. T Manning, *The Crisis of the Old Order in Russia: Gentry and Government* (Princeton: Princeton University Press, 1982); Allan Wildman, *The End of the Imperial Army*, 2 vols. (Princeton: Princeton University Press, 1979, 1980); David MacLaren McDonald, *United Government and Russian Foreign Policy, 1900–1914* (Cambridge: Harvard University Press, 1992).

5.   Leopold H. Haimson, "The Parties and the State: The Evolution of Political Attitudes," in Michael Cherniavsky, ed., *The Structure of Russian History: Interpretive Essays* (New York: Random House, 1970), pp. 309–340; idem, *Politics of Rural Russia*; idem, "The Problem of Social Identities in early Twentieth-Century Russia," *Slavic Review* 47, no. 1. (Spring, 1988): 1–20, and a reconsideration of his "social stability" articles from the 1960s, "'The Problem of Political and Social Stability in Urban Russia on the Eve of War and Revolution' Revisited," *Slavic Review* 59, no. 4 (Winter 2000): 848–875. The note material at the beginning and end of this discussion contains references to Haimson's considerable publications in Russian-language journals over the previous decade.

term "noble" meant "landowner" in representations from such groups as the Nationalist fraction or the United Nobility. Likewise, the peasantry nurtured its own separatist grievances after the reformed constitutional order failed to yield the land they sought, while lending ever increasing support to the *pomeshchiki* who owned it.[6] The scions of the Old Believer merchant families in Moscow created their own political party and saw themselves as an incipient "third estate."[7] From Poland, through the Pale, Ukraine, the Caucasus and into Central Asia, nationalist activists seeking self-determination entered tactical and often contentious relationships with their erstwhile allies among Russia's liberals. Within the intelligentsia itself, debates raged over the very identity and historical utility of this amorphous grouping and the make-up of the Russian "nation" whose birth had appeared imminent in 1905.

For its part, the imperial government could no longer claim to serve as a disinterested structure overarching the manifold estates, groupings, confessions and nationalities constituting the Russian empire. Officials differed fundamentally over virtually every question but the paramountcy of state power—the Council of Ministers could not even agree within its ranks on the legitimacy of the post-1905 constitutional accommodation, including the central issue of whether the Duma should continue to exist. Through his increasingly frequent intervention in the day-to-day working of government, Nicholas II confirmed a lack of confidence in his own administration, sapping in turn his officials' faith in the order they had sworn to uphold.[8] The composition of the Fourth Duma, fractured along the entire political spectrum, only reflected the extent of disunity in imperial society.

In these circumstances, the issue of political power and its sources became a matter of pervasive concern among all the empire's subjects. Liberals and revolutionaries debated loud and long over what the post-autocratic order would look like and how history's discernible laws [*zakonomernosti*] would bring it into being.[9] State officials debated less publicly but no less urgently the meaning and durability of the post-1905 order. And every group sought a

6. See the chapters on the peasantry and the nobility in *The Politics of Rural Russia.*
7. On this group, see the dissertation by Haimson's student William R. Duggan, *The Progressists and Russian Politics, 1914–1917,* Columbia University in the City of New York, 1984.
8. See *Krizis samoderzhaviia;* McDonald, *United Government.*
9. Haimson noted this debate and its importance in "The Parties and the State," p. 331. The clearest statements in this vein came from P. B. Struve in his leaders for the journal *Russkaia mysl'*. He published many of these writings in the collection *Patriotica: politika, kul'tura, religiia, sotsializm; sbornik statei za piat' let* (St. Petersburg: Izd. D. E. Zhukovskago, 1911).

social base for power, whether in Stolypin's outreach to landowning nobles and an emergent yeoman peasantry or the reconstituted and integral individual sought by most of the contributors to *Vekhi*.[10] Ironically, P. N. Durnovo and his allies on the extreme right, virtually alone among observers of the period, recognized the looming catastrophe facing those who sought the transformation of the existing order. Lacking any real social base, the intelligentsia and the Duma opposition would undo the autocracy only to leave the path to power open to the elemental forces of the proletariat and the peasantry.[11]

Concentrating on the urban working population, Haimson uses the Lena case and its aftermath to illustrate both sides of this process. In doing so, he powerfully refutes the hopeful new vein in Russian historiography that seeks alternatives to the catastrophes of 1917 and its aftermath in the emergence of an embryonic "civil society" whose growth appears to some to have promised a political alternative to the decay of autocracy and the grim simulacrum of socialism that supplanted it. On one hand, he portrays the isolation of state officials forced to defend the use of military force to suppress a strike by workers whose exploitation drew disapproval from across the spectrum of political commentators, from Social Democrats to that undisguised reactionary Prince V. M. Meshcherskii. At the same time, he demonstrates the surprisingly rapid subsidence of the Lena incident in the Duma as other matters moved to the center of political attention. Most of all, however, he shows how the Lena massacre served as a catalyst for the articulation—in both words and deeds—by Russia's industrial workers of a sense of class solidarity, which increasingly entailed a fierce rejection of any attempt by outside groups to harness the workers' support to their own political ends.

In a series of statistical studies, Haimson and various partners have demonstrated the growth of this new workers' movement as it burgeoned through the prewar years and resumed its momentum after the hiatus of late 1914, gathering impressive strength during the war years. In this volume, however, through close study of workers' testimony in the press and in police files, Haimson examines the subjective or psychological mechanisms that imparted to this movement the revolutionary potential recognized dimly by Durnovo and much more concretely by Social Democratic and Social Revolutionary activists. To this end, he fleshes out much more than in his

---

10.   *Vekhi: sbornik statei o russkoi intelligentsii* (Moscow: I. N. Kushnerev, 1909).
11.   See his famous "memorandum," published in English by F. A. Golder, ed., *Documents of Russian History*, 1914–1917 (New York: The Century Co., 1927), pp. 3–23.

earlier work the centrality of notions of the dignity and autonomy that underlay workers' demands for *vezhlivoe obrashchenie*—i.e. polite treatment and polite address. He also demonstrates clearly the growing sense of class solidarity expressed by Russia's industrial workers in several arenas, including the norms that defined their "shaming" of strikebreakers and their encounters with other inhabitants of the urban space, most notably in St. Petersburg.

This renascent workers' movement came increasingly to represent an autonomous source of power, as the events of early 1917 conclusively demonstrated. By then they could mobilize sufficient political, social and rhetorical resources to claim persuasively such demands as a shorter workday and "polite address." As the months of *dvoevlast'e* demonstrated, they could also make their will felt through the network of Soviets devised in part as a vehicle for their political might.

Indeed, to the extent that they and their contemporaries—*intelligenty* of all political stripes—identified them with the Soviets—as opposed to the "bourgeois" groupings represented in the Provisional Government—the workers appeared to constitute the embryonic rudiments of a state. Since the 1840s, a period one might term the Hegelian revolution in Russian thought, dissident intellectuals had criticized the autocracy as a morally and historically *ersatz* state. Rather than embodying the historical will of a self-conscious and self-determining people/nation, the autocracy imposed its own arbitrary will—and that of a small elite—upon a *narod* deliberately kept benighted in the toils of serfdom or, later, the social regime that arose from the unsatisfactory terms of its abolition.

In opposition to this order, generations of intelligentsia thinkers and activists across the spectrum of theoretical persuasions had sought to place Russia back on the rails of proper historical development. Since a proper state embodied the codified will of a self-determining people, it was necessary to elicit the collective self-consciousness and will of this people as a historical agent to establish an alternative, legitimate political order. These variables of will, collective self-consciousness, and the state developing through historical processes in accord with *zakonomernosti* pervaded Russian political and historical thought. In the early twentieth century, these categories framed the analyses of writers and thinkers as diverse as Kliuchevskii, the *Vekhovtsy*, and even Lenin, in his study of the state and revolution. Thus, when revolution came, as in 1905 or in 1917, politicians and revolutionaries alike sought to ride and harness the forces of the emerging future. The failure to do so in 1905 gave way to the bitter debates that split liberals and revolutionaries alike, whether in the furor provoked by the publication of *Vekhi* in 1909 or in the fitful conflicts that roiled Social Democrats and Socialist Revolutionaries over participation in the post-1905 quasi-constitutional regime or, later, in the imperial war effort.

The strange hybrid of *dvoevlast'e* that eventuated from the events of February 1917 brought a sharp focus to these debates. This was especially the case for revolutionary actors, who found themselves confronted with the task of applying their theoretically-derived knowledge of history's proper course to an explosive revolutionary situation. They had to prosecute this task while also contending with two acute challenges shaping their political environment: on one hand, the continuing war against the Central Powers and its impact on all questions of Russian life, from the rural population through the integrity of the empire's boundaries to the disintegration and politicization of the armed forces; and on the other, the "bourgeois" Provisional Government which alternately threatened the revolutionary forces represented in the Soviets—in the July Days and the *Kornilovshchina*—and yet placed the question of political power on the order of the day, with the growing weakness that it demonstrated in its attempts to contain the Soviets and their supporters.

This was the situation that faced Lenin and Martov during the months between their return to Russia from exile in the spring of 1917 and the *coup d'état* that took place at Lenin's energetic insistence in late October. In this volume's first essay, Haimson analyzes each individual's reactions to these serial challenges, thereby extending and deepening a scholarly vein in his career that originated in the 1950s and has continued to the present with his recent publication of Menshevik documents from 1917.[12] Effacing the traditional line that divides political from intellectual history, Haimson mines the publications and private papers of both revolutionaries to analyze the attempts by both Lenin and Martov simultaneously to master their respective fractions in Russian social democracy and, more importantly, the revolutionary force embodied by the workers' movement.

To this extent, the mutual confrontation of the revolutionary intelligentsia world-view with the symptoms of social unrest amid the collapse of the *ancien régime* forms the connective tissue binding the two halves of this

---

12.   L. Haimson, Z. Galili, A. Nenarokov, *Men'sheviki v 1917 g.*, 3 vols. (Moscow: Progress-Akademiia, 1995–1997). See also, his earlier work on the Mensheviks, including: Haimson, Galili, and R. Wortman, eds., *The Making of Three Russian Revolutionaries: Voices from the Menshevik Past* (New York: Cambridge University Press; Paris: Maison des Sciences de l'Homme, 1987); and Haimson, ed., *The Mensheviks: From the Revolution of 1917 until the Second World War* (Chicago: University of Chicago Press, 1974).

book. In another sense, despite the methodological differences between these two parts, this confrontation and its historical consequences—for Lenin, Martov, and for Russia—unify the diverse *corpus* of Haimson's scholarship into a comprehensive whole.

This first essay presents an entirely different sort of historical analysis than the one Haimson offers in his discussion of worker identity and mobilization. Here, he examines the interplay between the conceptual armature provided by the world-views of his two principals and the rapidly changing circumstances that saw the opening of a power vacuum in revolutionary Russia through the summer and autumn of 1917. With admirable clarity and rigor, Haimson underscores the consistency of Lenin's and Martov's adherence to ideological premises they had first developed in response to their encounter with the revolutions of 1905–1907. At the same time, he highlights the interesting parallels in the two men's experience and perceptions of the unfolding revolution in 1917. Indeed, Haimson notes an intriguing symmetry between the situations of the two leaders—each focused on the other, contending for sway in the various organs associated with the soviet structure, while likewise fighting for control over policy and direction within their respective party fractions.

Certainly, much united the leaders of the two factions, beyond their shared affiliation with the Russian Social Democratic movement and their earlier collaboration on *Iskra*. Both understood history through categories derived from Marxian—and ultimately Hegelian—thought. Both agreed in large measure on where the law-governed historical process was headed—a classless self-determining communist society, built on the productive base of an industrial economy. Each, too, recognized the revolutionary character of the situation that took shape during the summer and early autumn of 1917. Both interpreted in surprisingly similar terms—and before many of their comrades—the folly of any cooperation with the "bourgeois" forces represented in the Provisional Government, a particular point of contention between Martov and other Menshevik leaders. Martov also parted company from these latter in his adamant opposition to Russia's continued involvement in the Great War. Most importantly, Martov immediately understood the dramatic implications of the peasant unrest that broke out with renewed vigor in Tambov *guberniia* in September 1917. The Tambov rising evoked in Martov an appreciation, surprisingly close to Lenin's own assessment, for the revolutionary potential of the peasantry as a social and political adversary to the crumbling bourgeois order.

Yet, as Haimson reminds us, Lenin and Martov premised their prescriptions for action on fundamentally divergent understandings of the appropriate means for the realization of their revolutionary goals. Equally important, these differences sprang from surprisingly solid ideological underpinnings that had become apparent as early as the beginning of the century. A proponent of *samodeiatel'nost'* [self-determined activity] among the revolutionary classes, Martov believed in acting through the crystallizing revolutionary forces represented in the soviets during the fall of 1917, allowing the revolution to create itself under the guidance and leadership of the workers' party.

From this point of view, the evolving soviet structure and the Constituent Assembly that succeeded it would serve as evolutionary stages in the creation of a truly revolutionary state that would reflect the will of Russia's "democratic" forces. Central to this vision were two related concerns. First, revolution could only come when the self-consciousness of social actors reached a proper level of maturity *and* power to overthrow the old order while creating the new one. Second, the ethical purpose of revolution—its liberating function—could only be served through a process in which power originated with the groups making up the new order. To refer yet again to the Hegelian underpinnings of this mode of thought, revolution could only fulfill its role if the rising classes acted as self-determining agents in creating the vessels—state, culture, political organizations—for their historical will. In its solicitude for the ethical element in the conquest of power, and for the *samodeiatel'nost'* of the "democratic" forces, Martov's view continued a deep-seated tradition in Russian revolutionary thought, extending back through "social" Populism to Herzen.

For his part, Lenin had long hewed to a very different and equally established tradition in Russian revolutionary thought, labeled Jacobin or Blanquist by its opponents. In this view, a variety of circumstances, most peculiar to Russia, required the seizure of the state apparatus as an instrument to pull society toward an end visible to those equipped to understand the laws of historical development. For Lenin, these circumstances included the overdeveloped tsarist state, Russia's economic backwardness vis-à-vis other industrial states, and the resulting distortions in Russia's social formations, which accommodated a stunted bourgeoisie alongside a persisting gentry/state hegemony over Russia's lower social strata, themselves undergoing fracture into petty bourgeoisie, proletariat, and *lumpenproletariat* in both industrial towns and peasant villages.

Lenin's thought, both during the years before 1917 and, as Haimson shows, in the fall of 1917, also reflected other traditions in Russian intellectual history. In justifying the inception of an international socialist revolution in Russia, the least developed capitalist state, Lenin recurred to a variant of what one might term the "advantages of backwardness" discourse in Russian thought. Both P. Ia. Chaadaev and Herzen had suggested that Russia's very primitiveness in comparison with western European societies would allow it to avoid their mistakes and to outstrip Europe in reaching the next phase of historical development. Radical populists had argued in a similar vein. In his famous pamphlet *Imperialism: The Highest Stage of Capitalism*, as elsewhere, Lenin depicted Russia as the "weak link" in capitalist development, and thus the easiest to break.

By the same token, Lenin evinced a visceral appreciation for state power as a lever for social and political transformation, an often-underappreciated element in his reflections on *State and Revolution*. Here, he brought out a peculiarly Russian note in Russian Marxism, with this insistence on the crucial significance of political power as the very motor of historical transformation, at the expense of the emphasis on the role of the productive and distributive infrastructure that typified most Marxist thought: "Russian" because his perspective on power and its uses, indeed the very conceptual topography of "above" and "below" that pervaded his terminology. This perspective reflected in its turn a representation of state power that had anchored two centuries of autocratic ideology and policy, from Peter the Great through the Great Reforms of the mid-nineteenth century. Seen this way, the autocracy deserved overthrow not for the power it wielded, but for the oppressive ends that its power had served. Turned to proper goals—the creation of a just society—and used in behalf of the oppressed majority, this power would gain legitimacy.

As Haimson's discussion shows, however, Lenin demonstrated throughout the summer and fall of 1917 an impressively broad and subtle appreciation of power and its application. Lenin also showed a remarkable consistency in the historical world-view through which he interpreted and organized his understanding of unfolding events. Thus, in an angry letter written in mid-October, urging immediate action on his recalcitrant comrades, Lenin alluded to each of the dynamic—and, to his view, evolving—forces shaping the current historical context: the workers' movement, now joined by the peasants deserting the army and fomenting rebellion in Tambov; the Bolsheviks' growing support in the army and among the workers in both capitals; the rising tide of economic want; and the obligation of the "vanguard" party of Bolsheviks to organize and channel these energies, through the seizure of power at a critical moment. Left unmentioned, however, in Lenin's letter was yet another problem that Haimson stresses as contributing to Lenin's furious insistence on a *coup*—the fact that Martov, having reached a similar interpretation of the historical importance of the moment, had strengthened his position, and that of his allies, within the Central Executive Committee of the Soviet. Lenin's furious advocacy of action drew its ardor from both sets of circumstances.

In the event, whatever one makes of the outcome, Lenin's judgment, forced on his colleagues by a set of actions he initiated without the approval of the Central Committee, proved correct: framed by an ideological vision that could make order out of the maelstrom of revolutionary Petrograd, the Bolsheviks acquiesced—sometimes slowly—in Lenin's *fait accompli* and maintained an organizational and logistical cohesion, undergirded by an unflinching view of the uses of state power and the support of "democratic" forces through the immediate travails of the revolution, as well as the Civil War. Out of a combination of tenacity, conviction in his own rightness, and an unwavering gaze at his surroundings, Lenin stole a march on his own Central Committee, on the Central Executive Committee of the Soviets, on Martov, and on history.

Taken together, these two essays trace important processes in the rise of what became the new regime from the wreckage of the old. They also attest to the consistency and originality of a historical vision that has defined Haimson's work since its very inception in the 1950s. Grounded equally in the analytical traditions of pre-revolutionary Russian historiography and the social sciences revolution that swept the American academy in the years after World War II, Haimson's interpretation of the processes that shaped the history of the late empire reconciles the tectonic forces that transformed Russian society in the late nineteenth century with the importance and indeterminacy of specific moments, whether the crystallization of worker militancy and consciousness in the post-Lena months or Lenin's preemptive *coup de main* in late 1917. If he accepts the argument that modernization doomed tsarism to collapse, he contends equally forcefully that specific events and specific actors intervened to lend unpredictable direction to unfolding processes.

In other words, Haimson argues that, even though the imperial order had lost its capacity to survive, there was nothing necessary in the specific outcomes embodied by the mass demonstrations and strikes of the post-Lena period or the success of Lenin's audacious *coup*. Rather, he seeks the sources of these *tournures* in a broader web of interactions, whose components include the formation of social identities, differing modes of self-expression and self-representation by social-political agents—whether social formations or individuals like Lenin and Martov—and, ultimately the centrality of language and perception as both catalysts and limiting factors in shaping these outcomes. To this extent, Haimson's historical vision stands out for the way in which it anticipated conceptually and methodologically many of the interpretive schools that now dominate the writing of social and political history. Well before historians began to incorporate the insights of Clifford Geertz or James Scott, Haimson drew on an interest in anthropology to explore the means by which power is constituted in social and political orders. He attested this interest when acknowledging his debt to Margaret Mead in his study of Russian Marxism; it is equally visible in his reflections on the importance of venue and performance when he roots worker identity in the social interactions of St. Petersburg or, in an earlier work, when he underscores the importance of worker protest spilling out of its traditional neighborhoods and into the central complex of the imperial capital in early 1917.[13] Equally, in the close attention he displays to the utterances of his historical actors—whether the languages of inclusion and exclusion he finds among strikers in post-Lena St. Petersburg or in the systematized world-views espoused by Lenin, Martov and other *intelligenty*—Haimson continues a practice that has characterized his analyses since the mid-1950s, what one might term the "linguistic turn" *avant la lettre*.

Taking for granted the transformative processes associated with Russia's modernization—from the Great Reforms through the crash industrialization of the 1890s—Haimson studies the various ways in which change tugged at and altered the material and conceptual fabric that made up the imperial order. While recognizing the material bases of these changes, however, Haimson seeks the sources of historical change in the experiential dimensions produced by these processes among groups of actors bound together by the political power of the imperial state, as well as by webs of traditional social practice and mediated by languages that more or less plausibly explained the existing order while seeking to legitimate it, or to critique its legitimacy by reference to shared assumptions about how society and power ought to be constituted. Two related sets of conceptual categories figure prominently in these analyses: the texture of social identity, alternating between ideas of class over against the older notion of *soslovie*; and the themes of particularity and universality as bases for claims to authority or as the bases for criticism of the existing order.[14]

13. Haimson and E. Brian, "Les grèves ouvrières en Russie impériale pendant la première guerre mondiale et le déclenchement de la révolution de février 1917," *Le Mouvement Social*, no. 169, octobre-décembre 1994, pp. 9–44.
14. See the related discussion in Haimson, "The Problem of Social Identities."

One finds these considerations reflected concretely in both essays presented in this volume. Thus, in examining the crystallization of a specific and self-assertive worker identity, Haimson combines two sorts of evidence. On one hand, in his appendices and in much of his earlier work, Haimson outlines the accretion of factors that combined to produce this new identity—the growth of industrial enterprises, the concentration of worker residency in specific neighborhoods, the increasing stratification of skills and wages among workers, the rising incidence of literacy, or the impact of the rapidly modernizing urban *milieu* on in-migrating peasants, displaced by land-hunger or the Stolypin reforms in the countryside. On the other hand, through a painstaking reconstruction of the terms in which they claimed "dignity," reflected in the workers' press and in police reports, he traces how workers experienced and explained the Lena massacre and its aftermath in the strikes and demonstrations that spread through the capital, even as debate subsided among "census society" in the Duma and the press.

Workers' demands for "dignity" and their use of shaming to isolate and stigmatize strike-breakers marked them as a new force and formation in Russian society. Certainly, in the starkness with which they drew boundaries of belonging, they spoke in terms that echoed the attributes of the older *soslovie* groupings—nobility, peasantry, clergy. But at the same time, the composition and emerging assertiveness of this new group bore the hallmarks of a new sort of social identity. Belonging depended on one's occupation, not birth, and on the acceptance of behavioral-moral norms related to the workplace and to solidarity vis-à-vis surrounding groups in urban society. Indeed, as Haimson suggests, continual interaction with nobles, officials, and *petit-bourgeois* helped concretize worker identity in opposition to these other groups. Moreover, membership in the working-class sprang from a distinctive orientation to the forces wreaking change in Russian society—a new type of city, the industrial economy, urban modes of consumption—and from a conscious rejection of what they saw as a backward and backward-looking rural past. Indeed, the political power that this class could exert—beginning with the strike waves that first swept over St. Petersburg from 1912–1914 and then with increasing force after the middle of 1915—sprang both from its self-consciousness and from its physical concentration in Russia's capital cities.

Yet, the sheer assertion of worker claims to dignity or an eight-hour day or, later, a voice in factory management did not suffice to create an alternative to the existing regime, whether the tsarist order or the caretaker effort embodied in the Provisional Government. Even the creation of the Petrograd Soviet and its cognates elsewhere constituted only the institutional expression of demands and aspirations to contend with those advanced by the Provisional Government. Haimson's account notes in passing the intermittent ambivalence felt by Lenin, Martov and other members of the Soviet with regard to this body's assuming power in the name of a new Russia. At the heart of this ambivalence—and of the decisions to act reached independently by Martov and Lenin after the eruption of the *Tambovshchina*— lies the last and most important theme running implicitly through these two studies and, indeed, the majority of Haimson's works on the revolutions of the early twentieth century: the tensions between the related dyads of particularity/universality and spontaneity/consciousness that served as axes for the rhetoric of political legitimacy in imperial and revolutionary Russia. For, in order to gain power even amid the tumult of 1917, it appears that all actors subscribed to similar conventions in their understanding of what would make that power legitimate. These conventions acted simultaneously in two ways: while they offered a means to justify the actions proposed alternatively by Lenin and Martov, they also drew on deep traditions of Russian political speech, and as such imposed limits on the alternatives perceived by political actors and ensuring on some levels strong continuities in how power was explained and justified.

The relationship between discourses of particularity and universality do not figure as prominently in Haimson's written work as his observations on the juxtaposition in Russian thought of spontaneity and consciousness, but it forms an important sub-theme in his work as well as constituting a point of emphasis in his teaching. Both sets of oppositions play a critical role in understanding the rhetorical or conceptual element in the taking of power that stands as the central theme in this volume. Beginning with the "men of the 'forties" the assertion that they possessed consciousness, over against the pre-conscious spontaneity [*stikhiinost'*] of the lower orders in society, anchored the revolutionary intelligentsia's fundamental claim to the role of political leader as an alternative or successor to the autocracy. This conceit served a variety of ends. The possession of consciousness implied an understanding of the laws of history—whether Hegelian historiosophy or dialectical materialism—and a concomitant awareness of where the possessor stood in relation to the historical process as it brought the future to life, in accordance with those same laws. This understanding brought in its train the claim to be able to direct and mobilize the spontaneous energies of the *narod* against the tottering edifice of the old order, while leading them in the construction of the new, in which conditions would develop that would allow in turn the transmogrification of popular spontaneity into one or another form of self-determining self-consciousness, be it class-based or national, and an end to the alienation or "one-sidedness" of the intelligentsia itself. Thus, Lenin and Martov continued a venerable tradition when seeking ways to channel the energies that had wrought such change since the early winter of 1916. Seen from this perspective, the Tambov rising portended a true point of departure, as well, since it demonstrated to each of these observers that the revolutionary energies had gained hold in the countryside, in opposition to the bourgeois Provisional Government.

Yet, the intelligentsia's claim to leadership of the nation or society-in-becoming also rested on an equally powerful and pervasive discourse, appropriated by Russian thinkers from the rhetoric of the autocracy itself. In this tradition, leadership gained legitimacy from the related facts that it played the roles of mediator among and director of the manifold groups making up the body politic, while using its superordinate position—and, later, the professional expertise of its officials—to mobilize the population in pursuit of one or another "state" interest. Since nobles, peasants, workers or clergy could by definition only articulate their own particular interests, none of them could take on the universalizing functions performed by the ruler and the state apparatus that served him or her. For instance, members of Alexander I's "Unofficial Committee" or officials preparing the abolition of serfdom routinely opposed noble defenses of the institution since they represented only the viewpoint of "selfish" nobles rather than the good of the state as a whole. Rebellious peasants could attack their masters or landlords for selfishly refusing to obey the orders of the good tsar to give the peasants what they sought.

For their part, those who opposed the arbitrariness of the bureaucracy began to argue in the late nineteenth century that officialdom itself had become a self-interested participant in the empire's political life, holding onto power for its own ends despite its obligations to obey the emperor or the law. Such a perspective informed, most notably, the resolution of the Zemstvo Congress of November 1904, or, as trenchantly, Marxist and populist broadsides against an autocracy that had allied itself with the nobility or the bourgeoisie. Of course, the most powerful and memorable expression of this vision—as a viable alternative to the universalism represented by the autocracy—came with the gathering "all-nation struggle" that provided the appearance of unity to the various movements that came together to propel the revolutions of 1905–1907. The memory of this moment continued in following years to offer hope and a sense of possibility to liberals and revolutionaries alike.

As much as the claim to possess a necessary consciousness, intelligentsia self-representation also claimed to rise above the mundane distinctions that divided Russian society. A famous article from the time, entitled "What *is* the Intelligentsia?" [*Chto takoe intelligentsia?*] founded that group's historical importance precisely on the fact that it formed a supra-class, supra-estate body; its members stemmed from all social groups, forming a community by their own shared, conscious, and freely chosen dedication to the betterment of their country and the enlightenment of its people.[15] One discerns a similar aspiration to universality in the *mythos* of *prishel raznochinets* that defined the intelligentsia interpretation of the 1860s. This view saw the importance of this period in the influx of non-nobles—most obviously Dobroliubov and Chernyshevskii, or the fictional character of Bazarov— into the previously gentry-dominated ranks of the intelligentsia. In fact, the noble-born continued to make up the majority of this movement; even modern readers often forget that Bazarov, or the figure of Rakhmetov in Chernyshevskii's *What Is To Be Done?* sprang from gentry roots. Equally interesting, one sees even in Lenin's own *What Is To Be Done?* a move in the same direction. Discussing the composition of his vanguard party, Lenin urged that it should unify in its ranks the most progressive and conscious members of all orders of society—gentry, students, workers, and even clergy. In all of these cases, intelligentsia speech satisfied the rhetorical rules of the game for political leadership in Russia by devising a new way of transcending particularity, grounding this new universality in the trump condition of consciousness. Precisely because the intelligentsia found unity in adherence to philosophies and an ethos that downplayed ascriptive status, it personified a legitimate alternative to the autocratic state.

Haimson's account of Lenin's and Martov's reactions to the turns of events in the fall of 1917 assumes new and interesting aspects in this context. Each actor sought the legitimate conceptual means to espouse consummating the next stage of the revolution and both relied, as Haimson argues, on the perceptual architecture provided by their ideological orientation. For Martov, the rising of the Tambov peasants put the problem of dealing with the bourgeoisie *hors de jeu*: the dawning democracy could now be found in the *samodeiatel'nost'* of the peasantry alongside the previously more conscious forces represented in the network of Soviets. This democracy and its

---

15. Ivanov-Razumnik, "Chto takoe intelligentsia?", first chapter in *Istoriia russkoi obshchestvennoi mysli*, 3-e izdanie, t. I (St. Petersburg: Tip. M. M. Stasiulevicha, 1911), pp. 3–12, also published separately as a pamphlet: (Berlin: Skify, 1920).

founding institutions would embody a new universalizing force, uniting through active political participation its various constituencies.

For his part, Lenin showed a consistency not often accorded him. In *State and Revolution* and in his exhortations to the recalcitrant Bolshevik Central Committee, he argued for the seizure of power as the only way consciously to guide the achievement of the future non-particularized society that the moment and his reading of history appeared to promise. Again, Lenin's ability to combine action with this powerful and coherent vision— regardless of its ethical content and consequences—gave him the means to persuade and command his comrades and to gain control of the social unrest that had made their coup possible in the first place.

Throughout his career, Leopold Haimson has reflected on power and its workings in late imperial Russia. These reflections are characterized by an arresting globality of scope and vision, combining methodologies drawn from anthropology and psychology, in addition to intellectual, political, social and labor history. His publications span areas as diverse as the history of Russian Marxism, the crises confronting rural Russia in the early twentieth century, and parliamentary fractions in Duma Russia. He has used quantitative analysis to trace the history of the workers' movement, complementing its findings with sensitive readings of the same population's everyday life. Throughout, as one sees in this volume, he relies on a close and tireless reading of primary sources, in an effort to reconstruct history, not "as it happened" but as its participants lived it.

As a teacher, Haimson has served as *Doktorvater* for four generations of graduate students, whose own work addresses such widely scattered subject areas as the army, the rural gentry, the bureaucracy, and the cultural-intellectual life of the late empire. These students—to this writer's own particularistic view—have formed an identifiable school in Russian historiography, but do not exhibit the lockstep conformity in methodology or emphasis that one usually identifies with most powerful mentors. The interests represented among students range from David Mandel's studies of labor history, to studies of rural reform and agrarian politics—in the work of such scholars as Roberta Manning, Frank Wcislo, David Macey—to imperial institutional history—represented by Alexandra Korros and Andrew Verner, among others—to the history of Russia's radicals and revolutionaries, as seen in the scholarship of Ziva Galili and Susan Heuman. Some of his earliest students helped shape new subfields in the American practice of Russian history—Allan Wildman's work on the late imperial army, Richard Wortman's studies of populists and Nicholaevan jurists, and Richard Hellie's penetrating studies of Muscovite law and society. In turn, a rising generation of scholars in twentieth-century Russian history—Peter Holquist, Jochen Hellbeck, and Frederick Corney, to name only a few—also show the stamp of Haimson's training. The larger field of Russian history has also benefitted from his contributions as a critic and interlocutor, as acknowledged by some of the leading practitioners of late imperial Russian history, including William Rosenberg, Reginald Zelnik, Geoffrey Hosking, Alfred Rieber and Laura Engelstein.

Most of all, Haimson continues to reshape the ways in which we understand what befell the Romanov empire in the early twentieth century. To be sure, he does not always address the issues that have moved to the center of our field today—Russia as a multinational empire or the problem of a Russian "modernity," the interaction of social status and gender during a time of sweeping change, or the material cultures of urban and rural life. Yet, one can also contend that historians cannot explain the last thirty years of the Romanov empire without having to address arguments Haimson first began to articulate fifty years ago. Indeed, much of the new and interesting historical work on civil society and political life under Nicholas II continues to seek a refutation for his claim, first made in the early 1960s, that, given the ways in which Russians thought and spoke and acted on their notions of who they were and given the cultural world in which Russia's rulers lived, the empire had to fall apart.

In doing so, he has suggested that his readers and students move beyond the pat categories within which generations of western and Russian observers alike have understood Russian history—the tyranny of the autocracy, the opposition of "state" and "society" or any operations of dialectical processes associated with Russia's exceptionality. As a student of revolution and its etiology, he recognizes the undeniable impact of the processes that created that phenomenon we now call modernity—industrialization, urbanization, professionalization, or the advent of mass culture, to name but a few. He also recognizes that these processes unfold in roughly predictable ways. But, ultimately, the arena where his history takes place is that of social psychology, of perception, of language—the realm in which power is constituted through persuasion, coercion and action.

In a sense, Haimson explores how the practices and claims of autocracy ceased to address or persuade its manifold audiences, who could no longer suspend disbelief enough to coexist under its aegis. Even under the duress of perceived agrarian crisis, and even after the upheavals of 1905, the imperial state could not recapture the trust of its traditional supporters among the rural nobility. The peasantry, long seen as the truest support of the dynasty, made its disaffection increasingly manifest after the turn of the twentieth century. Nicholas II's efforts to assert his reading of his autocratic prerogative alienated many of the best and brightest officials who had built their careers and their identities in defense of that autocracy. And, of course, this order appeared oppressive or outmoded to the new social groups that had arisen from the effort to modernize: workers, professionals and the urban classes.

Haimson's emphasis on these groups' language, mutual perceptions and self-representation at a time of social ferment allows him to demonstrate both how the old order fell apart and how the order that replaced it took the form it did. In that arena, as Haimson shows in this volume, identity and the action it produces or the interaction between an individual personality and the mandates of ideology can produce unexpected effects, much like the unseen collision between natural law and the circumstances of a specific moment that confounded Macbeth as he reflected on which seeds would sprout and which not.

ACKNOWLEDGMENTS

I have dedicated this volume to the memory of the late Valentin Semenovich Diakin, who more than any other scholar influenced the approach reflected in the research that I conducted in primary sources in St. Petersburg's historical archives on the themes addressed in these two essays and indeed, on all of my historical work. My relationship with Diakin was a close professional as well as personal one. As it developed and deepened during the years that I conducted my research in the St. Petersburg archives (in particular, the Russian State Historical Archive, RGIA), Valentin Semenovich increasingly impressed on me a lesson he himself had drawn from previous generations of the so-called St. Petersburg historical school—generations that stretched back to the late nineteenth century. It can be summarized in the following formula: the original source of the significance of any truly original and important historical work is to be traced—first, and foremost—to its author's original selection of the primary sources on which he elects to focus attention in his research. To this I would add that its essential value will ultimately depend on the degree of precision and insight with which these sources are penetrated and analyzed. I can only hope that my own selection of primary sources, and especially the care with which I have attempted to analyze them in the essays that compose this volume, testifies to the permanent stamp Valentin Semenovich has left on my studies. His untimely death because of the lack of adequate medical treatment continues to anguish his many former colleagues and friends.

It is also important for me to emphasize the significance of the work of those Western historians who, in a more general, but no less significant way—contributed to the shaping of my research and the approach used in my explorations of the themes addressed in this volume. Here, particular mention must be made of E. P. Thompson, whose conceptualization of a "moral economy" influenced my approach to labor protests among Russian industrial workers, particularly in the wake of the Lena gold fields massacre in 1912; and of Michelle Perrot, whose two classic volumes on strikes in France helped shape my understanding of this complex element of labor activism. The impact of these two fine historians was all the greater because both offered comments directly on my own work on labor unrest in early twentieth-century Russia at the colloquia organized by the Maison des Sciences de l'Homme in Paris, for many years my second scholarly home.

From the 1960s onward, the colloquia were also where I felt the impact on my scholarly work of Fernand Braudel, who was then Director of the M.S.H., and responsible for the organization of these colloquia. Readers of my other scholarly writings will already know the profound influence Braudel's emphasis on the processes of "long duration," and their interplay with processes of "shorter duration," has had on me for many years. Indeed, I must confess to having appropriated, or to put it more precisely misappropriated them, in my own studies in Russian history of what I have termed the "interplay" of roles of structural factors, conjunctures, and events, as well as with their counterparts in the mentalités, attitudes, and behavior of individual and collective actors.

I also need to mention a less evident aspect of Braudel's influence on my scholarly work and, through me, on that of my graduate students. This is the influence he exercised on my recognition of the significance of language used by historical actors in the actual shaping, as well as the eventual articulation, of their ideas and attitudes. Readers will possibly observe Braudel's influence in this regard in my treatment of the attitudes articulated by Russia's industrial workers in their wave of labor protests during and after 1912. Let me note that I owe, at least in part, my concern for the significance of language in the actual shaping as well as the articulation of the mentalités of individual and collective historical actors to a seminar that Braudel organized for the presentation of my views on the ideological evolution of the nineteenth-century Russian intelligentsia. He continuously peppered my presentation in this seminar with questions about the "semiotics" of discourse, or to put it simply, the language of the actors whose behavior I was discussing. Students in my own graduate seminars in later years will recall my frequent interruptions of their presentations, with questions of the same nature about the language used by the historical actors whom they discussed.

One of the most brilliant of the graduate students with whom I was blessed was David McDonald, now Professor of History at the University of Wisconsin at Madison, and a major specialist on the internal policies and diplomatic history of early-twentieth-century Russia. In acknowledging now the contributions of other persons who, in a variety of ways, contributed to the preparation and completion of this work, let me start by expressing my profound gratitude to David for contributing his penetrating, and, not least, exceedingly generous introduction, as well as for the place he assigns to the essays here in the corpus of scholarly work that I have conducted over the past fifty years. I wish to express as well my gratitude to my close friend and colleague at the University of Michigan, Professor William Rosenberg, for his patient and prescient readings and valuable comments on the various drafts of these essays, and to Professor Mark Steinberg, Professor of History and Director of the Russian Center at the University of Illinois, who served as one of the manuscript's outside readers for Columbia University Press. In this capacity, Professor Steinberg offered valuable suggestions for its improvement, especially regarding my concluding comments to the essay on "Lenin, Martov and the Issue of Power." Professor Steinberg made these helpful suggestions even while he was pursuing his own scholarly research in Russian historical archives, and he continued to do so after his return, when I burdened him with yet another version of my conclusion to this essay for his review. Let me add that his very generous comments about my general contribution to studies of the history of pre-revolutionary and revolutionary Russia that he also included in his report for the Press sounded all the more like music to my ears, given that I have now reached—in my view, but not in those of my dear wife Natasha—the venerable age of 77.

I also need and wish to express my heartfelt thanks to Elizabeth Robeson, my wonderful "girl Friday," who diligently and intelligently recorded on the computer each and all of the various drafts that culminated in the final versions of these essays, and who took scarce and valuable time away from her own scholarship and family to give me such splendid assistance; and to Peter Dimock, the executive editor of the Columbia University Press, who afforded me in so touching a form (perhaps because of my advanced age?) his personal attention during the remarkably rapid process (so I am told) of the review of the manuscript for publication.

Finally, may I say here how deeply grateful I am and will always be to my wife Natalia, who was herself trained as a professional historian, for her loving care and patience as well as the insights she has always brought to my research and writings. Her pointed comments and supportive criticisms, not to mention her profoundly touching concern for my general well-being, have unquestionably contributed very greatly to the completion of this work.

RUSSIA'S REVOLUTIONARY EXPERIENCE, 1905–1917

PART I
LENIN, MARTOV AND THE ISSUE OF POWER

I

Undoubtedly the most novel and important of the findings presented in the volumes devoted to the revolution of 1917 in the new documentary history of Menshevism, made possible by the opening of hitherto secret archives after 1991, is the account that it provides of the political journey that Iulii Osipovich Martov, the leader of the Menshevik Internationalists, traveled during the period from the July Days of 1917 up to Vladimir Lenin's seizure and consolidation of his power in October 1917.[1] The significance of Martov's political evolution during this period, which has been ignored even in his most recent biographies, lay in his conversion to the view that the existing coalition government should be replaced by an "all-democratic" regime, consisting solely of representatives of parties and factions supporting the rule of "revolutionary democracy," and resting in addition to the support of Russia's working class, on that of its "petty bourgeoisie" of city and country—including most notably the masses of the peasantry, which constituted the vast majority of the Russian people.

Most remarkable and important from a political standpoint, this evolution of Martov's political views, under the impact of the crisis of the July Days of 1917, would culminate in his formulation in early October 1917 of a platform to guide the delegates of the Menshevik Internationalists at the Second Congress of Soviets, which called for the immediate formation of an "all-democratic" government, resting first and foremost on the support of the masses of the peasantry. The political significance of this new platform was that it appeared to have every chance of mobilizing broad support among the delegates to the Second Congress of Soviets, including the Bolshevik opponents of Lenin's pressure for an armed uprising to be conducted even before the opening of the congress.

As the date set for the opening of the congress approached, Lenin's pressure would become more and more insistent. But so would the resistance to his pressure even among Bolshevik leaders, who found Lenin's warnings of impending doom, unless they followed his will, less and less persuasive. By the same token, by the eve of the congress, it appeared that Martov's platform for the formation of an "all-democratic" government was likely to attract a broad range of support among the delegates, including many of those who had been nominally elected on Bolshevik lists.

We shall focus particular attention below on the dramatic confrontation that eventuated in October 1917 over Lenin's plans for the Bolshevik seizure of power. But before doing so, we shall examine a far more sweeping historical question about Lenin's and Martov's respective conceptions of the nature and sources of political power, and the uses to which it should be put in a revolutionary situation. How did Lenin's and Martov's views on this issue evolve from the issuance of the October Manifesto of 1905, which enabled them both, upon their return to Russia, to participate directly in the further unfolding of Russia's first revolution, through the decade of political exile in Western Europe which both of them experienced after Stolypin's *coup d'état* of June 1907, until the February Revolution of 1917? And how did these views eventually come to assume increasingly important parts in the events that culminated in the Bolshevik seizure of power?

To understand more fully the sources of the conflict that emerged between Lenin and Martov during this earlier period, we need to recall the nature of the consensus that had originally prevailed among the editors of the "old" *Iskra*—future Bolsheviks and Mensheviks alike—which had been articulated in their struggle against their "revisionist" and "economist" opponents. This consensus had rested on the shared assumption that Russian Social Democracy and its working class followers would need to exercise "political hegemony" in Russia's "bourgeois" revolution. Because of the political backwardness of the Russian bourgeoisie, stemming from its traditional dependence on autocracy, the exercise of political hegemony by Social Democracy was imperative to ensure the success of Russia's bourgeois revolution. But it would also greatly benefit Russia's industrial workers, since they would gain through this leading role of Social Democracy the most favorable conditions for their subsequent political and economic development, which would culminate in the overthrow of capitalism and the establishment of socialism. This view, shared by all the editors of the "old" *Iskra*, provided the rationale for their original support of Lenin's vision of a centralized underground party to provide the leadership of the nationwide struggle for political freedom.

Even more important was an issue which arose more and more insistently by the eve of Russia's first revolution in 1905. What was to be done if, in the course of this revolution, the liberal bourgeoisie failed to keep faith with the proletariat in pursuing the goal of achieving full political freedom and establishing a democratic political, social, and economic order following the overthrow of the autocracy (as the leaders of Russia's liberal movement had promised to do in their meeting with the representatives of Russia's socialist parties in Paris in November 1904)? Specifically, what were the Social Democrats to do if the leaders of the liberal movement sought to reach a compromise with a tsarist regime, short of the establishment of a democratic republic?

After the inception of the Revolution of 1905, this issue became a major preoccupation for both Mensheviks and Bolsheviks, especially after the decision of Paul Miliukov and his liberal allies to take part in the elections to the so-called Bulygin Duma although the *ukaz* that the tsar had issued in the summer of 1905 stated that this Duma would play only an advisory role. Neither did this *ukaz* indicate how these elections were to be conducted, and specifically whether their members were to be selected in accordance with the principle of "four tail" suffrage (calling for universal direct, equal, and secret suffrage) which had been sanctified in the platform jointly endorsed by the liberal Union of Liberation and its revolutionary allies in November 1904.

Lenin, who had believed from the outset that the liberal bourgeoisie would seek to achieve a compromise with the autocracy, proposed already at the beginning of 1905 an alternative scheme: the establishment of a dictatorship of the proletariat and peasantry (or more precisely, an alliance of the proletariat with the "middle" and "poor" peasants). The most important of

Lenin's writings advocating this course were his "Tactics of Social Democracy in the Bourgeois Revolution," published in 1905, and his "Economic Program for Russian Social Democracy," in 1906. These two works outlined the platform for nationalization of land, designed to win support of the "middle" peasants for the conquest of a power by the proletariat. But while seeking to achieve this political objective, Lenin also argued in these two works that this nationalization of the land would provide ideal conditions for the rapid and successful development of capitalism in Russian agriculture, similar to the conditions that had been achieved for the rapid development of capitalism in American agriculture in the nineteenth century by the passage of the Homestead Act.

Martov was opposed from the very outset to the proposal that Lenin had already formulated in "What Is to Be Done?", and stubbornly pursued at the Second Party Congress in 1903, that the party organize and mobilize all its resources on the preparation and conduct of an armed uprising to overthrow the autocracy and establish a democratic republic in its stead. Neither did he share the fascination that his brother-in-law Fedor Dan and his colleague A. Martynov displayed during the brief period of their editorship of the Menshevik legal newspaper *Nachalo* in October 1905, under the influence of the exhilarated mood induced by the success of the nationwide general strike, with the theory of "permanent revolution" originally articulated by Parvus and subsequently by Trotsky.

Contrary to the insistence originally enunciated by Plekhanov and Akselrod during the days of *Ozvobozhdenie Truda* in the 1880s on the necessity that a proper historical interval separate the launching of Russia's bourgeois and socialist revolutions, Parvus and Trotsky argued in 1905 that the revolutionary process set in motion by the Russian Revolution would provide the catalyst for a socialist revolution in the industrially more advanced northern countries of Western Europe, whose industrial workers would then come to the assistance of their Russian comrades to ensure the success of a socialist revolution on Russian soil. Dan and Martynov quickly recovered from this intoxicating conception when Russia recovered a measure of political stability in the wake of the issuance of the October Manifesto. They repented publicly their "revolutionary excesses" at the Stockholm Congress of the RSDRP in June 1906, after being subjected to the strictures directed at them by Plekhanov and Akselrod.

At no time during the period of Russia's first revolution did Martov succumb to the intoxicated mood briefly displayed by his Menshevik comrades. This is not to say, however, that he failed to recognize the possibility that the leadership of Russia's liberal movement would seek to achieve a compromise with the tsarist regime that would leave the proletariat far short of the political, social, and economic gains they were to achieve through a democratic revolution. Indeed, of the leaders of the Menshevik movement, Martov was the first to envision this possibility, as well as the dilemma that it would pose for Russian Social Democracy and its working class followers. He did so in a series of articles published in the spring of 1905 in the Menshevik-dominated "new" *Iskra*. In these articles he explicitly envisaged the possibility—indeed the likelihood—that Russia's liberal movement would strike precisely such a compromise with the tsarist regime.

What was to be done in this eventuality? Martov replied that Russia's Social Democracy and its working class followers would have no alternative but to pursue their revolutionary struggle—without the aid, and possibly against the opposition, of Russia's bourgeoisie. Martov admitted that under these conditions, the struggle of Russia's proletariat would be successful only if it provided the catalyst for a socialist revolution in the West, whose workers would then be able to come to the assistance of their Russian comrades. But unlike Parvus and Trotsky (and the Menshevik editorial board of *Nachalo* in October 1905), Martov considered this an unlikely eventuality. Far more likely, in his view, was the prospect that Russia's workers would remain isolated in this revolutionary struggle, and inevitably experience, as a result, a crushing defeat. As he wrote in the new *Iskra*, however, even in this most likely perspective, their pursuit of this struggle, however hopeless, would leave for future generations of Russian workers a heroic memory, comparable to one that the Paris Commune had left for subsequent generations of French workers.[2]

II

The political amnesty issued under the terms of the October Manifesto in 1905 enabled both Lenin and Martov to live openly in the capital upon their return to St. Petersburg, and thereby *experience directly* the impact of the mass labor protests which had brought the autocracy to its knees. This experience had a profound psychological effect on the perceptions that both entertained of the character and dynamics of Russia's revolutionary processes. In Martov's case, the effect was especially significant, and largely irreversible.

The pathos with which Martov's last contribution to the new *Iskra* had been infused was swept away immediately upon his return to the capital, and he experienced first hand the ongoing labor unrest, which had not subsided notwithstanding the issuance of the October Manifesto. Indeed, under the impact of this experience, the strategy that Russian Social Democracy should follow now appeared self-evident to Martov: it was to exploit all the opportunities generated by the legal concessions of the tsarist regime, granted under the pressure of the workers as well as the hesitations and contradictions resulting from the weakening of its capacity for repression, to build a mass labor movement and mass labor party in Russia. The emergence of such a mass labor movement and labor party would accelerate the development of the political self-consciousness and organization of Russia's working class, and most importantly its ability to exercise the independent initiative (*samodeiatel'nost'*) that would enable it to become a mature political actor in the Russian Revolution. From this time on, *samodeiatel'nost'* became a key term in the Mensheviks' references to the emergence of a mature working class on Russian soil.

Following a suggestion by P. B. Akselrod, Martov proposed that a workers' congress be convened without delay to undertake, even under the conditions of the revolution, the task of creating such a mass labor party and labor movement. We should note, however, that it was also under Akselrod's influence that Martov committed his gravest tactical error of the prewar period. He called for the conclusion of an accord with the Kadet party in the elections in the St. Petersburg labor curia to the Second Duma, should such an accord prove necessary to forestall the possibility of a victory of the reactionary "Black Hundreds." The advocacy of this course, loudly denounced by the Bolsheviks, caused the Mensheviks to suffer an unprecedented and humiliating defeat in the election returns from St. Petersburg labor curia, as they came in *third* behind the Bolsheviks as well as the PSR [Socialist Revolutionary Party].[3]

Notwithstanding the fact that he occasionally committed such tactical errors, Martov left no doubt in subsequent years about his commitment to the emergence of an independent and mature labor party and labor movement on Russian soil, indeed, even at the height of the popularity of "Liquidationism" in 1909, when his friend A.N. Potresov and his own younger brother, V.O. Levitsky, advocated the "liquidation" of the party's underground organizations. In view of their well-publicized excesses (such as the "expropriation" of private banks that they committed with the support of the Bolsheviks), Martov resisted the "Liquidators'" appeal, considering that the preservation of the party's underground organizations was a prerequisite for the success of the democratic revolution necessary to achieve the conditions required for the rapid growth of a mass labor party and labor movement. And at all the party's congresses and conferences of the prewar period, Martov religiously reiterated the appeal that a workers' congress be convened to create a mass labor party.

Martov's skepticism about the prospects for a permanent revolution that would enable Russia's workers to seize and hold onto power did not abate at any time during Russia's first revolution, and thus unlike Dan and Martynov, he had no cause to repent for revolutionary excesses when the Stockholm Congress of the RSDRP convened in the summer of 1906. But he and most of his associates in the party's Menshevik faction drew certain basic conclusions from the experience of the Revolution of 1905, which appeared to have become firmly rooted by the eve of the war in Menshevik political culture. (As we shall see, however, Martov turned out to be the only major figure in the Menshevik party who consistently remained faithful to these conclusions in the course of the Revolution of 1917.) These conclusions rested on two major propositions that put Martov and his followers sharply at odds with Lenin on the crucial issue of the character and sources of political power.

The first of these was that the conquest of political power was not to be viewed as an independent factor in the dynamics of a revolutionary situation. Rather, the possibility of attaining and holding onto political power was to be viewed as a reflection, a "function," of the struggle between the *social groups* competing for power in a revolutionary situation, whose outcome would be largely dictated by the degree of political consciousness, self-organization, and independent initiative (*samodeiatel'nost'*) that these groups displayed in their struggle for power.

This was reinforced by a second, corollary proposition. It was that in revolutionary situations new relationships and institutions of power could emerge *de facto*, *sui generis*, as a result of the degree of political consciousness, and capacity for political initiative and organization, displayed by the social groups competing for power.

The French Third Estate, reflecting chiefly the interests of the French bourgeoisie, had displayed this capacity at the opening of the French Revolution, when it had transformed the Estates General convoked by the monarchy into a Constituent Assembly. And so had Russia's industrial workers, during several episodes of Russia's first revolution. In certain of these episodes, such as the calling of the Shidlovskii Commission to consider labor reforms, Russia's industrial workers had exploited concessions made by the frightened tsarist regime. In other cases, most notably that of the creation of the St. Petersburg Soviet, they had been impelled simply by the evidence, provided in this case by the success of the general strike of October 1905, of the weakening of the autocracy's hold on power and of its loss of legitimacy in the eyes of the Russian people. The Revolution of 1917 would demonstrate, however, that, of the major figures in the Menshevik party, only Martov and his followers continued to follow faithfully these precepts, drawn from the experience of the Revolution of 1905, much to the growing puzzlement and irritation of other leading Mensheviks.

III

The opportunity that the political amnesty issued under the October Manifesto afforded Russia's political émigrés to return to the capital, and experience directly the pulse of its mass labor movement, also exercised a profound effect on Lenin's political views (although less irreversibly so than was Martov's experience of these events). Perhaps the most accurate and significant barometer of this experience in Lenin's case was the evolution of his attitudes toward the character and role of the St. Petersburg Soviet.

To be sure, even before his return to the capital, Lenin had dismissed the criticisms addressed by the Bolshevik *komitetchiki* (the leaders of the party's underground organizations in Russia), to the effect that the St. Petersburg Soviet constituted a diversion from the task of organizing an armed uprising to overthrow the tsarist regime. Indeed, already during a brief stopover in Stockholm, before his arrival in the capital, Lenin wrote a glowing article about the St. Petersburg Soviet on the basis of his reading of newspaper reports.[4] Lenin asserted in this unpublished article that, while he did not have as yet any direct immediate impression of the situation in the capital, it appeared to him "that the St. Petersburg Soviet of Workers' Deputies should be viewed . . . and should proclaim itself as quickly as possible, Russia's Provisional Government, or to put it another way, that it should establish a Provisional Revolutionary Government."

Lenin decisively dismissed in this connection the complaint voiced by the Bolshevik *komitetchiki* that the St. Petersburg Soviet had not subordinated itself to the control of the Bolshevik party. On the contrary, he wrote:

The Soviet must include in its ranks representatives of all revolutionary parties and all revolutionary . . . democrats. We do not fear, but on the contrary welcome, the fact that it should assume such a broad and variegated character, because, in the absence of a militant rapprochement between the proletariat and peasantry, and between the Social Democrats and revolutionary democrats, the complete success of the great Russian revolution cannot be ensured. This will be a temporary alliance for the achievement of specific, practical tasks, even while an independent and principled RSDRP continues to stand firm for the realization of the proletariat's ultimate objectives.

Continuing in this vein, Lenin added:

The objection may be raised, whether such a broad and variegated composition can be sufficiently consolidated to provide an effective leadership. I will answer this objection with a question:

What has the October [1905] Revolution taught us in this regard? Has not the strike committee [from which the Soviet emerged] proven, *in practice*, to be the universally recognized center, the real government? And has not this committee welcomed into its ranks representatives of those unions and of the union of unions that are genuinely revolutionary and supportive of the proletariat in the struggle for political freedom? The only qualification to the inclusive character of this provisional revolutionary government is that workers constitute its core, so that, by way of illustration, it includes hundreds of workers, soldiers, and peasants, as against dozens of representatives of the revolutionary intelligentsia. I think that the proletariat itself will prove capable to determine in practice the correct proportions in this regard.

The question may also be raised whether such a government is capable of advancing a program sufficiently coherent to ensure the victory of the revolution, and yet sufficiently broad to make possible the creation of militant alliances devoid of contradictions, silences, and hypocrisy.

[The answer is that] such a program is already accepted in principle by all conscious elements of the population, including even Orthodox priests. [This wide consensus is that] such a program must include in the first place, political freedom, freedom of conscience, of expression, of association, as well as freedom to strike, as

well as the elimination of all institutions that now restrict these free-
doms. This program must also include the calling of a constituent
assembly truly representative of all the people, the liberation of all
national minorities currently oppressed by the tsarist regime, including Poland, for whose freedom, just as for Russia's freedom, the
Russian people will fight arms-in-hand.

This program must also include the legalization of the eight-
hour day, which the workers have already won *de facto*, and other
immediate measures to eliminate capitalist exploitation. Last but
not least, it must include the transfer of all the land to the peasantry
(while not fostering the illusion that the exploitation of the land can
be 'equalized'), as well as the establishment of peasant land committees, which have already begun to emerge spontaneously. . . .

Of course, such a program can only be achieved by an armed
uprising, and a provisional revolutionary government is to constitute precisely the organ of this already-growing and maturing uprising. . . . It is now imperative for the provisional revolutionary
government to organize this uprising, which will ensure its support
by the whole people. . . . [5]

Lenin's inebriation with the spontaneous labor movement reached new
heights after his arrival in the capital on November 8 (21), 1905. Upon receiving the reports of the mutiny of the sailors of the battleship *Potemkin*, of
the victories of the revolutionary movement in Finland, and of the spread of
the revolutionary unrest from St. Petersburg to provincial Russia, he concluded that the general strike had "magnificently fulfilled its task of laying
the grounds for an uprising. The ranks of the revolutionary army are growing everywhere; its forces are becoming battle-hardened, the red banner is
being raised higher and higher over the new Russia."[6]

However, the most striking illustration of the intoxicating effect that the
spectacle of the St. Petersburg labor movement exercised on Lenin's political attitudes at this moment was the dramatic changes that it induced in his
views about the organization of the party, and indeed, about the process of
reunification of its Bolshevik and Menshevik factions. These changes were
articulated in a series of articles entitled "About the Reorganization of the
Party," which Lenin published in *Novaia Zhizn'* in mid-November 1905.[7]

Lenin proposed in one of these articles that the "narrow" formulation of
the definition of party membership on which he had insisted at the Second
Party Congress (provoking thereby the schism between Bolsheviks and

Mensheviks) be eliminated. He now proposed that *all workers* be entitled to join the party, and not merely members of the party's underground organizations, and that all workers, therefore, should enjoy the right to take part, on an equal basis, in the elections of delegates to party congresses, and all other organizational matters.

The party had nothing to fear from such a full participation in its ranks of all members of the proletariat, who were "demonstrating by deeds, and not merely by words, their capacity to struggle, without let-up, in a purely social democratic spirit." "The working class is *instinctively, spontaneously* Social Democratic" [my emphasis L.H.], Lenin now stated, as if he had always entertained this point of view. The work that Social Democracy had conducted for over a decade had contributed no little to the transformation of this elementalness [spontaneity, *stikhiinost'*] into consciousness: "The underground is breaking apart. Move forward boldly . . . broaden the base of the party . . . include Social Democratic workers by the thousands in the party's organizations. Let us throw all petty considerations aside in the conduct of this imperative reform of the party," Lenin concluded. "Let us enter without delay on this new path. . . . It will furnish us new, young forces from the only consistently revolutionary class, which has already won for Russia part of its freedom, will conquer full freedom on its behalf, and bring it through this conquest to the achievement of socialism."[8]

In the third of this series of astonishing articles, infused with the spirit of *stikhiinost'* that he had absorbed from his immediate perceptions of the mass labor movement in the capital, Lenin tackled in the same spirit the issue of party reunification: "It is no secret," he wrote,

> that the great majority of social democratic workers greatly disapprove of the split in the ranks of Social Democracy and demand reunification. It is also no secret that they have no faith in the ability of the party's hierarchy to achieve it.
>
> Since both the majority and the minority of the party's leadership now accept the principle of the immediate introduction of elections of the party's leading organs, the working class members of Social Democracy, who so overwhelmingly favor the reunification of the party, should be able to achieve it.
>
> After all, the relationship between the factions of the intelligentsia and the working class in the social democratic movement could be summarized on the basis of the following formula: the intelligentsia can decide issues in principle, on the basis of abstract

schemes, but it is the workers who bring these great theoretical schemes to real life. And I will not be minimizing the significance of Marxist theory . . . if I now say:

We drew up great theoretical schemes for the restoration of party unity. Comrade workers! Help us turn these great theoretical schemes into real life! Join our party organizations in overwhelming numbers. . . . Help us to turn . . . the issue of reunification from a predominantly theoretical, ideological, issue into a practical question.

We 'theorized' (sometimes, we should not keep this a secret, in a complete vacuum), in the atmosphere of the emigration. It would do no harm, for God's sake, to turn the bar a little the other way, and bring to bear practical considerations on the issue of reunification, on which so much ink and paper have been wasted. Such an approach would be particularly appropriate. In particular, we in the emigration [did not use] a practical approach. To be sure, we drew up on paper a very good and complete program for a democratic revolution. Let us now unite for the sake of achieving this revolution.[9] [My emphasis L.H.]

The last significant piece that Lenin contributed during his stay in St. Petersburg, while less innovative than the other articles that he published during this period, was an outline of the agrarian program for Social Democracy that he would publish in 1906. "The issue of translating the appeals of the revolutionary proletariat to the revolutionary peasantry into a fully spelled revolutionary program has now assumed the most immediate practical significance," he noted in his introduction to this article, written, he emphasized, at a moment when the peasantry was emerging as a conscious actor in the revolution. The very course of the Russian revolution would hinge to a considerable degree on the growth of the consciousness of the Russian peasants:

What does the peasantry want from the revolution? What can the revolution give to the peasantry? These are the two questions that now need to be answered by every conscious worker.

The peasantry wants land and freedom. This cannot be disputed, and by the same token, all conscious workers are supporting the revolutionary peasantry with all their might. . . .

All the land means no compromises with the *pomeshchiki*, the elimination of all gentry property, the support of all the peasants' revolutionary demands, including the confiscation of all privately owned land. Both factions of the RSDRP concur on this point.

All freedom means the destruction of the institutions of the state order which do not emanate from the will of the people. While not all peasants demand a democratic republic, the underlying democratic character of the peasants' movement is indisputable.

The proletariat will support the peasants in their struggle to eliminate all surviving remnants of serfdom. [However,] it not only supports the peasantry's struggle for land and freedom, but also struggles against the rule of capitalism. Hence, the second question is: What can the peasantry contribute to the revolution? Even the complete abolition of private ownership of the land and the elimination of all bureaucrats will not eliminate the rule of capital, and the poverty of the masses. For even if land belongs to all the people, its exploitation will be controlled by those who own capital: that is, those who have equipment, capital, grain, etc. Those who do not will remain slaves to capital, even if the land belongs to all the people. Thus, among the masses of the peasantry, those who own capital will be able to exploit the peasants who don't. This is why the Social Democrats argue that while they support the struggle of all of the peasantry against the *pomeshchiki* and the *chinovniki*, they support, in addition, the struggle of agricultural workers against the capitalists. This is why, while warmly supporting the peasants' struggle for land and freedom, we must not forget to keep in mind the struggle for the emancipation of all laboring people from the exploitation of capital.

Forward, workers and peasants, in the struggle for land and freedom! Forward, proletarians, under the banner of international social democracy, in the struggle for socialism![10]

Peter Garvi, then as in subsequent years a leading *praktik* of the Menshevik movement, has left us an indelible impression of Lenin's ability as a speaker, or more precisely, of his exceptional capacity to persuade his largely plebeian audiences during this period. He noted about the tone of his speeches:

There was nothing resembling oratorical skills, the use of gestures, the raising of his voice to achieve oratorical pathos. He spoke . . . completely quietly, without any oratorical modulations in his voice, and exceptionally clearly, in a business-like fashion, which could reach the simplest minds [in his audience]. And he also impressed them by his quiet self assurance, by his ability to impart, without a dose of self-flattery, a feeling of the superiority [of his arguments], which convinced [his listeners] that truth was on his side, and only on his side, and that everyone else [among the competing speakers] was either in error, over-simplified, complete idiots, or intent on deceiving the working-class, and more generally all laboring people, and should be therefore be exposed mercilessly . . . and chased away.

Garvi commented on another of Lenin's addresses:

His speech produced a great impression, and not only on party members and advanced workers who knew the identity of the speaker, but also on other members of the audience. I remember that at the very heart of Lenin's address, I felt a warm breath behind my back, and turned to see the face of a bearded man, with an excited and heated expression in his eyes. His appearance was that of a small merchant, or a well-to-do peasant. Apologizing for inconveniencing me, he stepped back a little, but said with great excitement: "*Vot zdorovyi muzhik, vot sila*" [figuratively, "Now there is a real fellow, a really powerful man."].[11]

IV

The Stockholm "Unification" Congress in the summer of 1906 marked the conclusion, rather than the consecration, of the phase in the evolution of Lenin's attitudes and views that had been opened by the Revolution of 1905. There were two major reasons for the conclusion of this phase in Lenin's development:

The first was the election of a large number of Social Democratic deputies from the Caucasus (largely from Georgia, as the Georgian Social Democrats, who had refused to boycott the elections, dominated Georgia's political life), as well as the significant number of deputies elected independently by the labor curiae of the major industrial provinces, who also joined the Duma's Social Democratic faction. Their presence made it impossible for either the Bolsheviks or Mensheviks to turn their backs to the

Duma's proceedings, notwithstanding their earlier concurrence (with Martov's exception) on the boycotting of the elections to the Duma.

The second reason why these elections marked a turning point in the evolution of Lenin's political views, however, was the glowing impression that he had already drawn from the behavior of the Duma's peasant deputies during the proceedings of the First Duma, notwithstanding the fact that the deputies elected by its peasant curia generally consisted of older and uneducated members of the peasantry. Even these deputies (usually the heads of peasant households) had assumed a quite independent position from the Kadet party on the crucial issue of land reform. Indeed, when they revolted against the Kadets' platform on this issue, which was confined to a demand for the expropriation of outmoded large estates with a provision for the compensation of their proprietors, the peasant deputies to the First Duma joined with the workers' deputies in demanding the expropriation of all gentry land, without compensation, and its transfer to the possession (not the property) of the members of village communes. (The distinction between possession and property was important, as it reflected the principle that peasants to whom these gentry estates were transferred would only be entitled to hold them as long as they remained members of village communes.)

Following the elections to the Second Duma, in which the peasant curiae elected notably younger, and better educated, deputies—representatives, in fact, of the peasant intelligentsia (including village teachers, clerks, and the like)—Lenin became even more enamored of the revolutionary potential of the peasantry. For these younger and better educated representatives of the peasant intelligentsia now organized themselves to form the *Trudovik* faction, which pursued, even more energetically than the peasant deputies to the First Duma, the goal of confiscating the estates of noble landowners without compensation, and of turning them over to the possession of members of the peasants' village communes. It was during this period that two basic premises hardened in Lenin's political views. These remained unmodified, at least in principle, up to the outbreak of the Revolution of 1917:

The first of these premises was that the objective for which the Bolsheviks should strive in the democratic revolution, which was to precede the struggle for socialism, was the establishment of a dictatorship of the proletariat *and* peasantry. The second, just as important, was that the Bolsheviks should exploit all available legal opportunities to spread their political message, including participation in the State Duma. Lenin held on to both of these conceptions, even after Stolypin's *coup d'état* of June 1907, and the drastic changes that it imposed in the processes of the selection of the Duma deputies.

To be sure, Lenin was profoundly disappointed that the peasants did not rise up in revolt against this *coup d'état*. Indeed, he had originally accounted for the peasants' failure to do so, notwithstanding the appeals of their own *Trudovik* deputies, with the rationalization that the peasants were busy with the collection of their crops and would revolt at the conclusion of the agricultural season. But notwithstanding his disillusionment when the peasants remained politically quiescent and indeed voted for right-wing deputies in the elections to both the Third and Fourth State Dumas in most of European Russia, and notwithstanding the outbreak in the spring of 1912 of the post-Lena wave of workers' unrest, Lenin continued to expound his platform of a dictatorship of the proletariat and peasantry. Indeed, Lenin could not have failed to do so, since the conception of a dictatorship of the proletariat and peasantry constituted the very *basis of the Bolsheviks' claim to political hegemony in the democratic revolution*, which according to the canons of orthodox Marxism was to precede, by a significant interval, the pursuit and achievement of socialism.

At the same time, the view that Lenin reached on the basis of the political experience of the First and Second Dumas—concerning the imperative need for the Bolsheviks to exploit all available legal opportunities to spread their political influence—also survived the shock of the experience of Stolypin's *coup d'état* of June 1907. Indeed, it was on these grounds that Lenin split with Bogdanov and his supporters among the Bolshevik intelligentsia, who had played so prominent a role during the Revolution of 1905, when they demanded a boycott of the elections to the Third Duma and eventually insisted on the recall of the Social Democratic deputies who were elected to it.

Both of these conclusions were emphasized in the resolutions passed at the conference of the Bolshevik Party Central Committee, held in Poronin in November 1913, at the height of the post-Lena strike wave. In fact, these resolutions included the provision that the deputies elected by the labor curiae of Russia's seven major industrial provinces, who had eventually joined the Bolshevik party, be included in the Bolshevik Central Committee. This initiative was all the more important because the political activities of these deputies in spreading the influence of the Bolsheviks in their respective provinces were protected by the legal immunities afforded to all deputies elected to the State Duma. Another of the resolutions passed by the Poronin conference also reflected Lenin's disillusionment with the revolutionary potential of the peasantry. It called for a general strike, followed by an armed uprising, leading to the overthrow of the tsarist regime, and the establishment of what Lenin termed "a firm democratic regime," but did not elaborate on the role that the peasantry might play in this revolutionary process.

V

The next important phase in the evolution of Martov's and Lenin's views on power began with the outbreak of the First World War. The initial psychological effects of the war on Lenin and Martov were, to a significant degree, quite similar. Both were profoundly upset by the inability of the member parties of the Second International to prevent the war's outbreak, or at least to put an immediate halt to it—through the general strike that the International had planned to organize to prevent such an eventuality. Both were even more deeply shocked by the decision of the majorities of the socialist parties represented in the legislatures of most of the belligerent countries to support unconditionally their countries' war effort, by voting, usually unanimously, to approve the budgetary requests that their governments submitted to sustain it. Both found even more intolerable the decision of the majorities of the socialist parties in a number of these belligerent countries to be represented in governments of national unity. Lenin was especially upset in this regard by the behavior of the German Social Democrats, since they previously had represented in his eyes veritable exemplars of a politically mature socialist party and of a mature and politically conscious working class. Yet, they too had voted unconditionally in support of their country's war effort.

Indeed, it was widely rumored that Lenin underwent a veritable nervous breakdown under the shock of this experience, and that he did not really begin to recover until 1915, after having settled in Switzerland, taking long walks in Krupskaya's company in the Swiss countryside, and seeking reassurance in the writing of his commentaries on Hegel's *Logic*. What does the evidence available to us suggest about the validity of this thesis, and more generally about the character of Lenin's response to the outbreak of the First World War?

Lenin was still living in Poronin, the town in Galicia (then, under Hapsburg rule) where he had settled in 1913. Upon the outbreak of the war, he was briefly put under house arrest as the subject of an enemy power, but quickly

released thanks to the intervention of Victor Adler, a leader of Austrian Social Democracy. Adler also obtained permission for him to go to Vienna
from where, following brief meetings with Adler and Hilferding, he traveled to Switzerland, where he remained until the outbreak of the Russian
revolution. During this initial period of little more than six weeks, Lenin
wrote very little (for habitually so copious a writer). Indeed, this was the
one real evidence of the shock that the war, and the circumstances under
which it had occurred, had inflicted on his psychological resources. Still,
what he did write about the war, the responses to it on the part of various
European socialist parties, and the tasks that Russian Social Democracy
now had to assume, outlined the major theses that he would later develop
about its fundamental causes, including the argument that the phenomenon of imperialism as the ultimate phase in the development of capitalism
had contributed to it through struggle among various capitalist countries
for colonies.[12]

We should also take note of the especially harsh denunciations that
Lenin delivered during these months of the leaders of German Social
Democracy, including Kautsky, whose words he had previously hailed as the
most important contributions to Marxist theory except for those of Marx
and Engels, and whom he had also praised to the skies for his contributions
to the development of German Social Democracy as the most advanced socialist party in Europe. Hence, the sense of bitterness that now infused his
denunciations of Kautsky for what he viewed as his betrayal of socialist internationalism, including the convictions that he had so sharply expressed
before the outbreak of the war about the development of a revolutionary situation in Europe that would culminate in the establishment of the dictatorship of the proletariat. Lenin extensively cited in this connection the theses
that Kautsky had expounded in his brochure, "The Task of Power," published in 1909, including his statement that while one could not predict precisely when the aggravation of class contradictions in advanced capitalist
countries would lead to a revolution, one could definitely affirm that in the
event of the outbreak of a war, a revolution would definitely occur "either in
the course of the war, or immediately upon its conclusion." Lenin further
cited Kautsky's statement in this pamphlet to the effect that a new era of revolution was approaching as a result of the growth of class contradictions, of
imperialist conflicts, and of militarism. "A world war is fast approaching,"
Kautsky had written, and "it will provide a catalyst for a revolution. This is
what Kautsky wrote, just five years ago. This is what German Social Democracy constituted, or more precisely, promised to become. This was a Social

Democracy which could only evoke admiration." But what had Kautsky become since the outbreak of the war? To illustrate his transformation, Lenin went on to list contemptuously a number of citations from the article "Social Democracy in the Period of the War" that Kautsky had published in *Neue Zeit* in October 1914.[13]

Most of the citations I have quoted up to this point about Lenin's responses to the outbreak of the war may well be viewed as a reflection of the sense of betrayal that was to be expected of any of the Social Democratic Internationalists in response to the cataclysm that the war had unleashed—except, perhaps for the stridency and hardly suppressed rage that distinguished many of Lenin's remarks. However, from the end of 1914, and especially the beginning of 1915 onward, an additional and distinctive new theme assumed growing importance in Lenin's speeches and writings as he sought to explain to his readers, and indeed to himself, the factors that had contributed to the betrayal by the majority parties in the various belligerent countries of the sacred principle of the international solidarity of the proletariat. Given his espousal of the principles of orthodox Marxism (at least in his own view) he predictably found one of those underlying factors in the attraction that these parties had already displayed before the outbreak of war to "bourgeois reformism." Lenin now followed this well-trodden path in his discussion of the background of those in Russia and international Social Democracy who had now deviated from international proletarian solidarity.

Lenin devoted most of the very substantial body of his writings during the six-odd months of 1915, preceding the conference organized by the remaining Internationalists in Zimmerwald, to the subject of the strategy and tactics to be adopted to bring the carnage to an end. The body of his writings during these months was especially voluminous, even for Lenin. It constitutes some 275 pages of the 26th volume of the fifth edition of his Collected Works. It also included a brochure of some 75 printed pages, entitled "Socialism and the War (The Relationship of the RSDRP to the War)," which he wrote in a period of less than six weeks in July-August 1915 to prepare its readers to support the arguments that he would advance at the Zimmerwald Conference, which convened on August 20, 1915.[14]

Notwithstanding the diffusiveness of "Socialism and the War," this important pamphlet clearly suggests the character of the conflicts that would emerge between Lenin and Martov at the Zimmerwald Conference. The irreconcilable character of these differences was also suggested by the ruthlessness of Lenin's critique of the positions that the Mensheviks had assumed during the war years—notwithstanding the fact that the Menshevik deputies in the State Duma had unanimously voted against war credits when the Duma had been called back into session in the summer of 1915.

But Lenin's brochure also brought out a more fundamental conflict between him and Martov. It was that, in contrast to himself, Martov had advocated since the outbreak of the war the broadest possible mobilization of opponents to the war in Russian Social Democracy, regardless of the sharpness of the conflicts between them before 1914. Martov had specifically suggested in this connection that the conflict over the issue of "Liquidationism" (i.e., over the suggestion that the party's underground organizations be dissolved because of the excesses they committed during the prewar period, such as the "expropriation" of private banks),[15] was no longer germane, in the face of the more fundamental conflicts that the war had created between Defensists and Internationalists in Russian Social Democracy.

It would have been difficult to argue who, between Lenin and Martov, presented the most persuasive argument about this issue. On one hand, there was some validity in Lenin's thesis that most of the prewar supporters of "Liquidationism" had become Defensists, supporters of Russia's war effort in the face of what they perceived to be German militarism and expansionism. On the other hand, it was not difficult to find exceptions to the linkage that Lenin emphasized between Internationalists and Defensists after the outbreak of the war and what he considered to be earlier deviations from Marxist orthodoxy.

The most striking of these exceptions was Eduard Bernstein, the most notable of the champions of "Revisionism" at the turn of the century, and who Lenin had so sharply criticized during the period of his administrative exile in Siberia. Bernstein's adamant opposition to the war undermined Lenin's thesis all the more, given the fact that Kautsky and other champions of Marxist orthodoxy in German Social Democracy, who Lenin had so greatly admired, emerged as supporters of the German war effort.

Lenin's brochure also suggested the issues that he would emphasize at the Zimmerwald Conference in his efforts to provoke a split between his supporters and their opponents. The list included an insistence on a categorical statement by the delegates to the conference from the various belligerent countries of their opposition to the war. Lenin argued, in this connection, that "defeatism," i.e., the advocacy of one's own country's military defeat, was the only stand calculated to contribute to the overthrow of these governments (and, in particular, of the tsarist regime), and to the spread of the international civil war, which he viewed as the only effective way to seek to overthrow imperialism, and to achieve socialism throughout the world.

Since the outbreak of the war, Martov had emphasized in his appeals to Socialist Internationalists in the various belligerent and neutral countries, the pursuit of a strategy and tactics precisely opposite to those advocated by Lenin: through the achievement of a universal peace "without annexations and indemnities." It was to seek to mobilize the broadest support for such a platform among both socialist and nonsocialist opponents of the war among the populations of all belligerent and neutral countries, a process which, in his view, was bound to be accelerated by the growing realization by the populations of those countries of the catastrophic losses of life as well as the economic suffering the war was producing. Thus, even before the opening of the Zimmerwald conference, it was abundantly clear that the most important issue that would emerge in the course of its proceedings would concern these differences between Lenin and Martov about the strategy and tactics to be adopted in the effort to bring the war to an end.

Indeed, from the very opening of the Zimmerwald conference, the argument consistently advanced by Lenin and his supporters was that precisely because the World War had broken out as a result of the contradiction in the development of imperialism, the last stage in the development of capitalism through the world, it could be brought to an end only through the successful waging of an international civil war. Russia had proven to be the weakest link in the development of imperialism, and by the same token, Russia was to lead the way in this international civil war, which would spread from less developed countries and their colonial dependencies to the more developed capitalist countries of the west. The catalytic role that Russia was destined to play in this regard demonstrated even more fully the crucial importance of taking power in Russia through revolution.

Martov was the principal spokesman for the opponents of Lenin's position. The essence of his argument was that the strategy outlined by Lenin was both immoral and impractical. It was immoral because socialism could not be built on the ruins that would be left of the civilized world at the conclusion of the international civil war that Lenin prescribed. But Lenin's position was also impractical because a far broader coalition could be mobilized among the citizens of belligerent countries to press their respective governments to bring the war to an end than for the purpose of achieving a socialist revolution, let alone one that would lead to the unleashing of an international civil war. An additional argument Martov used in this connection was that victory in the struggle for peace would constitute the most effective way to launch a successful struggle for socialism.

In their response to Martov, Lenin and his supporters argued (both in Zimmerwald, and in Kienthal, where they met subsequently to articulate their political strategy) that it was the position advocated by Martov and his allies (among the delegates who became identified as members of the Zimmerwald center) that was detached from any political realities, given the deep involvement in the war of the bourgeois governments of the various belligerent countries. Consequently, a universal peace without annexations and indemnities could eventually be attained only through the successful prosecution of an international civil war.

Thus, the debates at the Zimmerwald Conference focused largely on the conflict between the positions advocated by Lenin and Martov about the most effective ways to bring the war to an end.

Even as the debates at the Zimmerwald conference unfolded, Lenin reportedly was already seeking to calculate, on the basis of the intervention of the various participants, how many of them would be likely to support his intention to provoke a split among the delegates between his own followers and Martov's. Lenin was aware that the decision of many of the delegates in this regard was likely to hinge on the definition of the major issues that he would emphasize in the debates. Further complicating his choice of issues was that they would have to transcend differences between the political attitudes and socioeconomic characteristics of the groups in the various belligerent countries represented by the participants at the conference, and in the first place, those representing Germany and Russia.

Lenin finally focused on the differences between the positions that he and Martov had articulated about the issue of restoring the international solidarity of the proletariat. Lenin demanded intransigently in this connection the liquidation of the still surviving bureau of the prewar Second Socialist International. Martov, on the contrary, favored efforts to restore it in order to facilitate the mobilization of the socialist parties, especially in the belligerent countries, to struggle for a universal peace without annexations and indemnities. It was ostensibly over this issue that Lenin now pushed for the split that he had planned since the outset of the conference between his supporters (who came to be called the "Left Internationalists") and Martov's.

Within a week of the conclusion of the debate at Zimmerwald, Lenin organized a conference to mobilize his supporters in the neighboring town of Kienthal. The proceedings of the conference in Kienthal did generally record support for the positions that Lenin advocated. However, as a biography of Martov published many years ago by Israel Getzler suggests, the proceedings of this conference *did not* register support for the proposal for the liquidation of the old, and the creation of a new, International. To be sure, one of the resolutions adopted at Kienthal denounced the Bureau of the old International, as "an accomplice in the policy in the so-called defense of the fatherland and of its civil peace." However, it spoke in favor of *"the recovery"* rather than the *dissolution* of the Second International.[16]

Getzler's also cites, in this connection, a statement that Martov directed at Zinoviev on the third day of the conference:

> If comrade Zinoviev were not opposed to the convocation of the International Bureau, we could see eye-to-eye. The main thing is that we do not repel those elements of the French or English parties, which disagree with the majority, but demand the *reconvocation* of the International Bureau (rather than its dissolution) [my emphasis LH].

This statement suggests that Zinoviev, who would emerge as one of Lenin's principal opponents in the Central Committee of the Bolshevik party in 1917, may already have displayed significant differences with him in the summer of 1915.[17]

Up to the outbreak of the February revolution, Martov would continue to advocate the position he had favored at the Zimmerwald Conference on the issue of the revival of the prewar Second International, although he introduced, or more precisely reintroduced, in his discourses on the subject, the distinction that he had already made in his writings in the (new) *Iskra* in 1905. It was that success in the struggle to achieve a universal peace without annexations and indemnities by a revived International would not only provide a catalyst for the overthrow of the tsarist regime, but was also likely to set off a socialist revolution in Western Europe. Martov did not include in his statement, however, the complementary thesis that he had advanced in October 1905 that in the event of a socialist revolution in Western Europe, the more advanced workers of these countries would come to the aid of their Russian comrades to achieve a socialist revolution on Russian soil.[18]

In the wake of the conferences in Zimmerwald and Kienthal, the letters of Martov to N.S. Kristi reflect a sense of initial excitement in what the conference had achieved. In a letter dated May 6, 1916, which recorded his

original reactions, Martov began with the observation that of the 40 delegates who had sought to participate in the Zimmerwald Conference, more
than 25 had either failed to obtain the passports required to attend it, or
had not been allowed to cross the Swiss border. The result was a lack of
comprehensiveness in the composition of the delegates attending the Zimmerwald Conference. This would have seemed to provide a favorable ter-
rain for the factional combinations conducted by Lenin and company, but
it had not turned out to be the case:

> Not only did Lenin prove unable to direct the proceedings of the
> conference, but after taking account of the situation, he and his
> supporters began to behave correctly, *"po Evropeiski."* This
> reached the point that by the conclusion of the conference we
> were practically being courted. In any case, we were able to work
> together without, or almost without, maneuvers on their part. . . .
> From a factional standpoint, the conference also turned out to be
> a great success. . . . The fact that the ex-Defensists (among the
> French, German, and Italian socialists attending the conference)
> signed the manifesto that we had drawn up radically changed the
> attitudes displayed toward us by the Leninists, who at the opening
> of the conference had sought, although unsuccessfully, to chal-
> lenge the mandates of Martov as well as P. B. Akselrod, to attend
> the conference.[19]

However, the delight apparent in this description in Martov's letter of
May 6, 1916, gave way rather quickly to depression during the subsequent
months of 1916 and early 1917. Reflected in this depression were two major
factors. The first was Martov's growing weariness of Lenin's accusations and
intrigues, and of the necessity of responding to them. Concerning the effects
of this factor on his psychological state, Martov commented in a letter to
Kristi, dated June 8, 1916, that "the unsavory events which infuse political life
from day-to-day ravage and embitter the soul. . . . These various political
polemics and intrigues cause me to break out in anger, and indeed to become enraged, whenever I am compelled to discuss them."[20]

In response to a letter from Kristi, in June 1916, in which she counseled
him, probably in response to the sense of depression he had expressed, to
turn away from party politics, Martov wrote that while he was currently
drawing great pleasure from reading Stendhal (and preferred him to
Balzac), he did not feel in a position to turn completely away from party

politics. After all, he noted, "the time is fast approaching when even individuals who by nature might prefer to be retiring scholars [*kabinetni*] have to plunge into the thick of political life. Besides, my feelings of accountability for my country and humanity as a whole make it psychologically impossible for me to follow your counsel. [Furthermore,] while it goes without saying that I share your antipathy for politics, [I do not consider that it] corrupts people any more than any other occupations, including those of artists and scientists."[21]

The other factor contributing to Martov's growing depression during these months was his yearning to go back to Russia, and the feeling that he would have to remain in Switzerland for a long time. It appeared to him that even after the conclusion of the war, a still dominant political reaction would seek to bar his return home because of the political stance that he had assumed during his stay in Switzerland.[22]

The evolution of Lenin's mood and political views in the aftermath of the Zimmerwald and Kienthal conferences is easier to follow from day-to-day from the writings assembled in his Collected Works. These reflect none of the doubts and psychological conflicts which plagued Martov. Lenin completed an extraordinary volume of theoretical writing between the conclusion of the Zimmerwald Conference in 1915 and the outbreak of the February revolution, the significance of which has often been overlooked or even cavalierly dismissed especially by recent commentators. Even more striking was the wide range of topics that Lenin addressed in this period, as well as the ambitiousness of the objectives he sought with these writings to achieve.

Readers may draw a sense of the range of Lenin's theoretical interests, as well as of his extraordinary industry in pursuit of them, from the fact that during these months he managed to complete a full study of the development of American agriculture after the emancipation of the slaves, drawing on a variety of American official sources, such as the reports of the Census Bureau and various publications of the Department of Agriculture. Lenin sought thereby to provide a solid scholarly basis for his conception of an "American path" to be achieved in the further development of Russian agriculture through the nationalization of the land (and its distribution to the peasants who cultivated it), which he had already compared in 1906 in its potential effects in Russia to those of the passage of the Homestead Act in the United States. From a political standpoint, however, the most important of the works that he completed during this period was clearly the study entitled, "Imperialism as the Highest Stage of Capitalism," which he wrote during the first six months of 1916 (although he did not succeed in publishing a Russian-language edition until 1917).[23]

In his foreword to the various editions of this work, Lenin emphasized the debt that he owed to the English scholar John H. Hobson for his study of the character of imperialism, which he noted had not received the attention that it deserved. Lenin's major debt to Hobson lay in the breadth of his analysis of the *internal* transformations that the economies of the major capitalist countries had undergone since the opening of the era of imperialism.[24] This was the thrust of Lenin's analysis. He sought to demonstrate, step-by-step, the processes of *internal transformation* that the more advanced capitalist countries had undergone as the result of the growing concentration of industrial production in large enterprises. This process had involved an even more disproportionate concentration of the steam and electrical power available in industry as a whole, for which Lenin provided statistical data to illustrate his thesis (e.g., he noted, consistently citing official sources, that in Germany, for example, large enterprises employing less than one percent of the total number of industrial workers were responsible for 39 percent of the steam power and 70 percent of the electrical power used in Germany as a whole, while the corresponding figures for the United States were even higher). Lenin then argued that the concentration of production, and even more substantially of steam and electric power, in this new stage of the development of capitalism, had laid the ground for the emergence of monopolies and oligopolies, as well as for an additional phenomenon: the concentration of production in large enterprises, which was also characteristic of the development of capitalism in this last stage of its development.

The economic crisis that Europe had undergone after the turn of the century had accelerated these processes of change, as cartels sought to control production in an effort to control the prices at which industrial products were sold. This crisis had also contributed to another aspect of the evolution of industry, especially in advanced capitalist countries: the growing financial control that commercial banks had assumed over industrial development through the conditions they set for the extension of financial credits. Last but not least was the control that banks in advanced capitalist countries had come to exercise over industrial development in less advanced countries through the growing share that they had assumed of their financial capital. The evidence that Lenin provided for each of the steps were drawn from official sources, and provided a seemingly indisputable demonstration of the accuracy of his thesis.

The conclusions that Lenin drew from his analysis (many of which, to this day, are shared by students of Russia's industrial development during this period) were particularly pleasing to Marxist readers, since they suggested that, notwithstanding the "order" that the various aspects that the development of imperialism had introduced in advanced capitalist countries, it had in fact contributed to the aggravation of the contradictions in the development of capitalism that would lead to its eventual demise. These conflicting and contradictory features did not stem merely from the uneven results of the process of colonial expansion of the capitalist powers, which Lenin had noted earlier, nor even from the more significant degree of economic exploitation that more advanced capitalist countries had come to exercise on less advanced countries. The broader and more fundamental problem lay, Lenin emphasized, in the contradictions between the more advanced and less advanced sectors of industrial development—even in advanced capitalist countries—and the precariousness of the economic situations in which the less advanced sectors found themselves as a result. Thus, notwithstanding the process of "*embourgeoisement*" that industrial workers of the most advanced capitalist countries had undergone as a result of the benefits they had drawn from their countries' exploitations of the workers of less advanced countries (including those of the colonies they had acquired), these contradictions of capitalism during the era of imperialism would contribute to its eventual demise.

Finally, Lenin stated in passing that the various aspects of the "generalization" of the character and organization of production that capitalism had undergone during the era of imperialism were also contributing to the creation of the objective conditions for the achievement of socialism. Presumably, Lenin did not chose to emphasize this point at this moment since it might have raised doubts about the thesis that he also advanced to the effect that the international civil war, which would lead to the overthrow of capitalism throughout the world, would be launched in Russia, the weakest link in the development of capitalism among the countries participating in the First World War.[25]

Thus, contrary to the opinion expressed by some commentators, Lenin did not significantly revise during these months the views on the process of world revolution that he had articulated at Zimmerwald and Kienthal. He continued to believe that the World War could be brought to an end only through the overthrow of imperialism, the last phase in the development of capitalism.[26]

VI

As soon as they received the news of the outbreak of the February revolution in Russia, Russia's political émigrés in Switzerland were understandably eager to return to Russia as quickly as possible. Through the intermediary of the Swiss and German Social Democrats, they were issued the invitation by the German government to travel through German territory by sealed train. In the discussions and public debates about this offer, which were attended by Russia's political émigrés in Switzerland, Lenin supported its acceptance unhesitatingly so that Russia's political émigrés could participate without delay in the further unfolding of the revolution. As soon as he was able to do so, he acted accordingly.

Martov was reluctant to do so, however, not because of the streak of "petty bourgeois morality" of which Lenin irately accused him in these debates, but because of his fear of the disastrous impression that the acceptance of the offer of the German government might produce on public opinion in Russia, even among members of the socialist parties. For this reason, Martov looked for more palatable alternatives. He tried to mobilize the Provisional Government, through the pressure of the Petrograd Soviet, to induce the British government to allow Russia's political émigrés to transit to Russia by sea, through Scandinavia. Upon failing in this attempt, he sought, equally vainly, to induce the Provisional Government, again through pressure from the Soviet, to offer in exchange for the return of Russia's political émigrés through German territory, the release of an equal number of German prisoners-of-war. And it was only after the failure of these additional efforts that he finally felt compelled to accept, without any modification, the German government's proposal.

Before setting off on his journey, Martov exchanged two significant letters with Kristi in which he outlined the principles that he intended to guide his political course upon his return to Russia:

> The events that we are witnessing brilliantly confirm the thesis that we advanced in 1905 against Lenin and Trotsky to the effect that a radical bourgeois revolution can unfold, even while the proletariat leaves the bourgeoisie in power, but is pushing it continuously forward through the exercise of its pressure and control. So long as events follow this course, the interest of the revolution and those of the working class would both benefit from the continuation of such

a state of affairs: those of the revolution because the elimination of the old order achieved most easily and fully through the combination of such joint efforts on the part of all classes of society, would enable the working class to organize itself to an unprecedented degree, to gain a colossal influence in the country as a whole, while pushing the government further and further to the left, even while refraining from becoming involved with it in any way. Even when the existing government no longer allows itself to be pushed any further, it can be replaced by another, more progressive, bourgeois government or by a coalition of the Kadets and the *Trudoviki*, or some other "social patriots." Only when the bourgeoisie and all of its fellow travelers have moved as far as they will go, even under the pressure of the proletariat, will Russia's workers have to accept the necessity of assuming the role of an opposition, since they constitute a minority of the population, while preparing their forces for the next revolution, which will see the overthrow of the bourgeoisie as a whole.[27]

By advancing the notion of a labor government in place of the existing one, the Leninists were seeking to overthrow it even before it managed to complete tasks which it was quite capable of performing (e.g., equal rights for minorities, agrarian and military reforms, etc). Thereby, they would deprive the proletariat of its current advantageous situation of being able to move the revolution forward, even while remaining out of the government, and in this way maintaining the most advantageous conditions for the growth of the strength and influence of the proletariat.

Upon receiving Kristi's answer to this letter, Martov, still in exile, wrote to her again on April 7 (20), 1917, elaborating, in response to her evident objections, his argument in support of the course that he would in fact pursue up to the July Days of 1917, once he returned to Russia.

There is a grain of truth in what you write about the seizure of power, but only a grain of truth. It is true that every party must seek to gain power. At issue, however, is under what conditions it should seek to attain it. At this stage of the revolution, the proletariat could come to power only with the support of the peasantry and the peasant soldiers, who are guided by other interests and expectations than the proletariat: the pursuit of the war to victorious conclusion;

the elimination of poverty in the countryside, even while preserving the peasants' existing small allotments of land, etc.

Under such circumstances, to seek power with the aid of the peasants would only contribute to confusing the revolutionary consciousness of the proletariat by infusing it with the peasants' illusions about the effectiveness of a peasant "bunt'," while contributing at the same time to the eventual disillusionment of the peasantry.

The workers should recognize that they are a minority of the population, and consequently seek to influence the course of the revolution, as they are now doing, through pressure from the outside, by the Soviet of Workers' Deputies on the Kadet party, but also on the peasantry, until the peasants mature to the point when their own party takes power from the Kadet party.[28]

VII

In contrast to Martov's cautious approach to the role workers should now play in Russia's revolutionary regime, the speech that Lenin delivered upon his arrival at the Finland Station on the evening of April 3 boldly addressed the issue of power by calling for "All Power to the Soviets."

Sukhanov has left us an amusing description of the shock that Lenin's statement produced among members of the Bolsheviks' Petrograd Party Committee who had come to greet him (no less than on Chkheidze, who welcomed him in his official capacity of chairman of the Menshevik-led Petrograd Soviet of Workers' and Soldiers' Deputies). Lenin was well aware of the reaction that he had evoked among his followers, who in the wake of his address sought to take him as quickly as possible to the Bolshevik headquarters at the Kshesinskaia Palace, there to enlighten him about the political situation in the capital and in the country at large of which they perceived him to be entirely unaware. But Lenin deliberately lingered behind them, engaging in an animated conversation with Nikolai Sukhanov (who had also been at the station in his capacity as a journalist and had introduced himself to Lenin), over the articles that Sukhanov had published after the outbreak of the war in Gorky's journal, *Letopisi*. Lenin criticized them vigorously for the neopopulist views they expressed on the land question. With Lenin's help, Sukhanov stuck to the group's heels until they were finally able to get rid of him upon their arrival at the Kshesinskaia Palace.

Moreover, on April 4, the day following his arrival, Lenin delivered, on the basis of notes that he had hastily prepared on his train trip from Helsinki to Petrograd, a version of what came to be known as his April Theses. He read these Theses twice that day at the Tauride Palace: the first time, at a meeting of members of the Bolshevik party; the second, at a joint meeting of the Bolshevik and Menshevik delegates to the All-Russia Conference of Workers' and Soldiers' Deputies.

Since most of the readers of this volume are likely to be familiar with the thrust of Lenin's April Theses, I will confine myself to observations about the emphases that distinguished Lenin's discussion of them. The full text is in the appendix.[29] The first of these concerns Lenin's statement to the effect that the distinguishing feature of the political situation in Russia at this moment is the fact that it constitutes a period of *transition* from the first stage of the revolution, which has given power to the bourgeoisie because of the inadequate degree of consciousness and organization of the proletariat, to the second stage of the revolution which will culminate in the transfer of power to Russia's proletariat and the poorest strata of the peasantry. This statement repeated, in a slightly different tone, the remark that Lenin had made in one of his "Letters from Afar" to the effect that, notwithstanding the bourgeois character of the Provisional Government, *power* really lay from the outset of the revolution in the hands of the Petrograd Soviet, which had conceded this power, *of its own will*, to the bourgeoisie.[30]

To be sure, Lenin recognized that the Bolshevik party constituted at that moment but a small minority, even in most of the Soviets of Workers' Deputies, a fact which he attributed to the influence exercised in the soviets by petty bourgeois elements, themselves under the influence of Russia's big bourgeoisie. Under the circumstances, the Bolsheviks should exploit the unprecedented degree of political freedom afforded to them by the existing equilibrium of forces to conduct patient, systematic work to explain, first and foremost to the proletariat, but also to the poorest peasants (*batraki*), that the Soviets of Workers' Deputies, along with the soviets of *batraki* that should be created in the countryside, were the only reliable forms of revolutionary government.

Thus, the special emphasis on the role to be played by the poorest peasants, and on the need to organize them in separate soviets from other peasants, already appeared in Lenin's April Theses, as did his reference to them as *batraki*. Lenin used this term to designate those peasants *who did not possess any land*, and drew their livelihood *exclusively* from the compensation that they received, whether in money or in kind, for the work they performed on the land possessed by other peasants.

Lenin's repeated insistence on the need to focus the major emphasis of the Bolsheviks' agrarian program on the organization of soviets of these *batraki*, separately from the Soviets of the Peasants as a whole, clearly suggested that he already viewed these poorest peasants (along with hired agricultural workers) as the only reliable allies of the proletariat in the countryside.

Also worthy of note was the assertion in the eighth of Lenin's April Theses that the task of the Bolshevik party *was not* to introduce socialism immediately but *to take intermediary steps toward* this goal, such as the transfer to the soviets of control over the production and distribution of consumer goods in the countryside.

Finally, we should take note of the significance that Lenin assigned in his list of the party's immediate tasks to renaming the Bolshevik party as the Communist party (on the model of the Paris Commune), as well as to the creation of a new Communist International, cleansed not only of the stigma of "social chauvinism," but also of those elements in international Social Democracy that were wavering between chauvinist and internationalist sentiments. Among these, Lenin included Chkheidze, currently the chairman of the Petrograd Soviet, as well as Kautsky.

Lenin had already presented certain of these points in his *Pis'ma o taktike*, of which he actually succeeded in publishing only the first, entitled, "*Otsenka momenty*," in time to submit it for discussion at the April Conference of the Bolshevik party. This document was especially interesting, however, because it spelled out Lenin's remarks about the differences of views that had arisen between him and Kamenev, when he had originally presented his April Theses. To this purpose, Lenin quoted a note that Kamenev, who was then serving as the editor of *Pravda*, had published in it, immediately following Lenin's return, expressing disagreement with his April Theses. This note had read in part: "therefore, c. Lenin's scheme appears to me unacceptable, since it rests on the thesis that the bourgeois revolution has already been *completed*, and is destined to turn *immediately* into a socialist revolution [my emphasis, L.H.]." "In this statement, Kamenev committed two major errors," Lenin observed:

> The first is that he oversimplified the issue of the completion of a "bourgeois revolution," when in fact we are dealing with a more complex reality, for on one hand, we have witnessed the completion

of a bourgeois revolution, which has brought the bourgeoisie to power; but on the other hand, the emergence of a revolutionary dictatorship of the proletariat and the peasantry, *which has conceded power to the bourgeoisie of its own will*, and thereby tied itself up to a bourgeois government. [My emphasis, L.H.]

Thus, Kamenev's formula to the effect that a bourgeois democratic government is now taking place, is out of date [since it has been completed already].

The second issue is a practical one. Whether a dictatorship of the proletariat can now be achieved is impossible to predict. What can be predicted, however, is that the only way to achieve it is to separate decisively the communist elements of the proletariat from the petty bourgeois ones. Only the consolidation of a proletarian communist party, free of the influence of the petty bourgeoisie, can heat the ground under the feet of the petty bourgeoisie sufficiently to compel it under certain conditions to take power. Indeed, it is not to be excluded that under certain conditions Guchkov and Milukov would favor the assumption of the full prerequisites of power ["*edinovlastie*"] by Chkheidze, Tsereteli, the SRs, Steklov, and co., because after all, all of them are Defensists.

C. Kamenev's error is that he considers the [issue of the] revolutionary dictatorship of the proletariat and peasantry in the [perspective of] the past, whereas a future has already opened in which the interests of the workers and property owners diverge on such a crucial issue as "Defensism"—i.e., on the position to be assumed toward the imperialist war.

"And here, I come to the second error in c. Kamenev's reasoning," Lenin continued:

He alleges that my scheme envisages the immediate transformation [of the bourgeois democratic] revolution into a socialist one. This is inaccurate. I specifically stated in my eighth thesis that our immediate task is *not* to introduce socialism. . . . I even stated that a state power on the model of the Paris Commune cannot be introduced until the majority of the deputies in "all," or at least "most," of the soviets have become persuaded of the harmfulness of the political course of the SRs, the Chkheidzes, the Tseretelis, the Steklovs, and co. And this can be achieved only through the patient work of enlightening members of the soviets.

Furthermore, and this was another major error on Kamenev's part, he failed to recognize that just as was the case with the Paris Commune, a new type of state power has emerged in Russia, with the Soviets of Workers' and Soldiers' Deputies. Instead of taking account of the significance of the soviets, and of their superiority over a parliamentary republic, he raised the dead academic issue of whether an immediate transformation is possible.

I am deeply convinced that the Soviets of Workers' and Soldiers' Deputies will help the masses of people to grow to independent existence, and help them *to take steps forward* [on the road] to socialism [my emphasis, L. H.].[31]

With this rebuttal of Kamenev's critique, Lenin now felt well prepared to respond to any criticism that might come his way at the Bolsheviks' Petrograd Conference, which was to open on April 14, as well as at the party's All-Russian Conference, scheduled to open some ten days later. At the Petrograd Conference, Lenin continued to hammer away at the criticism that Kamenev had directed against his April Theses for abandoning the advocacy of a dictatorship of the proletariat and peasantry as the next stage of the revolution. On this occasion, however, Lenin focused greater attention on the petty bourgeoisie's support of "Defensism" which demonstrated that it had parted ways with the proletariat and joined forces with the big bourgeoisie on this most fundamental issue.[32]

Because of the peasants' support of the war, Lenin argued, even the big bourgeoisie could now make its peace with the peasants' demand for the nationalization of the land. Under those circumstances, it was all the more important for the proletariat to focus its efforts in the countryside on winning the support of the poorer peasants and agricultural workers.

An additional indication of the paramount importance that Lenin assigned to the issue of the war *in his approach to all major problems* appeared in the resolution that he submitted on the attitude that the Bolsheviks should assume toward the PSR, the Mensheviks, and related political currents. Predictably, this text emphasized that any positive attitude on the part of the Bolsheviks toward Revolutionary Defensism as well as Defensism was out of the question. However, Lenin added, in an open invitation to Martov's followers, if not to Martov himself:

As for local groups of workers associated with the Mensheviks, but supporting an internationalist rather than a "defensist" position, our party favors a rapprochement with these groups, and indeed unification with them, on the condition that they break unconditionally with the petty bourgeois traitors to socialism.[33]

Finally, the resolution that Lenin submitted on relations with the Provisional Government reemphasized the need to conduct long and patient work to enlighten the proletariat of city and country, and to strengthen the organization of the internationalist elements in the soviets and other organs of the people's will "to ensure that the new revolutionary wave would unfold under the flag of revolutionary Social Democracy."[34]

VIII

The resolution adopted at the Bolsheviks' Petrograd City Conference on relations with the Provisional Government also provided the platform that Lenin submitted on this issue at the party's All-Russian Conference, which opened on April 24. Indeed, Lenin had originally intended to confine himself on this occasion simply to the delivery of that resolution, but was compelled to amplify his remarks because of questions from the floor concerning a variant—differing on certain major points from his text—that had been endorsed by the Moscow Party Committee.

Lenin's comments on the Moscow text articulated his differences with Kamenev even more sharply:

To state, as does the resolution adopted by the Moscovites, that the Provisional Government is counter-revolutionary because the bourgeois phase of the revolution is already completed is incorrect, while it would be premature to refer to the establishment of a dictatorship of the proletariat and the peasantry, since the peasantry has adopted a Defensist position, and concluded a whole series of agreements with the Kadets. . . .

We would like the peasants to go further than the bourgeoisie and to seize the land of the *pomeshchiki*. But at this moment, we cannot say anything conclusive about [the peasants'] future conduct. . . .

We therefore carefully omit phrases like "revolutionary democracy," because the use of such expressions at this moment is extremely deceptive. . . . Our task is to enlighten those who now stand at the tail of the bourgeoisie.

The Moscovites added the word "control" [over the Provisional Government] to the third point of the resolution. But one must hold power in order to control. . . . Otherwise, this expression is an empty charade.[35]

Rebutting Kamenev's critique in his concluding comments, Lenin further re-emphasized:

It would be insane to introduce socialism at this point, but *the soviets can take the first steps toward the introduction of socialism* [my emphasis, L.H.]. The first of these steps would be the nationalization of the land, which, although favored by most of the people, can only be carried out by the soviets. Similarly, banks can be established in every village to finance improvements in agriculture. . . . The syndicates of sugar producers could be nationalized and so on.

Rykov [a prominent member of the Moscow Party Committee] argues that socialism must first be achieved in the more developed countries. *But no one can say who will start and who will finish* [my emphasis, L.H.]. Rykov also said that there will not be any transitional period between capitalism and socialism. This is also untrue.[36]

This was the most forceful and optimistic statement that Lenin had yet issued about the role that the Russian revolution could play in the struggle for socialism. Its optimism rested first and foremost on Lenin's confidence in the ability of Russia's urban proletariat to draw to its side the rural proletariat and semi-proletariat in the unfolding of the Russian revolution.

For this reason, while struggling with all its might for the complete confiscation of all gentry land and its immediate transfer to the peasantry, it is imperative to undertake immediately, everywhere, the organization of the agricultural proletariat in the form of separate soviets of agricultural workers and semi-proletarian peasants, as well as the independent organization of these groups in all existing soviets of peasant deputies and other organs of local self-administration.[37]

The concluding resolution that Lenin presented at this conference reemphasized these points, arguing that while the Russian proletariat, living in one of the most backward countries of Europe largely inhabited by small peasants, could not assign to itself the task of achieving socialism immediately, it would be the greatest error not to advocate *a series of practical measures to open the way to socialism* [my emphasis, L. H.].

> Foremost among these is the nationalization of the land, which would constitute a major blow against private ownership of the means of production, as well as strengthen the influence of the socialist proletariat and semi-proletariat in the countryside.
> The second [such measure] would be the establishment of state control over all banks and their consolidation into a single banking system, as well as the establishment of state control over the largest capitalist syndicates, such as the syndicate controlling the production and distribution of sugar.[38]

Lenin once again reiterated in his concluding statement the caution that these measures should be carried out with great care, winning prior support for them among the vast majority of the population, by making it clear to them that these measures would enable them to gain control over their own lives in place of the control held over them by the bureaucratic state.

In addition to the sharpness of these statements, Lenin's presentation to the April Conference of the Bolshevik party provides a striking example of the ways in which, even in such formal settings, he occasionally "thought out loud" in discussing Russia's revolutionary processes. In the course of the discussion of the soviets, for example, he observed that, whereas in the capital and other major cities the soviets had effectively surrendered their power to the bourgeoisie as a result of the process of bureaucratization that the revolutionary movement had undergone, due to the power of the big bourgeoisie and the influence of petty bourgeois elements in its midst as well as of the unpreparedness of the proletariat to assume responsibilities on a state-wide basis (actually Lenin appeared uncertain at this point how to explain this phenomenon), a contrary process was taking place in the localities, as the soviets were extending their influence in local towns and villages. Consequently, it was in the localities that it was now possible to move the revolution forward, and indeed to achieve "All Power to the Soviets," by drawing on the revolutionary energy of the workers and peasants to carry out such measures as soviet control over the production and distribution of commodities.

As was typical of him when he "thought out loud" and his ideas flowed so quickly as to appear to be running away from him, Lenin sought to contain them by numbering them (or on other occasions bracketing them, as well):

> Conclusion: a) 1. Prepare for new revolution; b) 2. Move revolution *forward* in the localities (*vlast'*?, land?, factories?); c) 3. In the localities, establish communes; c) 4. Without police, without bureaucracy, All Power to the armed worker and peasant masses; d) 4. Struggle against all *chinovniki* and petty bourgeois elements; d) 5. Accumulate experience in the localities to *push the center forward;* the *localities* become the model; e) 6. Explain to the masses of workers, peasants, and soldiers that the cause of the success of the revolution in the localities *is* the *edinovlastie* [monopoly of power] and dictatorship of the proletariat; f) 7. Of course, in the center, it is more *difficult,* more time is needed; g) 8. Develop the revolution forward in *communes,* in the neighborhoods of large cities; g) 9. While in the capitals, the proletariat has been transformed into a further servant of the bourgeoisie.[39]

One of the major advantages involved in the more rapid spread of soviet power in the localities, Lenin now clearly felt, was that it was there that the process of nationalization of the land was to be carried out. This process would necessarily inflict a major blow against the principle of private property on which capitalism rested. And the effects of this process would be accentuated by such measures as the establishment of state control over capitalist syndicates (such as the syndicate controlling the production and distribution of sugar), the introduction of progressive taxation, and other measures to improve the lot, and by the same token win over the support, of the peasantry. All of these measures could be undertaken by the local soviets, as organs of revolutionary power, and while not constituting the immediate introduction of socialism, their undertaking would signal that in the localities, at least, Russia was taking a major step forward on the road to socialism.

Lenin's concluding statement at the Bolshevik April Conference was delivered in the context of the crisis set off by the leaking of Milukov's note to the Allied Powers, seeking to reassure them that Russia would remain faithful to its commitments.

> But Russia's soldiers do not want a continuation of the war. They are profoundly aware that the war is being waged in the interest of the capitalists. . . . Besides, the signs of an economic crash, famine, and economic disintegration, are looming in Russia as in other belligerent countries. . . . Russia is undergoing a situation of unprecedented difficulty. There is one and only one way out. The transfer of all state power, from top to bottom, into the hands of the soviets of workers, soldiers, peasants, and other deputies in all of Russia. Only if power is transferred to the working class with the support of the majority of the peasantry can one expect a potent revolution to break out in Western Europe, which will destroy the yoke of capitalism and bring the war to an end . . . The war has brought all of humanity to the edge of extinction. The capitalists are incapable of finding a way out of it. Only the workers, with the aid of the poorest peasants, are capable of finding a way out. But this will require not only heroism, but also organization, organization, and more organization on their part.

The resolutions of the party conference had clarified the position and distribution of forces of the various classes. Now the time had come to organize.

> Comrade workers! We call on you to work untiringly to unite and consolidate the revolutionary proletariat of all countries. This is the only way leading to the salvation of humanity from the horrors of the war and from the yoke of capital.[40]

Never before had Lenin laid the achievement of these tasks on the shoulders of Russia's workers and poorest peasants. And this, in essence, was the appeal that Lenin intended to issue to the delegates at the First Congress of Soviets, which was to assemble in June 1917, and which he now expected would resonate among them, notwithstanding the platforms espoused by their leaders in the Menshevik party and the PSR. The formation in early May of a coalition government, including in its ranks representatives of the Menshevik party and the PSR, only strengthened Lenin's determination in this regard, since it constituted in his view a glaring confirmation of his thesis that the Petrograd Soviet had surrendered its dominant power in the capital into the hands of the bourgeoisie.

IX

Because of the delay that he had incurred in his vain search for more palatable alternatives to an unconditional acceptance of the commission granted by the German authorities for the return of Russia's political émigrés by sealed train through German territory, Martov arrived in Petrograd only on May 9, more than two weeks after Lenin's return. This turned out to be a fateful delay. It profoundly affected Martov's relations with his old party comrades, and the spirit in which he had to pursue his political journey through the remaining course of the revolution.

Immediately upon the completion of the welcoming ceremonies that greeted his own arrival at the Finland Station, including Chkheidze's speech as Chairman of the Petrograd Soviet, Martov was told by the comrades who had come to meet him that on the very eve of his arrival, the majority of the delegates assembled at the opening session of the All-Russian Conference of the Menshevik party had voted (in accordance with the calendar set by the party leadership) in favor of the formation of a coalition government with the participation of Menshevik representatives.

The existence of support in the ranks of the Menshevik party for the formation of such a coalition government hardly came as a total surprise to Martov, since on the eve of boarding the train for his return to Russia, he had sent a telegram from Zurich expressing his categorical opposition to such a step.[41] Indeed, the text of this telegram had been read to the delegates, who were closely divided on this issue, on May 2, 1917, and following a heated debate, they had rejected Menshevik participation in a coalition government by a vote of 59 against, 55 for, with 2 abstentions.

In the light of this fact, it seems evident that the genuine sense of shock that Martov experienced upon being told of the resolution passed by the majority of the delegates attending the Menshevik conference, on the day before his expected arrival, probably stemmed even more from the timing than from the substance of this decision: i.e., from the fact that the vote on this decision had been scheduled by the party leadership (which controlled the agenda of the conference) in a way that effectively foreclosed any possibility of his own participation in the debate on this crucial issue.

Thus, with a sense of shock compounded by the fatigue accumulated from his journey to the capital without allowing himself a minute's rest, Martov and the comrades who had accompanied him headed for Smolny, where the Menshevik party's conference was being held. By the time of his arrival in the late afternoon, the delegates were already debating the second item on the agenda: the issue of the war.

Upon the appearance in the conference hall of the new arrivals who included besides Martov his fellow Menshevik Internationalists, A.S. Martynov and Kh. G. Rakovskii, and the revered Pavel Borisovich Akselrod (as well as the Swiss Social Democrat, Robert Grimm, who had negotiated the arrangements for their return), they were greeted by prolonged applause, unanimously elected honorary chairmen of the conference, and invited to address the delegates. Both Martov and Martynov immediately seized this occasion to denounce the decision the day before.

It is unlikely that whatever Martov might have said on this occasion could have shaken the bloc of provincial delegates and delegates from the front who had voted massively in support of coalition. For independently of the circumstances of the political crisis that had precipitated it, the formation of such a coalition government represented, in the view of these delegates, the recognition of an already established fact: that it was a coalition of socialists and nonsocialist representatives of the democratic intelligentsia who had taken charge of the administration of the cities and towns of provincial Russia, as well as of the army organizations that sustained through their political leadership the morale of the soldiers at the front.

However, what both Martov and Martynov failed to accomplish was to provide to the assembled delegates an adequate explanation for their appalled reaction to the decision the conference had made, and indeed to account in any way that these delegates could really understand the significance that they assigned to the issues at stake. Instead, most of the remarks that Martov delivered on this occasion sounded like (and probably constituted) a continuation of the oral argument that he had launched with the party leaders who had greeted him after his arrival at the Finland Station, when they had sought to explain to him the considerations that had induced them to support the formation of a coalition government.

By the same token, Martov's statement strongly emphasized that he had been totally unimpressed by the basic argument advanced by his colleagues. In response to Prince L'vov's ultimatum that the members of the Provisional Government would resign unless they were joined by representatives of the socialist parties in the formation of a coalition government, the Menshevik party's representatives should have let the Kadets and their allies assume responsibility of forming a new Provisional Government. Instead, in exchange for the meager share of political power that the one seat (out of eight) assigned to them in the new coalition government afforded them, the Mensheviks had surrendered their ability to control the policies of the Provisional Government which the system of Dual Power had afforded them. Admittedly, the leaders of the party had been faced with a critical situation, but the choice that they had made in seeking to find a way out of it had been worse than a crime; it had amounted to political idiocy.[42]

Curiously absent in Martov's remarks on this occasion was any reference to the major argument that he had presented with such effectiveness at the Zimmerwald Conference. This argument, it will be recalled, was that because of the impeccable record of opposition to Russia's war effort that the RSDRP had displayed, beginning in the summer of 1915 when the State Duma had convened, when the deputies representing the Menshevik party and the *Trudoviki* had voted against war credits (the Bolshevik deputies having been deported to Siberia shortly after the outbreak of the war), Russia's Social Democrats had been in an ideal position to press the socialist parties of all other belligerent countries to follow their example by repudiating any form of support for the war effort. This was the opportunity that the Menshevik party had largely, if not entirely, dissipated by joining in the formation of a coalition government.

Martov and his fellow Internationalists would not find a new opportunity to provide this clarification about the character and sources of their basic conflict with the supporters of coalition in the Menshevik party until later in the spring of 1917, when after overcoming great financial difficulties to do so, they managed to launch an organ of their own, *Letuchii Listok Men'-shevikov Internationalistov*, to spell out their platform and its underlying rationale. (The Menshevik party's official organ, *Rabochaia Gazeta*, edited by Martov's brother-in-law, Fedor Dan, advocated the views of the party's majority of Revolutionary Defensists.)

In a letter to Kristi, dated May 22, Martov commented on the difficulties he had had to overcome to finance the publication of the new journal. But as this was his first opportunity to transmit a letter to her since his arrival in Petrograd, he sought to record for her his most important impressions. Significantly, Martov noted that only Chernov had come to meet him at the Finland Station, although Tsereteli, Skobelev, and Gvozdev had visited him at the Tsederbaums' apartment shortly thereafter. Martov continued:

A brief exchange of views confirmed the impression that we had already drawn in Switzerland that something irreparable had occurred: that those in our midst who, since the outbreak of the revolution had deviated from the Zimmerwald line by calling for "the defense of the revolution" and for "remaining faithful to the Allies," had committed the ultimate idiocy of joining the government, merely on the basis of a promise to call on the Allies to "review the aims of the war," rather than of a clear-cut agreement to call for an immediate peace.[43]

When Martov and his fellow Internationalists had appeared at the All-Russian Menshevik Conference, they had been greeted with enthusiasm, but as Martov's letter to Kristi continues, the mood of the delegates—especially that of the mass of the provincial ones, who were convinced that only by joining a coalition government could a civil war be avoided—had drastically changed, as soon as they discovered that Martov was opposed to their views. Thus, by the next day, Martov had already been greeted by shouts of "*Doloi!*"

One would assume that Martov spelled out more clearly in his discussions with his former comrades, who had now assumed the leadership of the new party majority, the reasons for his vehement opposition to the formation of a coalition government. In his letter to Kristi, however, Martov did not seek to recount, however briefly, any exchange of views that he might have had with the new party leaders on this crucial issue, while describing at length their efforts to conciliate him. He drew a sharp contrast, in this regard, between their behavior toward him and that of the majority of the rank-and-file delegates at the Menshevik Party Conference:

On the other hand, the leaders—all of them, my personal friends, and until then my fellow Internationalists—sought to reason with me, to persuade me that they remained Internationalists, and that I simply did not understand the situation.

They begged me to preserve the unity of our faction, to join the O.K. [Organizatsionnyi Komitet], as well as the editorial board of *Rabochaia Gazeta*. On the other hand, most of our Petrograd supporters demanded that we break immediately with the party, and join up with Lenin and Trotsky. . . .

We decided not to take either of these extreme courses of actions—not to carry out an immediate schism but to come out

openly against the course taken by the O.K. and to decline any official responsibilities, while making the Petersburg Committee (two-
thirds of whose members support us) our political base. . . .

The leaders of the majority, in turn, proposed to call another
conference in two months, at which all the issues at stake would be
brought up and reviewed anew. Evidently, at that conference a
raskol will take place, as the extreme right . . . are as irreconcilable
as we are. The only issue is whether Dan, Tsereteli and company, or
at least the masses supporting them, will go over to our side, or will
be drawn to the "social patriots." And that will depend a great deal
on the skill that [we manage to display]. Most of the workers who
support the Mensheviks are clearly drawn to our side, except for the
older and most influential ones. . . .

Overall, my general impression is not a cheerful one. It is that
the revolution, which began so brilliantly, is going down the drain,
because it cannot get anywhere if the war continues. The country is
in very bad shape (prices are incredibly high and rising, the ruble is
now no more than 25–30 kopeks, not more). The city is in an awful
state of neglect and the members of the population live in fear about
everything: civil war, famine, the millions of unemployed, etc.

If peace is not achieved very soon, a catastrophe is inevitable.[44]

In the first issue of the Internationalists' new journal, *Letuchii Listok*,
Martov and his collaborators explained far more lucidly and compellingly
than they had managed to do at the Menshevik Party Conference the reasons
for their vehement opposition to the decisions ratified by the majority of the
delegates to support the formation of a coalition government. The core of
the their argument was a restatement of the basic argument that Martov and
his allies had advanced at Zimmerwald about the leading role that the Russian revolution could play in the struggle for peace. The enthusiasm the outbreak of the Russian revolution had evoked among the peoples of other belligerent countries, Martov had argued at Zimmerwald, stemmed from the
Russian socialists' consistent record of opposition to Russia's participation
in the war, including the votes that their deputies had recorded against their
government's budgetary requests for military appropriations when the State
Duma had been called back into session in the summer of 1915. This had
been the source of the appeal by Russian socialists to socialists in other belligerent countries to follow their example. The decision of the Revolutionary Defensists to join in the formation of a coalition government with bour-

geois parties in support of Russia's war effort had crippled the effectiveness of this appeal in the struggle for peace.

In this first issue of *Letuchii Listok* Martov thus restated the argument he had previously advanced at Zimmerwald with a militancy that infused it with a new sense of immediacy and purpose, if not an entirely new logic. The sufferings and dislocations inflicted by the war on the peoples of all belligerent countries would lead to revolutionary upheavals, culminating in the establishment of a dictatorship of the proletariat and the transformation of the existing economic order. The outbreak of the Russian revolution had been the first manifestation of this process, and the dynamics that it had assumed could accelerate the mobilization of revolutionary forces in all civilized countries. But the opposite was also the case. The future of the Russian revolution would hinge on its liberation from its political dependency on the imperialism of Britain and France, as well as from the threat to its survival posed by the German imperialists.

Muted in the formulation of these propositions was the distinction that Martov had made at Zimmerwald, and consistently reiterated up to this moment, between the timing of the struggle for peace and the inception of the struggle to overthrow capitalism and to establish a socialist order. This shortening of the time perspective for the overthrow of capitalism in the various belligerent countries was coupled with—and indeed largely influenced by—a growing sense of alarm about the prospects of the Russian revolution. This stemmed in part from the immediate threat that the policy of "active defense" propounded by the Revolutionary Defensists would be translated momentarily into the launching of new offensive operations by the Russian army. At the most recent meeting of the Organizational Committee of the Menshevik party, which Martov had attended, a majority of its members had voted in support of such an offensive, and so had a majority of the Central Committee of the PSR. It was to be expected, therefore, that the majority of the delegates to the First Congress of Soviets, scheduled to convene in early June, would follow the example of their parties' leaderships.[45]

To restore the ability of the Russian revolution to provide an effective political and moral leadership in the struggle for peace, and to stake out their own claims in this regard, the Menshevik Internationalists also presented in this first issue of their new journal a platform resting on three major planks:

The first was a reassertion of the demand for the restoration of an "independent class line" in all organs of Russian Social Democracy, and for the strengthening of its ties with those socialist parties and factions which supported the Zimmerwald platform, to press forward toward the realization of the objective of achieving a democratic revolution in all belligerent countries.

To assist the mobilization of public opinion in the various belligerent countries against the war, the second plank called for the immediate conclusion of an armistice on all fronts, as the first step toward the achievement of a universal peace without annexations and indemnities.

Finally, the third plank advocated the formation of a new Socialist International, whose membership would be confined to those socialist parties and factions that were prepared to struggle for the immediate conclusion of an armistice among all belligerent countries. The conclusion of such an armistice was also to facilitate the mobilization of revolutionary pressures on the governments of the belligerent countries to bring the war to an end.

Notwithstanding the bravura that it sought to display, the new platform of the Menshevik Internationalists reflected, more than its authors would have been prepared to admit, an underlying pessimism about the prospects of the struggle for peace, at least in the near term. This pessimism stemmed in part from the expectation that the majority of the delegates to the First Congress of Soviets would vote in support of a new military offensive by the Russian army. Even more fundamental, however, was the realization that the majority of Russia's petty bourgeoisie, and in particular, the masses of the peasantry, were still animated by Defensist sentiments. As long as such sentiments prevailed among the vast majority of the Russian people, they would continue to present an insurmountable obstacle to the struggle for peace.[46]

Shortly after its opening session on June 3, the First Congress of Soviets did indeed endorse, by a substantial majority, the launching of a military offensive by the Russian army. This offensive began on June 18, on the Southwestern Front, and repeated a scenario that should have become familiar, given the unfolding of similar military operations from the summer of 1915 onward: following initial successes won against Austro-Hungarian troops (consisting largely of Czech soldiers sympathetic to the Russian cause), the Russian offensive turned into a rout after German troops were dispatched as reinforcements. Before this disastrous, if familiar, scenario began to unfold, however, the various factions of Russian Social Democracy (the Bolsheviks were still included under this label) had assembled for a two-day meeting to debate the issue of the war and the issue of power. On the first day, June 1, the speakers for the Menshevik Revolutionary Defensists (Dan and Liber), for the Menshevik Internationalists (Ermansky), and for the Bolsheviks (Trotsky) reiterated the official positions of their respective factions on the issue of the war and the struggle for peace. Martov did not intervene in this debate until the next day, which was devoted to the question of power. In his brief intervention, he sought to rebuff the positions articulated by the spokesmen for the Bolsheviks (Kamenev) and for the Menshevik Defensists (Voitinsky and Liber), by reiterating his own, now familiar, position that the Menshevik party should have left in place the system of "dual power," and not committed the sin of joining the coalition government:

> *Is it correct that the Socialists need a powerful government? No, we need an organized will, which would assist the development of the class definition of the proletariat* [my emphasis, L.H.] . . . In this regard, it was a fundamental error for Socialists to join in the formation of a coalition government. Power should have been left to the bourgeoisie, under the strictest control of the soviets. This was, and remains, the only correct position."[47]

Martov felt his moral authority grew steadily in the course of this meeting and the subsequent Congress of Soviets, as he noted with pride in a letter to Kristi on June 17. He had managed to retain a humane relationship with both the Revolutionary Defensists and the Bolsheviks, even while throwing darts at them. In this regard, he observed, he now occupied a very privileged position in the revolutionary camp, both sides listening attentively to his delivery of bitter truths which they would not have heeded from anyone else.[48]

In fact, Martov did manage to influence the decisions of the Congress in the course of its debates. For example, after the majority of the delegates had rejected his resolution that they now consider the State Duma as no longer existent (i.e., no longer a legitimate organ of government), and had greeted his coming to the platform to further discuss this issue with the outcry, "*Doloi!* We don't want to hear any more of this," they had finally voted in support of his proposal that the Social Democrats recall their representatives from the Provisional Committee of the State Duma, which still sought to play the role of a super government, because they could not reject this resolution without displaying a glaring contradiction between words and deeds. On the other side of the aisle, the Bolsheviks greeted the address that Martov delivered against Tsereteli with applause, Trotsky even rising from his seat and shouting, "Hail to Revolutionary Social Democrat, Martov!" As Martov wrote to Kristi, "This despite the fact that I continued to reject their slogan in favor of the transfer of the power to the soviets."[49]

Notwithstanding these notes of self-congratulation, Martov concluded his letter to Kristi in a more somber vein:

> We are driven by a sense of the extreme provisionalness of every-thing that is happening, including that of the revolution that we have experienced. Tomorrow, if not today, something new will emerge in Russia; either a sharp turn back, or a display of red terror by some regiment or other, which proclaims itself Bolshevik, while in fact be-ing animated by the state of mind of a *Pugachevshchina*. Every day during the past two weeks has been filled with rumors about upris-ings (*bunty*) of individual regiments and the preparation of new out-breaks. All this, while imperceptibly but inexorably a counter-revolution is being organized and mobilizing accordingly.[50]

X

Until he learned of the endorsement in mid-May by the leaders of the Men-shevik party and the PSR of the Provisional Government's decision to launch a military offensive (the first such offensive since the outbreak of the revolution), Lenin had planned to exploit the convocation of the First Con-gress of Soviets to issue an appeal calculated to win wide support among the masses of the population of rural as well as urban Russia. As we have seen, this was to involve a call on the soviets, as currently constituted, i.e., with their existing majorities of Revolutionary Defensists, to assume all the pre-rogatives and responsibilities of power.

The platform that Lenin elaborated in support of this appeal had essen-tially rested on a twofold argument. The first was that the experience of the exercise of soviet power would provide for the masses a valuable, indeed an indispensable, schooling in the exercise of democratic rule. As a result, even on the issue of the war, about which the soviets, just as the masses of the pet-ty bourgeoisie who had elected them, were likely to be dominated at first by Defensist majorities, they would have the opportunity to learn from the mis-takes they committed in their exercise of power. Besides, by the time of the completion of the first phase of the revolution (as Lenin defined it), the so-viets as currently constituted could be counted upon to achieve significant institutional changes, including the repartition of land among the stratum of the peasantry identified by Lenin as "middle peasants," i.e., peasants who cultivated the land they had acquired in private title in addition to the allotments they possessed as members of village communes.

This was the platform that Lenin had drawn up, and to which he had won over most of the members of his party since the issuance of his call for "All Power to the Soviets" upon his arrival at the Finland Station. It was also a platform that he calculated would appeal to considerable numbers of the members of the petty bourgeoisie of rural as well as urban Russia when he issued it over the heads of their would-be representatives at the First Congress of Soviets. However, this scenario lost its legitimacy in Lenin's eyes as soon as he learned that the Defensist majorities of the Organizational Committee of the Menshevik party and of the Central Committee of the PSR had approved the offensive—an approval which seemed to ensure that the Defensist majority of the delegates to the Congress would also endorse this decision.

This prospect consternated Lenin no less than it did Martov, notwithstanding the quite different strategies that they advocated in order to bring the war, and the reign of imperialism that had brought it about, to an end. For in Lenin's scenario, the soviets were assigned the crucial role of issuing a call to the masses of the peoples of all countries, beginning with those which were bled by the war, to join in the international civil war through which the rule of imperialism could be eradicated from the earth.

Obviously an endorsement by the First Congress of Soviets of the launching of a military offensive by Russia's armed forces would destroy its ability to play such a catalytic role in the unleashing of a world revolution, and indeed, in furthering the progress of Russia's own revolution. Did this suggest, by the same token, that the first phase of the revolution (as Lenin had hitherto defined it) had now come to an end, thus setting the stage for the second phase of the revolution, which was to culminate in the Bolshevik seizure of power?

This was the basic issue that Lenin had to address in his speech at First Congress of Soviets on June 4 which was to be devoted to a discussion of the political situation. The rambling character of the address that Lenin delivered on this occasion reflected his hesitations about the political strategy that he should adopt at this turning point of the Russian revolution. But notwithstanding its groping character, Lenin's speech already included motifs which clearly indicated how his thinking about the dynamics of the revolution and the strategy that the Bolshevik party should pursue as a result, had been affected by the pending military offensive.

Lenin opened on the already familiar note of a eulogy of the soviets as the type of revolutionary institution characteristic of periods of great revolutionary upsurges, such as had been the case of the Convention of 1792, and the Commune of 1871 in France, and the original emergence of the soviets during the Russian Revolution of 1905. In the Russia of 1917, however, such a revolutionary institution could not continue to co-exist side-by-side with a bourgeois government. Either the soviets would assume the full prerogatives of power, or they would be repressed by the counter-revolutionary generals who held Russia's armed forces under their control.

After uttering these prophetic words, Lenin addressed the statement of the "Minister of Posts and Telegraphs" (as he contemptuously referred to Tsereteli) to the effect that there was no political party in Russia prepared to assume the full responsibilities of power:

> I answer: Yes! Not a single party can turn them down, and our party does not turn them down. It is prepared at any moment to assume all power [applause, laughter]. You may laugh as much as you want, but the citizen [not the comrade] minister, who raises this issue before us would receive an identical answer from a right-wing party. Not a single party can turn this [responsibility] down and at a moment when freedom is still in existence, and the threat of arrest and deportation to Siberia remains only a threat, every party can and must say: Show us your confidence, and we will offer you our program.[51]

Following this ringing (and famous) statement, Lenin spelled out the program adopted by the Bolshevik party at its April Conference (including the imposition of controls on profits made on military production), as well as the proposal for workers' control over the enterprises in which they were employed, which had just been adopted by the First Conference on Workers' Control. Then came the phrase, "Arrest 50 or 100 of the biggest millionaires. It will be enough to hold them for a few weeks . . . to expose all the dirty deals which cost million of rubles to our people, profits which they will continue to make, as long as they remain in power."[52]

Preceding this phrase and the flood of revolutionary rhetoric that followed it (and probably ignored for this reason by most commentators), had been a crucial statement of Lenin's diagnosis of the dynamics of the revolutionary situation in Russia and his preview of things to come:

> To object that this would mean to establish socialism in Russia is empty rhetoric. . . . Pure capitalism turning into pure socialism does

not and cannot occur anywhere in the world in wartime. Best, something in between, something new, something unheard of—because hundreds of millions of people who have been drawn into this criminal war among the capitalists are dying.[53]

Only in the concluding part of his speech did Lenin provide a systematic statement of changes that had now taken place in his position about soviet power. He reminded his listeners that he had believed previously that the establishment of soviet power in Russia could be achieved through a peaceful revolution on the grounds that no group, no class, could successfully resist it, and that he had also believed that when, after the establishment of soviet power, revolutionary Russia appealed to the peoples of France and Germany to overthrow their governments and their capitalist class, the masses of the peoples of these two countries would respond in short order, because they were dying by the millions as the result of the war. However, the existing soviets could retain this ability to lead their revolutionary struggle for peace successfully only so long as a military offensive was not launched. An offensive would constitute a turning point in the entire course of the Russian revolution, a shift from the expectation and the preparation of a revolutionary uprising from below to a renewal of the war. Only if power was now taken by a revolutionary organization to lead the struggle against Russia's capitalists would the toilers of other countries believe in the appeal of revolutionary Russia to follow its example: "This is why we assign such fundamental importance to the announcement of an offensive. It will constitute a turning point, a fundamental break (*perelom*) in the history of the whole revolution, a breaking point of not only strategic, but also political, and economic significance."[54]

And then came the concluding statement which was as pithy and succinct as the discussion leading up to it had appeared long-winded:

> The transfer of power to the revolutionary proletariat with the support of the poorest peasants constitutes the transition to the revolutionary struggle for peace in the most objective, the most painless form known to mankind, the [most effective] transition to securing power and victory for the revolutionary workers in Russia and throughout the world. [Applause by part of the audience][55]

To anyone familiar with Lenin's terminology, this last paragraph suggested quite unambiguously the point that he had now reached in the evolution of his views about the dynamics of the Russian revolution. For the reference it made to the transfer of power to the proletariat with the support of the poorest peasants, as the most objective and effective way that was now open to pursue the revolutionary struggle for peace in Russia and throughout the world, clearly indicated that Lenin now considered that the first phase of the Russian revolution had now indeed passed, or more precisely had aborted, and that its second phase, which was to culminate in the Bolshevik seizure of power through an armed uprising, was now at hand.

XI

At first glance, this observation would appear to support the position that Tsereteli articulated in the debate that opened within the leadership of the Central Executive Committee of Soviets (TsIK), when it learned in the early morning of June 10 of the Bolsheviks' plan to conduct an armed demonstration in Petrograd. This report immediately induced the TsIK to issue a prohibition against all armed demonstrations, and after the adoption of this resolution, to issue a broader prohibition against the conduct of *any* demonstrations (including peaceful ones) while the Congress was in session, without the TsIK's express authorization.

Tsereteli found even this resolution inadequate. He believed the Bolsheviks' plan actually masked a plot to seize power. He therefore called on the presidium of the Congress to order that the workers and soldiers of the capital be disarmed, by force if necessary. On this issue, however, Dan, considering Tsereteli's proposal an unnecessary provocation, parted ways with him (for the first time since the inception of the revolution), and with the support of the representatives of army committees, succeeded in defeating Tsereteli's resolution by the slimmest margin of one vote.[56]

The story of the Bolsheviks' plans at the time of the First Congress of Soviets, and of Lenin's involvement in them, has been very ably recounted in Alexander Rabinowitch's monograph on the July Days, with which most of the readers of this study are likely to be acquainted.[57] I will confine myself therefore to an analysis of Rabinowitch's major points, with special emphasis on those that require, in my view, some additional observations and/or reservations about the conclusions that the author draws from them.

As Rabinowitch recounts, the idea of conducting an armed demonstration originally began to float in early May among soldiers of the Petrograd garrison in response to the efforts of the government to restore military discipline among them, and was soon reinforced by reports of the plan to transfer soldiers of the garrison to the front to participate in the new military offense. On May 23, upon hearing of the growing unrest among soldiers of the garrison, and of their readiness to demonstrate on their own if a positive decision were not taken at the center, the Military Organization of the Bolshevik Petrograd Committee endorsed the idea of the demonstration on the condition that the sailors of Kronstadt also agreed to participate. After representatives of the sailors did so on June 1, the Petrograd Military Organization submitted to the Bolshevik Central Committee a list of the soldiers and sailors who could be counted upon to participate.

On June 4, the first full day of the Congress, sailors of the Baltic Fleet and soldiers of the Petrograd garrison gathered on Mars Field to show their revolutionary spirit, and two days later, on June 6, at a joint meeting of the Military Organization and the Bolshevik Central Committee voted to endorse an armed demonstration. The reporter for the Military Organization, Podvoiskii, justified the demonstration on the grounds that it would increase the party's influence in Petrograd, and serve as a battering ram to effect a breach at the Congress. No reference was made in his speech to the potential effects of this demonstration on the Bolsheviks' chances of gaining power.

Nonetheless, in striking contrast to the positive consensus that the idea of conducting an armed demonstration had evoked within the Petrograd Party Committee and its Military Organization, Podvoiskii's proposal set off a heated controversy within the Bolshevik Central Committee. This controversy brought out, really for the first time since the inception of the revolution, conflicting views between two camps in the Central Committee, which remained divided about the strategy and tactics to follow during the subsequent unfolding of the revolution right up until Lenin's seizure of power in October.

The first camp, led by Lenin, strongly favored an armed uprising at this time to prevent the launching of a military offensive, to effect the transfer of power to the soviets, and to immediately propose peace terms. Reportedly, Lenin feared most, in this connection, a successful military offensive, which he considered would drastically retard the opportunity for revolution. The opposing point of view within the Central Committee, represented at this time by Kamenev (and less consistently at this point by Zinoviev), as well as by Nogin, speaking on behalf of the majority of the Moscow City Committee, strongly opposed Lenin, arguing that such an action would be tantamount to a revolutionary insurrection at a time when the party's strength in the country as a whole did not yet justify it, and therefore would cause the party to risk its life. Zinoviev strongly supported Nogin's position, believing that even the workers of the capital were not as yet ready to engage in insurrection.

In contrast to the divisions within the Central Committee, no opposition to the conduct of an armed demonstration was manifest among the members of the Petrograd Party Committee. At a meeting of this Committee, also held on June 6, V. I. Nevskii argued that unrest among the soldiers of the garrison had now become so intense that they were likely to launch an armed demonstration even in the absence of an endorsement by the Bolsheviks. Nevskii also argued that the risk that such a demonstration would backfire could be minimized by keeping the preparations for it secret. At the conclusion of the meeting, the Petrograd Committee decided to postpone a final decision until an expanded session of its members with representatives of the rank and file was convoked on June 9.

In the interval, pressure mounted for an armed demonstration as the militant workers of the Vyborg district went on strike to protest against the government's threat to expel the Anarchist Communists from Durnovo Village. The strike action of the workers of this district, the most militant supporters of the Bolsheviks among the workers of the capital, prompted a rescheduling from June 9 to June 7 of a joint meeting of the Central Committee, the Petrograd Committee, and its Military Organization, now including representatives of trade unions and factory organizations. This expanded meeting passed on June 8 a resolution in support of an armed demonstration under the direction of the Executive Commission of the Petrograd Committee and its Military Organization by the overwhelming vote of 131 to 6, with 22 abstentions. On June 10, special issues of *Pravda* and *Soldatskaia Pravda* appeared, listing the route and order of march of the proposed demonstration, as well as the slogans to be used by the marchers: "Down with the Bourgeois Ministers!" "Bring the War to an End!" "All Power to the Soviets!"

As we already noted, rumors of the impending demonstration reached the Central Executive Committee of the Petrograd Soviet and the presidium of the Congress on the evening of June 9, eliciting indignant reactions from the delegates, including those representing the Bolsheviks, who had been kept in the dark about it. On the strength of these protests, Lunacharskii and Nogin demanded that an emergency meeting of the Central Committee, the Executive Commission of the Petrograd Committee, and its Military Organization be convened to reconsider the decision. Notwithstanding the protests of the Bolshevik delegates at the Congress, fourteen of the sixteen participants at this emergency meeting voted to go ahead with the demonstration.

The support for the conduct of an armed demonstration within the Bolshevik Central Committee began to unravel only after the Congress adopted in the early morning of June 10 a resolution prohibiting an armed uprising, which was passed unanimously with only the delegates of the Bolsheviks and *Mezhraiontsy* abstaining. Thereupon, the proposal to cancel the demonstration was brought up again at a rump meeting of the Bolshevik Central Committee, at which Zinoviev now joined Kamenev and Nogin in voting to cancel it. Lenin and Sverdlov abstained. To add insult to injury, the Bolsheviks' Petrograd Committee, which was to have been responsible for the organization of the demonstration, was not even informed of its cancellation, a neglect about which they bitterly complained to the Central Committee, and to which Lenin, in turn, responded with an unconvincing and unsatisfactory excuse.[58]

What questions are we to pose, and what inferences and conclusions are we in a position to draw, from this episode, which Rabinowitch has so elaborately reconstructed for us? The most important question, of course, is what objective was Lenin seeking to achieve by means of this armed demonstration? Clearly, it was no longer to bring the Congress of Soviets, which was about to ratify the launching of a military offensive, to power. But neither was there any convincing evidence (and none would be forthcoming after the fall of the Soviet regime) to support Tsereteli's thesis that the conduct of this armed demonstration was designed to bring the Bolsheviks themselves to power by an armed uprising. To be sure, Lenin now considered that the second phase of the revolution, which was to culminate in the Bolsheviks' seizure of power, was at hand. But the ambitious scope of the changes that the seizure of power would bring, as Lenin now outlined them, clearly required a preparatory phase of political propaganda, agitation, and organization on the part of the Bolshevik party.

What, then, was the objective to be achieved by the armed demonstration which Lenin, since mid-May, had been seeking to promote? Rabinowitch prudently skirts the issue (since Lenin never gave a straightforward answer to it), and confines himself to citing E. H. Carr's phrase about "testing the state of mind of the worker and soldier demonstrators," adding, quite wrongly in my view, that Lenin viewed this demonstration as a means for pressuring the Soviet Congress to take power in its own hands.[59]

Actually, the pithiest as well as most persuasive phrase to describe the demonstration's objective had been used on June 6 by Podvoiskii, the reporter for the Military Organization of the Bolsheviks, at a joint meeting with the Executive Commission of the Petrograd Committee. In this report, it will be recalled, Podvoiskii had justified appealing to the Central Committee to approve the demonstration on the ground that it would increase the influence of the Bolshevik party in Petrograd, and serve as a battering ram to achieve a breach at the Congress.

This was the real point. Given the impending ratification by the Congress of Soviets of the launching of a military offensive, it was imperative to shatter its political and moral authority. The "battering ram" of an armed demonstration was needed at this point not only to destroy the reputation of the Congress, but also to preserve, as much as it could possibly be preserved, the political appeal of the notion of soviet power, as a rallying point in the further unfolding of the Russian and world revolutions.

The story of the aborted armed demonstration is also instructive in at least two other respects. The first was that it caused to surface, really for the first time, the core of the opposition that emerged among the leaders of the Bolshevik party to the tactics to which Lenin now turned in his struggle for power: the majority of the Moscow Party Committee (represented on this occasion by Nogin), Zinoviev (notwithstanding his flip-flops), and Lunacharskii and other representatives of the former *Mezhraiontsy* among the representatives of the intelligentsia at the Congress. But secondly, and just as important, this episode exposed Lenin's total disregard for institutional niceties in the functioning of the Bolshevik party, when the issues at stake appeared to him politically crucial. Both of these features would continue to mark the internal politics of the Bolsheviks up to Lenin's seizure and consolidation of power in October.

The prohibitions that the leadership of the Congress had issued against the conduct of any demonstrations while the Congress was in session had specified that a unity demonstration in honor of the Congress was to be held on June 16 to celebrate the conclusion of its proceedings. The presidium of the Congress obviously expected this demonstration to be a harmonious affair, which would bring out the support of the soldiers and workers of the capital. However, according to most accounts, including Sukhanov's, Bolshevik slogans ("Down with the War!" "Down with the Bourgeois Ministers!" "All Power to the Soviets!") predominated on the posters carried on June 16, suggesting that notwithstanding Lenin's tactical blunders the Bolsheviks had emerged from the experience of the Congress considerably strengthened in the eyes of the more militant soldiers and workers of the capital. There was, in this fact, little cause for surprise, for aside from the growing popularity of the Bolshevik slogans, the more militant workers and soldiers of Petrograd had obviously interpreted the prohibitions that had been imposed on the conduct of demonstrations while the Congress was in session as restrictions on their own right to express their will and seek to influence the course of events. The loss of popularity that the Revolutionary Defensists, who had shaped the decisions of the Congress, suffered as a result would become even more glaringly apparent by the end of June, as the initial successes of the military offensive on the Southwestern front were followed by resounding defeats. If Lenin had indeed been most concerned about the potential effect of a successful Russian's military offensive on his revolutionary designs, he no longer had a cause of alarm, as by the end of June, the potential for any further Russian military offensive was effectively erased.

XII

For both Martov and Lenin, the crisis of the July Days was a largely unexpected and ultimately searing experience, which profoundly affected their respective views of the dynamics of the revolution, and consequently their prescriptions for the strategy and tactics to be pursued in order to achieve their respective political goals. Notwithstanding Lenin's emphasis at the Congress of Soviets on the Bolsheviks' readiness to assume the responsibilities of power, and Martov's warnings against the premature and potentially catastrophic consequences of pursuing such a course, Martov proved in fact psychologically better prepared and quicker to respond to the character of, and indeed the opportunities to be found in, the outbreak of the July Days. To understand the nature of Martov's response, it is necessary to bear in mind that the workers' and soldiers' demonstrations that broke out in the afternoon of July 3 were launched in the context of a major political crisis which suddenly exposed a power vacuum in Russian politics. By the same token, this crisis brought into question the legitimacy of the political order that had come into being with the formation of the coalition government.

The power vacuum, as well as the crisis of legitimacy that underlay it, was precipitated by the resignation on July 2 of the representatives of the Kadet party from the Provisional Government. This resignation was attributed by the Kadets to the concessions that a delegation to Kiev, led by

Tsereteli and Nekrasov, had made to the demands of the Ukrainian *Rada* for political autonomy. There were other contentious issues involved as well, as demonstrated by the resignation of Prince L'vov as Chairman of the Council of Ministers on July 8, in protest against what he denounced as the infringement by the Minister of Agriculture, Chernov, on the property rights of the owners of private land. L'vov specifically denounced Chernov's proposal for the placement of privately owned land under the control of land committees in each province, with the requirement that this land could not be sold without the committees' approval.[60]

Martov, now living in the spacious apartment belonging to the Tsederbaum family, which was also occupied by his sister Lydia and her husband Fedor Dan (Boris Nicolaevsky occupied the maid's room), had learned of the resignation of the Kadet ministers from his brother-in-law on the morning of July 2. This news caused Martov to make a psychological leap from the passive political position that he had hitherto felt constrained to observe. For in Martov's view, the resignation of the Kadet ministers demonstrated that the bourgeoisie—all the elements of the bourgeoisie—had already gone over to the camp of counter-revolution.

Martov therefore concluded that there was no longer time to procrastinate (although he in fact would continue to do so), and on the morning of July 3 , before the outbreak of the workers' and soldiers' demonstrations that afternoon, he drafted a resolution calling for the formation of an "all-democratic" government. The introduction to Martov's draft stated, *inter alia*, that

> the resignation of the representatives of the Kadet party from the Provisional Government signifies the repudiation of the revolution by the last organized group of the bourgeoisie. Revolutionary democracy responds to this challenge by taking state power in its own hands. It is assuming power in order to lead Russia to the Constituent Assembly, and most importantly, to tear Russia away from the deadly embrace of the war, which is stifling the revolution.[61]

The workers' and soldiers' demonstrations which broke out quite unexpectedly for Martov in the afternoon of July 3—i.e., well after he had written these lines—hardly provided an ideal setting for the presentation of his resolution, although they added to the sense of urgency which had induced him to write it.

The opportunity to present his resolution arose in the chaos created by the demonstrations, during an interval of relative calm created by Dan when he succeeded in persuading the soldiers of a reserve regiment, who had arrived from Tsarkoe Selo to call for all power to the soviets, to surround the hall to protect the members of the Petrograd Soviet from outside interference while they settled the issue of power. During that interval, Martov finally had the opportunity to come to the platform. He followed Tsereteli's presentation of the official resolution endorsed by the Central Executive Committee of Soviets. This resolution called for a two-weeks' delay before reaching a decision on the question of power, to enable the executive committees of the workers', soldiers', and peasants' soviets to assemble in Moscow, in a calmer political atmosphere and reach a considered decision.

Martov followed Tsereteli to the platform, and after fiercely denouncing this appeal for delay, read the text of the resolution that he had drafted that morning:

> With the resignation of the Kadets, all the responsibility of [governing] falls on our shoulders. History demands that we take power into our own hands. I believe that revolutionary democracy will support us. . . . Yes, we must establish a government of the Third Estate. . . . A two weeks' delay would be fatal. It would lead to an elemental upheaval (*smuta*). . . . One must act immediately to create an organ of power (*vlast'*) that will lead the revolution forward. . . . [62]

This was a remarkable psychological leap, because, as Martov subsequently explained (most fully at the Unification Congress of the RSDRP, at the end of August), he already had in mind, notwithstanding his somewhat confused reference to the French Third Estate, the formation of an "all-democratic government," in the language of the times. This was a social as well as a political and moral construct. It automatically excluded the bourgeoisie, while including the industrial proletariat and the petty bourgeoisie of urban and rural Russia, and most importantly, the masses of the Russian peasantry. As Martov's critics at the Unification Congress of the Menshevik party would not fail to point out, this political leap was all the more notable in view of the emphasis that he had laid consistently up to this point on the political, cultural, and economic backwardness of the peasantry, which, just as other Russian Marxists, he had denounced since the 1890s as a social stratum representative of an earlier age, devoid of class consciousness, and destined to polarize into a rural bourgeoisie and a rural proletariat as capitalism developed in the countryside. For this reason, Martov had been one of the most vocal critics of Populist and neo-Populist ideology throughout the pre-revolutionary period, and indeed, had criticized almost equally sharply Lenin's advocacy, from 1905 onward, of a dictatorship of the proletariat and of the peasantry.

Because of the onset of the period of reaction that followed the July Days, Martov did not have the opportunity to answer his party critics until the convocation of the Unification Congress in late August. But even at this point, although unbeknownst to both Lenin and Martov (as they remained ignorant of the changes in each other's views until the eve of the October Revolution), it appeared as if, by a supreme irony of history, under impact of the same events, Martov had now come to espouse the position that Lenin himself had ostensibly assumed upon his return to Petrograd on the question of power during the first phase of the revolution, while Lenin, who repudiated this position when the issue of the military offensive had come to the fore on the eve of the First Congress of Soviets, had now come to adopt the more jaundiced views that Martov had entertained up to the July Days about the revolutionary potential of the Russian peasantry.

XIII

It is important to emphasize that Lenin took no part in the preparations for the conduct of the demonstrations of the July Days, or indeed in the agitation conducted in their support by the Bolshevik's Petrograd Committee, and after their outbreak, even by members of the Central Committee.

Lenin was not even in Petrograd when the demonstrations broke out, having taken a few days vacation to rest up from the fatigue he had accumulated since his return to Russia. He returned to Petrograd only on the evening of July 3, when the demonstrations were well underway. No evidence has emerged before or since the fall of the Soviet regime that Lenin was at all cognizant during the period of his absence from Petrograd of the agitation conducted in favor of the demonstrations among the workers of the capital. Indeed, the only publication reflecting his state of mind during this period was an article about the resignation of the Kadet ministers, which suggested that Lenin did not even appreciate at the time he wrote this commentary the gravity of the crisis to which it had given rise. This article suggested, in fact, that while the reaction of the Kadets undoubtedly reflected broader conflicts, most notably over the land question, than the concessions made to the demands of the Ukrainian *Rada* for autonomy, the Kadet resignations actually constituted an ultimatum which would quickly be met by concessions on the part of other members of the government.[63]

Lenin returned to the capital on the evening of July 3. He immediately issued a statement to an assembled crowd of his followers, praising them for their militancy, but also urging them to display vigilance and restraint in the face of provocations. And the next morning a joint session of the Bolsheviks' Central and Petrograd Party Committees, convened at his initiative, called for a halt to the demonstrations.

However, one of the first acts of the Provisional Government after the demonstrations subsided that same afternoon was to order the arrest and prosecution of the entire leadership of the Bolshevik party, including Lenin, which was held responsible for the outbreak of the disorders. Lenin considered that it would be the height of folly for Bolshevik leaders to subject themselves to arrest and prosecution by a counter-revolutionary government because of some mistaken sense of honor. Other leaders of the Bolshevik party did so, however, making an exception for Lenin in view of his indispensability to the cause of the revolution. Lenin, needless to say, agreed with this last judgment, and thereupon went into hiding, with the approval—indeed under the express orders—of the Bolshevik Central Committee, until the Bolshevik seizure of power in October.

Contributing to Lenin's bitterness at this moment was a report fabricated by the ex-Bolshevik deputy to the Third Duma from Petrograd, G.A. Aleksinskii, alleging that Lenin had been receiving money from the German government for his services in conducting defeatist propaganda and agitation. (The report even specified the sums of money regularly paid by the German government to Lenin for this purpose.) The Provisional Government did not question the authenticity of the report. Indeed the only organ to do so at the time was a court of honor organized at Lenin's request by the leaders of the Menshevik party to look into its authenticity, and which dismissed it as a complete fabrication.[64]

It was with the feelings of bitterness and resentment induced by this series of events that Lenin wrote, in mid-July, an article seeking to summarize for the benefit of his Bolshevik followers the political lessons to be drawn from this experience. Given the significance that he assigned to the definition of political situations, and hence to the role of language in the shaping of political action, Lenin titled his article "On Slogans."[65] In this piece, and in a more summary version in which he outlined its theses, Lenin came bluntly and directly to the point as was characteristic of him in times of crises. The slogan "All Power to the Soviets," which the Bolshevik party had adopted at its Sixth Party Congress, when it had officially endorsed Lenin's April Theses, was now out-of-date. The slogan had been appropriate at a time when a peaceful transfer of power appeared conceivable, but the peaceful phase of the revolution had come to an abrupt end with the July Days. As a result of their involvement in the suppression of the soldiers' and workers' demonstrations, the Mensheviks in charge of the soviets had effectively surrendered their power to the counter-revolutionary bourgeoisie.

The period of dual power was also over, now that the counter-revolutionary bourgeoisie had gathered all power into its own hands. Its overthrow would require a new revolutionary upsurge, culminating in an armed uprising and the establishment of the dictatorship of the proletariat with the support of the poorest strata of the peasantry. The soviets would eventually play a significant role in this new revolutionary upsurge, *but only* after the majority of their members rallied in support of the Bolsheviks' platform. In the meantime, in order to avoid any political confusion, the use of the slogan, "All Power to the Soviets," should be suspended, and replaced by a slogan calling for an armed uprising leading to the establishment of a dictatorship of the proletariat and poorest peasants.

This change of slogans also brought to the forefront a major change in Lenin's diagnosis of the dynamics of the revolution, which had already been suggested at the First Congress of Soviets. It was that the Russian revolution had now entered what Lenin defined as its "second phase," which was to culminate in the Bolshevik seizure of power. During this second phase, the representatives of the petty bourgeoisie, who were held chiefly responsible for the disaster of the July Days, were not to be afforded any concessions by the Bolsheviks, even about the land question. For upon the Bolsheviks' seizure of power, the land holdings not already in peasant hands were to be confiscated and redistributed exclusively to the peasant poor, who would provide the core of the Bolsheviks' support in the countryside. Thus, Lenin now unambiguously emphasized the need for the establishment of a dictatorship of the proletariat and the peasant poor as the goal to be achieved at the culmination of this second phase of the revolution: "The proletariat must independently seize power. In the absence of its victory, there cannot be a victory of the revolution. Power to the proletariat, supported by the poorest peasantry, or semi-proletariat. This is the only way out."[66]

Beginning at the First Congress of Soviets, Lenin had used the term *batraki* interchangeably with that of "poorest peasants." We should note that the word *batraki* was commonly assigned to those members of the peasant population who supported themselves *exclusively* by working the land owned or possessed by others, in exchange for a share of the crop. Given the significance that Lenin consistently assigned to the land question as one of the keys to the understanding of Russia's revolutionary process, the emphasis that he now came to assign to the poorest peasants as the Bolsheviks' chief allies in the countryside in the second, culminating, phase of the revolution suggested how deeply his vision had been affected by the developments that had occurred, beginning with the reports that had emerged on the eve of the Congress of Soviets about the launching of a military offensive. Most notably of course, these developments, as well as the character and outcome of the July Days, brought out more sharply than ever, in Lenin's view, the importance of the seizure and consolidation of power by the proletariat (and by the same token, of the Bolshevik party speaking in its name), against all its active and potential adversaries in rural as well as urban Russia.

As was frequently the case with Lenin, he also contributed during this period with the publication of *State and Revolution* (which he took the time to write in September 1917), a theoretically oriented explanation and justification of the importance that he now assigned to the seizure and full exploitation of its power by the proletariat, and hence by the Bolshevik party, as a prerequisite—indeed the indispensable precondition—for the eventual establishment of a classless society. Readers will be familiar with Lenin's essential argument in support of this proposition: that only the creation of a dictatorship of the proletariat and the full use of its power would make possible the destruction of all the institutions and webs of social, political, and economic relations on which capitalism rested, down to their foundations.

However, fewer readers are likely to be familiar with the original manuscript of this text. As was his wont, Lenin numbered and underlined in this text the major propositions it advanced, and cited the various classics of Marxist literature (especially the writings of Engels), on which he was drawing in their support. The manuscript dramatically brought out the theoretical importance that Lenin assigned to its preparation, which he took the trouble to write just as he was beginning his complicated maneuvers for power. It provides an additional illustration of the seriousness that Lenin assigned to his theoretical concerns as a guide to political action, for himself as well as for his followers, throughout the entire course of the revolution.

XIV

Martov delivered a friendly address to the Bolshevik party's Sixth Congress, held in early August, which clearly indicated that he was totally unaware of the changes that had occurred in Lenin's views since the July Days. Both he and his own opponents in the Menshevik party were still clearly unaware of these changes when the Menshevik party's so-called "Unification Congress" convened on August 19. This gathering gave Martov the first real opportunity to present, *in extenso*, before an audience dominated by his Menshevik opponents, the platform that he had originally drawn up on the morning of July 3 in the Tsederbaums' family apartment, and which he had originally outlined under such difficult circumstances that afternoon following the onset of the July Days disorders.

As will be recalled, the first part of the twofold argument on which Martov's new platform rested emphasized that by the time of the July Days, the Russian bourgeoisie—*all* of Russia's bourgeoisie—had gone over to the camp of the counter-revolution. Thus, after five months, the most basic problems confronting the revolution would have to be resolved without the bourgeoisie, and to a significant extent against the bourgeoisie.

Under the circumstances, what social force was destined by history and the structure of contemporary society to become the moving force of what Martov still insisted on calling "the bourgeois revolution"? What force, in the place of the capitalist class, which dominated capitalist society, was now destined, if the revolution was to be victorious, to resolve its social and political tasks? "It is the rural and urban petty bourgeoisie, what we usually call the non-proletarian part of revolutionary democracy," was Martov's answer.[67]

To be able to play this role, however, the petty bourgeoisie would have to become conscious of its own interests, and to identify them with the interests of the country as a whole, on all major issues of domestic and foreign policy, including first and foremost the issue of the struggle for peace. To achieve this objective would require in turn that the petty bourgeoisie be liberated from the political and moral influence that the bourgeoisie itself had exercised on it up to this point in the revolution. However, there was an obvious prerequisite for the pursuit and eventual realization of this objective. It was that Russian Social Democracy, the party of the proletariat, recover its own political independence by breaking completely with the bourgeoisie and asserting its own independent platform. Only under these conditions could Social Democracy confront the petty bourgeoisie, and the country as a whole, with a clear alternative vision of Russia's domestic and foreign policy resting on the articulation of the proletariat's class-consciousness.

The reassertion by Russia's Social Democracy of its own independence, and its clear articulation of the class interests of Russia's proletariat, thus constituted *the prerequisite* for the liberation of the petty bourgeoisie of city and country from the sway held over it by Russia's capitalist class. By the same token, it was also the prerequisite for the eventual establishment of an all-democratic government dominated by the petty bourgeoisie of rural and urban Russia.[68]

My summary of the core of Martov's argument does not reflect the drawn-out character of his presentation of it at the Menshevik congress, and indeed his inability to spell out the conclusions to be drawn from it, as clearly as he would have wished, notwithstanding the several extensions of time that he received for its presentation. This was a clear sign that Martov did not as yet feel sure of the ground under his feet, and in particular of the ways in which he should phrase his argument before the majority of the delegates whom he knew to be hostile to his views. Indeed, as soon as he concluded (or more precisely was forced to conclude) his remarks, they were subjected to sharp criticism by his opponents in the party.

Martov's most scathing critic was Potresov, who had been his closest political associate during the period leading up to the creation of the old *Iskra* at the turn of the century, and with whom he had remained closely in touch by correspondence from Western Europe following the Stolypin *coup d'état* of June 1907, while Potresov stayed in Russia. On this occasion, Potresov sharply emphasized that he found Martov's new platform not only untenable, but actually ridiculous. Untenable, because Martov now dared to assert that the Russian bourgeoisie—in Potresov's view, the most significant and progressive force in Russia's economic, and, ergo, political development—had now turned into a counter-revolutionary force. Ridiculous, because Martov dared to suggest as an alternative to the central and progressive role played by the bourgeoisie in Russia's development, that of the urban and rural petty bourgeoisie, which Martov, along with other Russian Marxists, had rightly identified since the 1890s as the most backward stratum of Russian society: so backward in fact that it had not yet begun to divide in the countryside into a rural bourgeoisie and a rural proletariat, and was thus devoid of the very prerequisites of class consciousness. It was on these grounds, Potresov recalled, that Martov himself had been so critical of the

Populists and Neo-Populists for their idealization of the peasantry, and on which, beginning in 1905, he had also criticized Lenin's platform of the dictatorship of the proletariat and the peasantry.

Martov patiently sought to rebut Potresov's critique. He argued that he had originally attacked Lenin's platform in 1905 because it had so fiercely denounced the Russian bourgeoisie at a time when the bourgeoisie was still capable of playing a positive role in the Russian revolution. But this was no longer the case, now that the bourgeoisie had emerged as a counter-revolutionary force.

What is even more striking about this debate, however, is that none of the participants in it, including Tsereteli, who sought to exploit Potresov's argument for his own purposes, displayed any awareness of the changes that had occurred in Lenin's views and in the Bolsheviks' platform since the First Congress of Soviets and the July Days. For indeed, these changes in Lenin's position made most of the arguments that the participants in this debate advanced against one another no longer germane. Yet, it could also legitimately be argued that the changes in Lenin's views made even more salient and urgent the adoption of the new platform that Martov now urged against the opposition of his opponents and their supporters, who constituted a majority of the delegates.

In the concluding part of his presentation, Martov observed that since the July Days, Russia's military had emerged as an independent force, which was likely to play an increasingly important role in the unfolding of the Russian counter-revolution. This was one more demonstration of the prescience that Martov was coming to display about the dynamics of the revolution, for the conclusion of the Menshevik party congress was followed, within a few days, by the inception of the *Kornilovshchina*: the decision made by General Kornilov (under the false impression created by Kerensky's seeming approval of his intentions) to dispatch armed forces under his command to seize Petrograd.

XV

The *Kornilovshchina* had political consequences—in the shorter as well as the longer terms—which profoundly affected the attitudes and perceptions of all socialist leaders, including Lenin and Martov. The first of these consequences was the dramatic recovery of the Bolsheviks' fortunes as a political and as a military force, as their supporters were allowed to re-arm by the Petrograd Soviet in its efforts to mobilize resistance against the advance of General Kornilov's troops on Petrograd, as well to thwart any attempt at a *coup d'état* in the capital itself. The second, no less important political consequence (or so it appeared in the short-run) was the dramatic loss of support, even among the Defensists as well as the Revolutionary Defensists in the Menshevik party and the PSR, for the Kadet party remaining a partner in the formation of a new coalition government, in view of the exposure of the support that its leaders had extended to Kornilov's attempt to seize power. Thus, the formation of the all-democratic government favored by Martov now appeared the most likely way to resolve the problem of power. This solution became all the more probable when the leadership of the soviets decided to address the issue in the wake of the *Kornilovshchina* at a Democratic Conference, whose participants would include only representatives of "democracy."

Indeed, in the wake of the *Kornilovshchina* even Lenin briefly entertained the notion that the Russian revolution had now taken such a sharp and original turn as to allow the Bolsheviks to conclude a short-term compromise agreement with a petty bourgeois government dominated by the SRs and the Mensheviks. This compromise would involve a return to the platform that Lenin had supported at the time of his return to Russia: all power to the soviets *as currently constituted*, and a government of SRs and Mensheviks accountable to them. Lenin elaborated on this notion in an article that he prepared for publication in the Bolshevik newspaper *Rabochii Put'* at the beginning of September:

> Only now and perhaps *for only a few days*, or one or two weeks, such a government could be established and consolidated completely peacefully. It would secure, in great likelihood, a peaceful path *forward* for the all-Russian revolution and much greater changes, indeed big steps forward toward the achievement of peace. . . .
>
> Only for the sake of such a peaceful development of the revolution—an *exceptionally* rare and *very* valuable possibility in history—the Bolsheviks, while supporters of world revolution and revolutionary methods, could and should make such a compromise.
>
> For the Bolsheviks, the compromise would involve . . . giving up the demand for the immediate transfer of power to the proletariat and poor peasants and of revolutionary methods to achieve these demands, under the condition of full freedom of agitation and

of the calling of the Constituent Assembly without any further delay. The Mensheviks and the SRs, as the governing bloc, would agree to form a government (assuming that this is a realizable compromise), accountable entirely and exclusively to the soviets, and to turn all power locally to the soviets.

What would both sides gain by concluding such a compromise? The Bolsheviks would gain the possibility of agitating completely freely for their views, and under the conditions of really full democratization, to gain influence in the soviets. On paper, all now concede such freedom to the Bolsheviks, but in practice this freedom would not be possible under a government in which the bourgeoisie participates; [it] would become possible under a soviet government. (We won't say guaranteed, but possible.) For such a possibility to be realized [at such a difficult time], it would be worth concluding a compromise with the present majority of the soviets. We have nothing to fear in a genuine democracy, because life is going in our favor, and even the present evolution of the currents within the PSR and the Menshevik party [that are] hostile to us is proving this point. As for the Mensheviks and the SRs, they would gain at once the full possibility of implementing the program of their bloc, on the basis of the support of the great majority of the people and the exploitation of this majority in the soviets.

However, the uncertainty of the situation and of the possibility of concluding such a compromise stems from the wide range of currents and voices represented in the "bloc" of petty bourgeois democracy, ranging from currents fully compatible with a bourgeois government to currents leaning, although not fully capable as yet, of going over to the position of the proletariat.[69]

By the time Lenin sent this article to press, on Sunday, September 3, 1917, he felt compelled to add the following postscript: "Upon reading Saturday's and today's newspapers, it appears that the proposal for a compromise is already too late. It would appear that the few days during which a peaceful development was still *possible* have *also* gone by."[70]

What caused Lenin to change his mind so abruptly at this juncture about the possibility of concluding a short-term compromise with the Mensheviks and the PSR, which would open a peaceful path to achieve his goal? It appears to have been the announcement of the formation of a Directory, which was to temporarily assume governmental responsibilities until the creation of a more long-term political authority. This Directory, whose membership was approved on September 2 at a joint plenum of the Executive Committees of the Soviets of Workers' and Soldiers' Deputies and the Soviets of Peasant Deputies, was to consist of the following persons: Kerensky; A.I. Verkhovskii as Minister of War; D.P. Verderevskii as Minister of the Navy; A.M. Nikitin as Minister of Posts and Telegraphs; and M.I. Tereshchenko as Minister of Foreign Affairs.

None of these men had been directly implicated in the Kornilov affair, and two of them were highly popular and impeccable nonpolitical figures: A. I. Verkhovskii, who had commanded the Moscow military district, and D.P. Verderevskii, who had commanded the Baltic Fleet. The same could not be said, however, of Tereshchenko, who had served Minister of Foreign Affairs since the resignation of Miliukov, and whose reappointment to this post indicated that the socialist parties would continue to be confronted with the same determined opposition in their struggle for peace.

The Bolshevik delegates to the Democratic Conference did not become aware of Lenin's change of views and of his consequent opposition to their participation in the Conference until after it had already opened. Following its opening, however, they began to receive increasingly insistent messages from Lenin demanding that they withdraw. (It is revealing of the tensions that had developed between them and Lenin that the Bolshevik delegates left other delegates to the Conference completely in the dark about the pressure that Lenin was placing on them.)

We should note, *inter alia*, that the decision of the Bolshevik delegates to continue attending the Conference, notwithstanding Lenin's increasingly insistent pressure, proved to be a factor of considerable significance in determining the character that the Conference assumed in its early sessions. Indeed, the divisions and contradictions that these early sessions exposed in the voting patterns of the delegates suggested that on the most important issue that it had to face—the character of the new political authority to be established in place of the coalition discredited by the *Kornilovshchina*—the Conference might prove to be hopelessly divided and effectively paralyzed.

This fact probably came as a surprise to most of the delegates, since it had appeared in the wake of the *Kornilovshchina* and of the exposure of the involvement of the leaders of the Kadet party, that a solid majority of the delegates to the Democratic Conference would support the formation of an "all-democratic government," i.e., of a government consisting exclusively, as Martov advocated, of representatives of the "democracy." Such a resolution of the problem of power appeared all the more likely since only representatives of the "democracy" (excluding, by the same token, any representation of the bourgeoisie), were to be allowed to take part in this Conference.

Yet, in the course of these early sessions, no majority emerged among the delegates in support of Martov's resolution in favor of the formation of an "all-democratic" government. Then, by an even more significant majority, the delegates rejected a resolution in support of the formation of a coalition government which would include representatives of the Kadet party. Finally, at the seventh session of the Conference, Martov submitted, in a tactical move uncharacteristic of him, a resolution in support of coalition without the Kadets (to which he was in fact opposed) in an effort to harden the opposition to coalition *with* the Kadets. This resolution was rejected by an even more overwhelming vote, as supporters of coalition *with* the Kadets joined forces with supporters of an "all-democratic" government to defeat it.[71]

Because of the deadlock that had emerged among the delegates on the issue of power, it was referred to the presidium of the Conference for its recommendations. I have recounted elsewhere in considerable detail the maneuvers that distinguished the negotiations that were conducted, largely behind the scenes under the auspices of the presidium of the Conference, between Kerensky, who was still Premier of the Provisional Government, Tsereteli, who led the bloc of Revolutionary Defensists, and leaders of the Kadet party.[72]

Despite the support that the leaders of the Kadet party had extended in varying degrees to the *Kornilovshchina*, Tsereteli continued to believe—with all the fervor that he had previously displayed on this issue—in the imperative of keeping together the "vital forces of the nation," jointly represented in his views by "revolutionary democracy" and the "progressive elements" of the bourgeoisie. More than ever, the preservation of the unity of these "vital forces" required, Tsereteli believed, that representatives of the Kadet party be included in the Provisional Government, since even the big industrialists who were being mentioned as possible alternatives to the leaders of the Kadet party as representatives of the bourgeoisie in a new coalition government had formally joined the Kadet party in the early summer, and obviously would not be willing to serve in a coalition government without the approval of its leaders.

Three basic issues were referred by the delegates to the presidium of the Democratic Conference for its recommendations: they were the character of the new executive organ to be created; that of the new representative institution to be established, and presumably stay in place, until the Constituent Assembly convened; and last but not least, the relationship between these new executive and representative institutions.

The decision on the first of these issues, announced on behalf of the presidium by Kerensky and Tsereteli, was that the character of the representative institution to be put in place in the interim period between the adjournment of the Democratic Conference and the convocation of the Constituent Assembly was to be determined by the new government (*prima facie*, a decision contrary to logic, but which would leave the resolution of this issue up to the discretion of the presidium after the delegates to the Democratic Conference adjourned).

The other decision left pending—whether the representative institution to be established for the interim period before the Constituent Assembly convened was to have legislative powers or be confined to a purely consultative role—had not been settled by the time Tsereteli left for Georgia to recover from an illness, and Dan had assumed his succession as leader of the bloc of Revolutionary Defensists. (The new provisional representative institution assumed the title of Council of the Republic, but was more commonly referred to as the Pre-parliament.)

On the eve of the opening session of this new body, Dan gave in to the Kadets' demand that it not be assigned any legislative authority, and be confined to a purely consultative role. Dan's argument was that the new government to be created would in fact never deviate from the views espoused by the majority of the members of the Pre-parliament. (This, as we shall see, did not turn out to be the case.) Thus, it was already clear at the time when the new government was created on the basis once again of a coalition with representatives of the Kadet party that—really for the first time since the inception of the revolution—this government would be able to rule, or at least formulate its policies, without any formal or informal institutional restrictions, including the views espoused by the majority of the members of the Pre-parliament itself.

The dimensions of this veritable debacle suffered by the representatives of the socialist parties and of the Soviets of Workers' Deputies to the Democratic Conference, which did not become fully evident until well after it had adjourned, had two irreversible political consequences, the significance of which also did not become immediately apparent. The first of these was the weakening of the political authority of those representatives of the Bolshevik party at the Democratic Conference who, because of their interest in the formation of an "all-democratic" government, had resisted Lenin's pressure that they leave forthwith. The second effect, no less important, was the catalytic role that it played in Martov's decision to launch a major new initiative which, while sharpening the split between the Menshevik Internationalists and the party's dominant bloc of Revolutionary Defensists, also contributed very significantly to Martov's ability to propose a convincing alternative to the strategy and tactics that Lenin was now espousing in the pursuit of his revolutionary goals.

The catalyst for these new political developments was the announcement by the Bureau of the Central Executive Committee of the Soviets of its decision to convoke the Second Congress of Soldiers' and Workers' deputies on October 20. This announcement steeled Martov to publish in his journal *Iskra* on September 30 an editorial which spelled out his proposal for a platform to be submitted to the Congress by the delegates of the Menshevik Internationalists. Martov's editorial was all the more dramatic, as well as significant, because it appeared just days after the publication in *Izvestiia* of an article written by his brother-in-law, Fedor Dan, the leader of the Menshevik bloc of Revolutionary Defensists in the absence of Tsereteli, warning the Menshevik delegates to the Second Congress of Soviets against any tendency to assume in their pronouncements and resolutions the prerogatives reserved to the Constituent Assembly in the shaping of Russia's future political, social, and economic order.[73] Yet Martov did precisely that in his editorial. It spelled out his proposed platform in considerable detail.[74]

In and of itself, the sweeping character of the platform that Martov outlined could be viewed as a challenge to the prerogatives that had hitherto been reserved to the Constituent Assembly. But the unprecedented character of this editorial also lay in the fact that for the first time, *it called without any qualifications for the formation without delay* of an "all-democratic" government to be confirmed by the delegates to the Second Congress. Just as important, given the consistent pattern of support for "All Power to the Soviets," that had emerged among delegates already elected to the Congress of Soviets, as well as in the reelections of members of local soviets, were Martov's subtle emphases in this editorial on the differences between the "all-democratic" government that he advocated and the call of the Bolsheviks and Left SRs for "All Power to the Soviets."

This was a formidable task, which Martov managed to cope with on this occasion in the most lucid and persuasive statement that he had formulated since the outbreak of the revolution. What was even more astonishing for him, Martov resorted in it to a skillful use of rhetorical devices to disarm his opponents, which had been so completely absent in his earlier statements in the course of the revolution as to appear contrary to his nature.

The first of these rhetorical devices appeared in Martov's very first paragraph, which suggested, or more precisely implied, that Martov's readers could take it for granted that by the opening of the Second Congress, the movement of events would have already turned the question of the survival of a coalition government into a dead political issue. On the other hand, the new threat that the Congress would have to face was the role that sectarian, utopian, adventuristic views might assume in shaping the new order that would replace the coalition.

In a further effort to disarm his potential opponents, Martov elected to raise the issue of power only in third place in the presentation of the slogans of his platform—following "Unity in the Organization of the Soviets under the Condition They Pursue a Genuinely Revolutionary Course," and "A Genuine and Unambiguous Struggle for Peace." (Martov could expect to win broad support for these first two slogans among the Bolshevik delegates.)

It was following the presentation of these two slogans that Martov opened his argument on the issue of power with the phrase: "Our third slogan is 'All Power to Democracy!'" Given the fact that the bourgeoisie had "lost all credit among the masses," the Menshevik Internationalists should direct their fire at the Congress of Soviets primarily against "utopian and adventuristic conceptions of the forms and the essence of democratic power or democratic dictatorship." Otherwise, the revolutionary movement would be confronted by the threat of moving from the mire of opportunism to the chaos of anarchism. "All power to democracy must not be interpreted to mean all power to the soviets" Martov continued. But aware that this statement would alarm the vast majority of the delegates to the Congress who instinctively supported the slogan "All Power to the Soviets," because they viewed the soviets as their own, Martov immediately followed up with an explanation designed to reassure these instinctive supporters of soviet power:

> The issue here is not who will formally stand at the head of democracy in its struggle for power. The soviets, which have organized the most *active* elements of the people will naturally assume the leading role in this struggle. If a revolutionary democratic government is formed, it will greatly resemble a "soviet" government, since its most active elements will be drawn from the same milieu as the soviets. But this is not to mean that the "dictatorship of *all* democracy," led by the soviets, should be replaced by the dictatorship of the

soviets in and of themselves over all the institutions of organized democracy.[75]

What is at issue here, Martov concluded, driving his point home, "is that the so-called dictatorship of the soviets not be turned into the dictatorship of only the *parts* of the proletariat, the army, and the peasantry which are prepared to seek to carry out, not a democratic, but a socialist, or semi-socialist revolution."[76]

Martov concluded with an apparent denunciation of the tendencies in Lenin's program toward the weakening of the democratic state, which he discerned in Lenin's emphasis on the autonomy of local soviets, as well as in his recent endorsement of workers' control over production in their enterprises. Martov stressed that on the contrary, the preservation of a strong democratic state was a precondition for the proper functioning of the Russian economy.

With the exception of this genuine or pretended misperception of Lenin's actual views on this issue, Martov had presented in this discussion a statement of his own views and a rebuttal of Lenin's position with a lucidity, decisiveness, and indeed rhetorical skill that he had not previously displayed in the entire course of 1917, or for that matter, since the Revolution of 1905.

Martov did not discuss in his statement the issue of the war because he had already addressed it with equal clarity and decisiveness in the debates held during the closed sessions of the Soviet Central Executive Committee on October 3–4. The chief objective of these sessions had been to clarify the position to be assumed by the representative of the TsIK who would be designated to join, in a consultative capacity, the Russian delegation which was to negotiate in Paris with the representatives of the Western allies the terms to be offered to the Central Powers for the conclusion of a peace agreement.

Two resolutions were submitted at the conclusion of these sessions, one by Martov in the name of the Menshevik Internationalists, and the other by Dan on behalf of the dominant bloc of Revolutionary Defensists of the Menshevik Party and the PSR. In the main, except in style (the language used by Martov was sharper and more decisive than Dan's, undoubtedly reflecting the sense of assurance he had gained about the validity of his position), the two resolutions basically overlapped in the lists of demands that they proposed that the delegates of the soviets seek to induce the Provisional Government to present at the meeting in Paris. Both included the demand that the governments of Great Britain and France remove all obstacles to the par-

ticipation by representatives of the more militant minorities of their socialist parties, along with the representatives of the majorities of these parties, in
the international conference of representatives of all socialist parties which
the Russian socialists were so insistently seeking to organize in Stockholm.

In fact, Martov's resolution differed sharply in its content from Dan's
on only one major point. It was a crucial one, however, and Martov brought
it out for emphasis in his concluding statement: "Revolutionary democracy
must mobilize all possible pressure on the Provisional Government to induce the Allies to agree to the opening of peace negotiations—including the
threat of revoking Russia's alliance treaties with them."[77]

Martov made it amply clear in the subsequent discussion of this issue in
the Pre-parliament that he meant precisely what he had emphasized in the
conclusion of his statement: that in the event that Russia's Western allies
failed to agree to this demand, he proposed that Russia repudiate its alliance
with Western countries, and confront the troops of the Central Powers
alone, until the governments of all other belligerent countries agreed to its
demand for the immediate proclamation of a universal armistice, to open
the way to negotiations for the conclusion of the universal peace without annexations and indemnities that Russia's socialist parties had been demanding since the days of Zimmerwald.

XVI

From the outset, the sessions of the Pre-parliament were marked by a series
of *coups de théâtre*, which contributed to shaping the scenario that would
eventually culminate in Lenin's seizure of power.

Even before the opening of the first session, Trotsky announced that the
Bolsheviks would not take part. His explanation, calculated to win wide
sympathy among many followers of the socialist parties, was that all of the
promises that had been made by the Presidium and the leaders of the majority bloc of Revolutionary Defensists at the opening of the Democratic
Conference had been betrayed. The *vlast'* that had finally emerged from
their intrigues included "open or masked Kornilovites," and the complete
absence of accountability of this *vlast'* had been confirmed by the announcement that the Council of the Republic would play a purely consultative role. Martov, who basically agreed with Trotsky's argument but for
whom the Bolsheviks' refusal to participate also signified the weakening of

the size of the opposition to coalition in the Pre-parliament, felt it necessary to explain why, under the circumstances, the Menshevik Internationalists had decided to stay:

> We consider it the obligation of all Social Democrats who have no confidence in this government, or in the majority of the Pre-parliament . . . to expose *from within* the political course pursued by the "census elements" and by those segments of democracy which cannot mobilize themselves to break with the principle of coalition and to support the creation for an all-democratic *vlast'*.[78]

Among the various Menshevik leaders, including Martov, who were interviewed after Trotsky's dramatic announcement of the Bolsheviks' decision to boycott the Pre-parliament, only one, Bogdanov, advanced the hypothesis that the Bolsheviks might have in mind an armed uprising to seize power. Bogdanov thought, however, that "in this event, they would achieve only temporary success, as they would isolate themselves and the workers who might follow their lead, not only from the bourgeoisie, but also from democracy and the front."[79] As we shall see, Bogdanov's analysis would prove to be partially correct, as the Bolshevik's decision to boycott the Pre-parliament was, in fact, the first fruit of Lenin's increasingly insistent pressure on the Bolshevik Central Committee to endorse the conduct of an armed uprising without delay.

The second, no less sensational, development on the opening day of the Pre-parliament came as a result of the issuance of an imperious set of rules (*"Reglament"*) drawn up by Fedor Dan, and endorsed by the Revolutionary Defensist majority of the Menshevik delegation. These spelled out in the most authoritative (and authoritarian) language the rules of conduct that all Menshevik delegates would be required to observe during its sessions. Indeed, the terms of this *Reglament* were unprecedented in the annals of Russian Social Democracy. It specified that Menshevik delegates were to be allowed to submit during the sessions only proposals and draft resolutions previously authorized by the majority of the delegation. Only speakers previously delegated by the majority of the delegation were to be permitted to take part in the discussion of these resolutions, and other members of the delegation were also prohibited from voting against resolutions previously approved by the majority and only conceded the right to abstain. This unprecedented *Reglament* was indignantly denounced and turned down by Martov and his supporters, a development which signaled an open schism in the Mensheviks' delegation.[80]

Actually, this outcome freed Martov to pursue throughout the agitated sessions of the Pre-parliament the tactics that he had already prescribed to his followers: to address fully all the substantive issues that came up and to present them in the form of resolutions according to the platform of the Menshevik Internationalists, but concluding in every instance that none of its prescriptions could be fulfilled in the absence of a fundamental political change—from coalition to an all-democratic government. These tactics kept the issue of power dramatically in the foreground of the debate, and also took the steam out of any possible objections by Martov's opponents that his proposals were politically unachievable. Martov and his followers put these tactics to good use during the extraordinarily charged sessions, beginning with the discussion of a report by the new Minister of War, Verkhovskii, that the Russian army was no longer capable in its current state of effectively pursuing the war.

Verkhovskii probably had in mind, when he issued this statement, to inject a sense of urgency in order to enact the passage without delay of military reforms that he wanted to carry out. But overlapping as it did with the German army's occupation of Riga, his address opened up a Pandora's box of mutual recriminations between the representatives of the socialist parties and the Kadets, as well as conflicting proposals within the socialist camp by the Revolutionary Defensists and the Menshevik Internationalists.

For Martov and his followers, this occasion also provided the first opportunity to present to the delegates of the Pre-parliament the proposal that the Provisional Government assume the initiative of announcing an armistice on Russia's western front, and call on all other belligerent governments, beginning with Russia's western allies, to join in this initiative to facilitate the opening of peace negotiations between the Allies and the Central Powers.[81]

This declaration, and the demand Martov coupled with it that if Russia's allies refused to endorse this proposal, a direct appeal be issued to the peoples of all belligerent countries to exercise decisive pressure on their respective governments to force them to give in to this demand, had been a long-standing plank of the peace platform of the Menshevik Internationalists. It was originally formulated by Martov at Zimmerwald in 1915, and had been reiterated time and time again by the Menshevik Internationalists since the inception of the revolution. Two factors, however, now added a new tonality and sense of urgency to it. The first was that the issues of war and peace were to be the principal topics of discussion at the conference of the allied governments in Paris, which Skobelev was to attend with the members of the Russian delegation in an advisory capacity as a representative of the soviets. The second and politically more important element in the equation was the insistence on the part of the Menshevik Internationalists that this step, no more than any other taken in the efforts to achieve a universal peace without annexations and indemnities, would have no chance of success in the absence of a radical change of government in Russia, involving the replacement of coalition by an all-democratic regime. This proposition now provided the clearest linkage between the issue of peace and the issue of power in the efforts to demonstrate that the struggle for peace could not effectively be pursued in the absence of a resolution of the problem of power.

One more highly unusual but significant proposal was submitted before the conclusion of the discussion of army reform. It was that the platform adopted on this topic include a proposal that further sales of privately owned land be suspended, and that all land in private hands be placed under the jurisdiction of land committees until their final disposition was decided by the Constituent Assembly. This proposal, in the radical form advocated by Chernov, had induced the Kadets to block his reappointment as Minister of Agriculture early in the summer, but it was now adopted by the Pre-parliament without much resistance under the impact of the peasant disorders. These disorders, involving the seizure of privately owned land, had broken out quite spontaneously in the course of the summer in Tambov *guberniia,* and were now spreading to adjacent areas of the Central Agricultural and Volga regions. They were contributing to the growing rate of desertion among the peasant soldiers at the front who had come from these regions, but who now wanted to take part in "Black Repartition" of the land.

Dan's reluctant support of this proposal was a pragmatic response to the threat to army discipline posed by the situation. (He originally wanted to confine its reach to the estates of noble landowners). In the view of Martov and his supporters, however, the behavior of the peasants of Tambov *guberniia,* and the response that it was evoking among the peasant soldiers originating from this region, demonstrated a fundamental, and highly positive, new development in the unfolding of the Russian revolution: *that the peasants of this region, and the peasant soldiers at the front who had deserted to join them, had liberated themselves from the influence of the bourgeoisie, not only on the issue of the land but also on the linked issue of peace, and were demonstrating thereby their readiness to assume the leading role that Martov had assigned to them in his vision of democratic revolution.*

XVII

The issues that had been implicitly raised in the discussions of army reforms were brought out with much greater sharpness in the course of the confrontational debates at the next session of the Pre-parliament, which was explicitly devoted to foreign policy. Opening this discussion was the speech of the Minister of Foreign Affairs, M. I. Tereshchenko, who had to address, among the issues up for discussion, the *Nakaz* that the Soviet Executive Committee had issued to Skobelev when it had designated him to represent it in a consultative capacity in the Russian delegation to the Paris Conference.

Tereshchenko's address constituted a veritable and undoubtedly deliberate provocation of the delegates of the socialist parties sitting in the hall—of those representing the Revolutionary Defensists no less than the delegates of the Menshevik Internationalists. Tereshchenko was especially harsh—indeed brutal—in his comments about Skobelev's *Nakaz*, stating *inter alia* that the conference the socialist parties planned to organize in Stockholm was "a private affair, and for this reason not a suitable topic for discussion among the representatives of the allied governments." And he concluded his address with the equally ringing and uncompromising declaration about the peace settlement to be offered to the Central Powers: "faithfulness to the allies constitutes a priority task, and the conclusion of a peace treaty at any price, especially one involving a deviation from the state's interest, would be impermissible."[82]

Believing that Tereshchenko's speech had incontrovertibly proven their case, the Menshevik Internationalists drafted a resolution summarizing their conclusion that only a radical break with coalition and the establishment of an "all-democratic" government could prevent a catastrophic outcome for the revolution. However, even before they and their opponents could submit their respective resolutions on the issue of war and peace, the regular schedule of the Pre-parliament was suddenly interrupted as a result of the publication on October 19 in *Novaia Zhizn'*, the Internationalist journal edited by Maxim Gorky, of an indignant note written by Kamenev (himself a member of the Bolsheviks' Central Committee) to the effect that the Central Committee of the Bolshevik Party had just voted in favor of a resolution calling for the immediate conduct of an armed uprising.

Despite their previous disagreements about the course of the Russian revolution and the strategy and tactics that were appropriate for its success, Martov and Dan (perhaps to their surprise) instinctively reacted to this in the same way. Even more surprisingly, they also reacted in the same way to the theatrical appearance of Kerensky before the delegates of the

Pre-parliament to demand their unconditional support for the measures to be taken by the Provisional Government to suppress the Bolsheviks' planned uprising by force of arms.

The joint [!] resolution that Martov and Dan submitted to the Pre-parliament about these developments resolutely condemned the decision of the Bolshevik Central Committee to sponsor an armed uprising, warning that even if it were to prove temporarily successful, it would open the door to civil war and an eventual counter-revolution. Martov and Dan warned equally strongly, however, against Kerensky's proclaimed intention to suppress the uprising by force of arms, warning that such a development would be equally likely to culminate in civil war and an eventual counter-revolution.

The only way to avoid such a catastrophic scenario, their joint resolution concluded, was through the achievement of a political solution of the crisis by the Pre-parliament and other organs of revolutionary democracy. In order to be effective, such a political solution would have to ensure that the basic demands of the people be fulfilled, including a guarantee that all private land be *turned over immediately* to the control of land committees, and that an ultimatum be issued to Russia's western allies to agree to the terms proposed by Russia's socialist parties for a peace agreement under the equally immediate threat that, otherwise, Russia would otherwise repudiate its alliances with them.[83]

This formulation was proposed on October 24 in a resolution sponsored *jointly* by the Internationalist and Revolutionary Defensist delegates of the Menshevik party and the PSR. It was adopted by a vote of 123 to 102, with 26 abstentions. The breakdown of the votes indicated that it had been supported by all Internationalists and Revolutionary Defensist delegates affiliated with the Menshevik Party and the PSR. The Popular Socialists (*Narodnye Sotsialisty*) and some other representatives of the *zemstva* and rural cooperatives had abstained. On the other side, as was to be expected, all supporters of the Kadet party had voted against this text, and for a resolution in favor of the demand of the Provisional Government for support of its decision to suppress the Bolsheviks' uprising by force of arms.[84]

XVIII

The development to which Kamenev referred with such indignation in his note to *Novaia Zhizn'* was the adoption by the Bolshevik Central Committee on October 10 of a resolution submitted by Lenin to the effect that a whole series of developments in Russia's international and domestic situation, some favorable to the Bolsheviks, others presenting a threat to the revolution, "placed an armed uprising on the order of the day." The text of the resolution continued:

> Recognizing, therefore, that an armed uprising is inevitable, and that the conditions for its success have fully emerged, the Central Committee proposes all party organizations guide themselves accordingly, and address and resolve from this point of view all practical questions (such as the Congress of Soviets of the Northern region, the transfer of the army from Petersburg, the demonstrations of the Moscovites, etc.).[85]

Notwithstanding the woodenness and ultimate ambiguity of its text, this was an important resolution, indeed the first tangible fruit of Lenin's unremitting pressure on the Central Committee since the end of September to endorse an immediate uprising. The catalyst for this call to arms, and for the victory Lenin had won in the Bolshevik Central Committee, *was probably, as had been the case of the steeling of Martov's position, the outbreak of peasant unrest in Tambov guberniia, the spread of this unrest among peasants of nearby regions, and the response it was evoking among peasant solders at the front originating from these regions.*

To be sure, other factors were cited as well in Lenin's September 29 article "The Crisis has Come to a Head,"[86] as contributing to his growing impatience about any delay in the Bolshevik seizure of power: the series of victories that the Bolsheviks had won in elections to local soviets, including the elections to both the Moscow and Petrograd Soviets, the evident polarization of the voters in the elections to the Moscow and Petrograd City Dumas, the radicalization and growing support for the Bolsheviks evident among the soldiers and sailors of Petrograd and Vyborg. But the development which Lenin, like Martov, put at the head of the list—calling it "the turning point of the revolution"—was that "*in a peasant country, ruled by a republican government supported by the SRs and the Mensheviks, which only yesterday ruled in the name of petty bourgeois democracy, a peasant uprising has broken out. This is incredible, but true.*" [My emphasis, L. H.]. Lenin elaborated:

> In and of itself it is clear that if in a peasant country, following seven months [of the rule of] a democratic republic, things should cul-

minate in a peasant uprising, it proves irrefutably [the emergence of] an all-national crisis of the revolution of unprecedented force, which is pushing the counter-revolution against the wall.[87]

A series of other symptoms also indicated that an all-national crisis had come to a head: the radicalization of Russia's minorities, already demonstrated at the Democratic Congress, at which the *curiae* of "nationalities" had voted against coalition in even higher proportions than the curiae of soldiers' and workers' deputies; the process of radicalization of the armed forces, which had been reflected not only in the repudiation of the existing government by the sailors of the Baltic fleet and the regiments quartered in Finland, but by a whole series of similar indications in other regions, including the endorsement of the Bolsheviks by soldiers of the Moscow garrison (by a vote of 13,000 out of 17,000). Indeed, even in the recent elections to the Moscow City Duma, the Bolsheviks won more votes than the Kadets (47%):

> If under these circumstances, the Bolsheviks allow themselves to succumb to constitutionalist illusions, to "waiting" for the Congress of Soviets to meet, and so on, there is no doubt that these Bolsheviks would prove themselves to be *sorry betrayers* of the cause of the proletariat.
>
> They would be betraying the German sailors who started a mutiny in the German fleet, so that, under the circumstances, to wait for the Congress of Soviets would mean to *betray the international revolution* . . . .
>
> They would be betraying the *peasantry* [allowing for] the suppression of the peasant uprising called for by *Delo Naroda*, which would constitute the murder of the revolution as a whole, forever and irreversibly. . . .
>
> The crisis has come to a head. The whole future of the revolution is at stake. The whole honor of the Bolshevik Party is at issue. The whole future of the international workers' revolution. . . . [88]

If this were not enough, Lenin added a concluding section which was to be distributed only to members of the Central Committee, of the Petrograd and Moscow Committees, and of the Soviets. What was truly unprecedented about the tone of this section was not only the inner stress, but also the anger that it expressed about the resistance Lenin was encountering among

leaders of his own party to what had become, for him and by the same token of many of his opponents in the party, the central point at issue: his insistence on carrying out an armed uprising *before* the date set for the opening of the Second Congress of Soviets. "To state things as they are," Lenin
opened this last section of his article, which, I repeat, was to be given only
restricted distribution:

> What is to be done? To tell things as they are, one must recognize
> that there is in our Central Committee and among other leaders of
> the Bolshevik party a current, or views, which favor waiting for the
> Congress of Soviets, and *oppose* the immediate seizure of power, *op-
> pose* an armed uprising. One must *defeat* this current of opinion.
> Otherwise the Bolsheviks would *disgrace* themselves for a century,
> and be reduced to *nothing* as a party. For to let such a moment go
> by, and wait for the Congress of Soviets to meet, is *complete idiocy*,
> or *complete betrayal*:
>
> Complete betrayal of the German workers! Should we wait for
> the *beginning* of their revolution!! By then, even the Liber-Dans
> would favor supporting it. But this revolution in Germany *cannot*
> begin, as long as Kerensky, Shiskin, and company are in power.
>
> Complete betrayal of the peasantry: at a time when the Soviets
> of *both capitals* are in our hands, to allow for the repression of the
> peasant uprising would mean to *lose, and deserve to lose*, any trust
> on the part of the peasants.
>
> To wait for the Congress of Soviets is complete political idiocy,
> because it means to let *weeks* go by, when a single week or even a few
> days, will decide *everything*. . . . It means to turn away in a coward-
> ly fashion from the seizure of power, because by 1–2 November,
> [launching it] will become impossible (both politically and techni-
> cally), as Cossacks will be assembled in the stupidly designated lo-
> cations of the uprising.
>
> To wait for the Congress is idiocy, because the Congress will
> not give anything. *It cannot give anything!*
>
> Moral significance? Amazing! What is the significance of con-
> versations with Liber-Dans when we know that the Soviets are *in fa-
> vor* of the peasants and that the peasant uprising will be *suppressed*!!
> We will reduce the *Soviets* to the role of pitiful babblers. First defeat
> Kerensky, then call the Congress together.[89]

At this point in the article, Lenin abruptly assumed the mantle of a military strategist:

> The success of an uprising is *assured* for the Bolsheviks (if we do not wait for the Congress of Soviets). 1. We can strike unexpectedly from three points: Piter [Petrograd], Moscow, and the Baltic Fleet. 2. We have the slogans which assure us support: "Down with the government, which is repressing the peasants' uprising against the *pomeshchiki* [the noble landowners]." 3. We are the majority *in the country*. 4. There is total disintegration among the Mensheviks and the SRs. 5. We have the technical capability of taking power in Moscow (which might even start the uprising), and thus disorient our foes by its unexpectedness. 6. We have thousands of armed solders and workers in Piter who can take *immediately* the Winter Palace, the General Staff, and the telephone stations and all the big printing presses; and we will be able to repel the opposition, as the agitation *in the army* will be such that it will be *impossible* to use it to struggle against this government of peace, land to the peasants, etc. . . . .
>
> If we strike immediately, unexpectedly, at these three points, Piter, Moscow, and the Baltic Fleet, there's a 99% chance that we will win with less victims than on July 3-5, because the army *will not move* against a peace government. Even if Kerensky should already have "faithful" cavalry in Piter, he will be forced to *surrender*. Given the chances for success that we now have, not to take power [would be] to turn the talk about all power to the soviets into a *lie*.
>
> Not to take power now amounts to engage in empty talk. To confine ourselves to a struggle to win a majority at the Congress of Soviets would be to turn our struggle into a *lie*. Not to take power, to wait, to engage in empty talk in TsIK, to confine ourselves to a struggle to win a majority at the Congress of Soviets means *to kill the revolution*.[90]

Lenin concluded this angry piece on an even angrier personal note:

> In view of the fact that the Central Committee has left *unanswered* my insistent pleas in this spirit since the beginning of the Democratic Conference, that the central organ [of the party] has *struck out* from my articles my remarks about such stinking errors on the part

of the Bolsheviks such as the shameful decision to take part in the Pre-parliament, in the Presidium of the Soviets, etc. etc., I must consider these as "subtle" hints that the Central Committee doesn't even want to permit me to discuss these issues, (i.e., that it wants me to shut my mouth), and as an invitation that I stand aside. . . .

I have decided [therefore] to *submit my resignation to the Central Committee*, in order to give myself the complete freedom to agitate in the party's *lower ranks* and at the party Congress.

For it is my most fervent conviction, that if we "wait" for the Congress of Soviets and let the present moment go by, we will *kill* the revolution.[91]

To reconstruct the evolution of the conflicts within the Bolshevik party that had led to Lenin's explosion of anger, we need to recall that the operative part of the resolution that the Bolshevik party's Central Committee had passed on October 10 (and which Kamenev had denounced to *Novaia Zhizn'*), did not even raise the issue of whether an armed uprising was to be launched before the Second Congress of Soviets convened. Neither had Lenin's speech introducing this resolution. Lenin had condemned in his introduction the apparent indifference with which the issue had been addressed since the beginning of September, and the lack of attention that had been paid to the technical aspects of the problem. He had noted the objections raised by Shotman and others about the apparent indifference of the masses, and dismissed them on the grounds that the masses were already weary of empty words and resolutions. But the closest that Lenin had come to the issue of the timing of an armed uprising had been to state that "to wait for the Constituent Assembly, which evidently will not be with us, is senseless, and would only complicate our task," adding the phrase that the Congress of the Northern Region and the proposal from Minsk should be used for the launching of a decisive action.[92]

Only Kamenev and Zinoviev had been recorded as opposed to Lenin's resolution, and we must recall that they had insisted that their vehement objections to the resolution be noted in the protocols of the Central Committee. Trotsky had presented a compromise proposal: that the launching of the uprising be timed to coincide with the opening of the Congress. But he did not insist that it be voted upon, and in the end had voted in support of Lenin's resolution.[93]

At Lenin's insistence, the Central Committee returned to this issue on October 16 (29), 1917. This was a particularly important and interesting meeting for a number of major reasons. The number of its participants was broadened to include, aside from the members of the Central Committee, representatives of the Executive Commission of the Military Organization attached to the Petrograd Soviet, as well as members of trade unions, factory committees, railroad unions, and of the Petrograd District Party Committee, by far the broadest representation that had been called upon to consider Lenin's proposal. Secondly, the accounts and source materials (provided largely by Lenin himself) on the proceedings of this meeting, give a much fuller account of the debates to which Lenin's introductory speech and the text of his resolution gave rise, including the nature of the objections made by his critics, as well as his attempts to refute them. Consequently, the reader is left with a much fuller sense of the attitudes of Bolshevik leaders at this point, or more precisely, of those who felt free to articulate their views at such an official meeting. (Included were Lenin's exchanges with Miliutin, an influential member of the Moscow Party Committee, with Shotman, a member of the Petrograd Party Committee reputed to be in close contact with Petrograd workers, and with Zinoviev who, along with Kamenev, continued to be the most articulate and irreconcilable critic of Lenin's position.)

Let us begin our analysis of these sources with Lenin's introduction to his resolution, the text of the resolution itself, and Lenin's responses to the criticisms of Miliutin, Shotman, and Zinoviev. In his prepared speech, Lenin read the text of the resolution adopted at the conclusion of the meeting of the Central Committee on October 10, and emphasized two major points. The first was that a compromise had been offered previously to the Mensheviks and the PSR, and that this compromise had been rejected by these two parties. The second point emphasized that since the rejection of this compromise, political developments had amply demonstrated that the masses supported the Bolsheviks. Lenin cited as evidence of this support the statistics of the municipal elections in Petrograd and Moscow, concluding from them that "the masses have invested their confidence in the Bolsheviks and demand of them not words, but decisive action. Even the recent anarchist outbreak confirms this fact."[94]

Along with confident assertions, however, came an uncustomary qualification: "One cannot be guided by the mood of the masses because it is changeable, and cannot be precisely calculated. We must guide ourselves by an objective analysis and evaluation of the revolution."[95] (This statement was in response to Shotman's emphasis on the lack of enthusiasm for an armed uprising to be observed among Petrograd workers.)

Lenin's remarks about the development of the revolutionary situation in Europe, were more inflated than ever: "If we strike now, we will have all of proletarian Europe with us." On the other hand, Lenin emphasized that the bourgeoisie wanted to surrender Petrograd to the Germans, and that the only way to keep this from happening was for the Bolsheviks to take power. Hence, an armed uprising was imperative to save the revolution.[96]

In his additional exchanges with Miliutin and Shotman, Lenin emphasized that the Bolsheviks would have to struggle only against part of the army, and that the facts showed that they would have the upper hand in this struggle. Furthermore, "the Bolsheviks could hold onto power," Lenin continued. "Objective conditions show that while the peasantry must be led, it will follow the proletariat."[97]

In the course of this debate, Lenin also concentrated his fire on Zinoviev, accusing him of repudiating the slogan, "All power to the proletariat," and of favoring instead "pressure on the government." "Furthermore, if we recognize that conditions had ripened for an uprising," Lenin insisted, "we can hardly speak about conspiracy. If an uprising is politically inevitable, one must address the issue of an uprising as an art, as politically, the conditions for it have already ripened."[98] Precisely because there was bread for only one day, one could not wait for the Constituent Assembly, Lenin concluded, and he called for the adoption of his resolution in favor of an armed uprising, leaving it to the Central Committee and to the soviets to determine its timing. Thus, the operative clause of the resolution that Lenin submitted expressed full confidence that the Central Committee and the soviets would determine the "appropriate moment" and the "appropriate means" for the conduct of an armed uprising.

The text of this resolution was adopted by a vote of 19 to 2 with 4 abstentions. Again, Kamenev's and Zinoviev's were the two opposing votes, but the four persons who abstained were not identified. We may presume, however, that they came largely from members of the Moscow Party Committee, such as Nogin, Miliutin, and Rykov, who had previously expressed reservations about an armed uprising, let alone one to be conducted before the Congress of Soviets convened.

The most detailed and revealing account that Lenin recorded about these deliberations of the enlarged Central Committee on October 16 was presented in a document entitled "Letter to Comrades," which he wrote on October 17 (30), and which appeared on 19, 20, and 21 October, i.e., almost on the very eve of the armed uprising.

This document opened with the assertion that while only a small minority of two (consisting of Zinoviev and Kamenev), had finally voted against the resolution adopted at this very important and representative meeting. The considerations that they had advanced had constituted such astounding manifestations of confusion, fearfulness, and disintegration of all the ideas of Bolshevism and proletarian internationalism, and might provoke such a degree of confusion, that it was imperative to decipher "the arguments of this miserly pair of comrades and the shameful loss of principles that they reflected." There followed an exposition summarizing the various objections raised by Zinoviev and Kamenev and Lenin's rebuttals of them, a useful way for readers to follow the essence of the debate, notwithstanding Lenin's biased presentation of it.[99]

"We don't have a popular majority in our favor, and without it the conditions for an uprising are hopeless . . . [the argument of Zinoviev and Kamenev]."

[Lenin's answer] People who speak like this are pedants who demand that the Bolsheviks receive in the country a majority of fifty percent plus. For reality shows that since July the majority of the people have rapidly gone over to the Bolsheviks. Even before the *Kornilovshchina*, in the municipal elections in Petrograd of 20 August, the percentage of Bolshevik votes rose from 20 to 33 percent, while in the elections to Moscow's District Duma, held in September, the percentage of Bolshevik votes had risen from 11 to 49 1/3 percent. (I was told by a comrade a few days ago that the precise percentage was 51 percent, as shown by the re-elections to the soviets.) By fall, the majority of the peasant soviets turned against the Kadets, and to be against coalition means in fact to be for the Bolsheviks. Furthermore, reports from the front show that the soldiers . . . are going over more and more decisively to the Bolsheviks, and finally, the biggest fact of contemporary life in Russia is the peasant uprising. . . . It shows that the majority of the people have gone over to the Bolsheviks. . . .

"We are not strong enough to take power, while the bourgeoisie is not strong enough to break up the Constituent Assembly [the argument of Zinoviev and Kamenev]."

The first question has already been answered. As for the second, if the present government is not overthrown, it can achieve this result by surrendering Piter to the Germans by opening up the front, by intensifying lockouts, sabotaging the delivery of bread. In part, the bourgeoisie has already begun to do this. . . .

"The soviets must be a revolver, aimed at the government's head, to demand the convocation of the Constituent Assembly and a rejection of any attempted *Kornilovshchina* [the argument of Zinoviev and Kamenev]."

One of the two pitiful pessimists spoke out in this vein, and it was necessary to point out to him that to reject an uprising meant to reject 'all power to the soviets,' and to leave the convocation of the Constituent Assembly entirely to the good will of the bourgeoisie. Either you go over to Liber-Danism, and renounce the slogan, 'All Power to the Soviets,' or an uprising; there is no intermediate choice. . . .

"The bourgeoisie cannot surrender Piter to the Germans even though Rodzianko wants this, because it isn't the bourgeoisie who is doing the fighting, but our heroic sailors . . . [the argument of Zinoviev and Kamenev]."

If the *Kornilovsty* (and Kerensky is one) wish to surrender Piter, they can do it in three ways: First, they can let the treacherous Kornilovite command open the Northern front to the Germans. Second, they can make a deal giving freedom of action to the Germans, or even to the English fleet. Third, through lockouts and sabotage of the delivery of bread, they can reduce the masses to complete despair and powerlessness. Therefore, we cannot wait until the bourgeoisie strangles the revolution to death. . . .

"We are becoming stronger as every day passes, and can emerge as a strong opposition in the constituent assembly. Why gamble everything on one card? [the argument of Zinoviev and Kamenev]."

Will everything remain at a standstill while we wait for the convocation of the Constituent Assembly? Famine doesn't wait, the peasants' uprising doesn't. The war continues. Conspiring criminals will not wait. . . .

"There's really nothing in the international situation to force us to act immediately. Rather we would harm the socialist revolution in the west, if we let ourselves be shot down [the argument of Zinoviev and Kamenev]."

Think for a moment: we will adopt a resolution in support of the German insurrectionists and reject an uprising in Russia. . . . The war has pushed the workers of all countries to the limit. There are more and more frequent outbreaks in Italy, Germany, and Austria. And we, who alone have Soviets of Workers' and Soldiers' Deputies, should wait, thereby betraying the German Internationalists, as well as the Russian peasants who are rising up against the noble landowners, and calling on us to rise up against Kerensky's government. . . .

"But every one is against us. We are isolated in TsIK. Even the Menshevik Internationalists, the supporters of *Novaia Zhizn'*, and the Left SRs have been issuing appeals against us [the argument of Zinoviev and Kamenev]."

. . . The essence of Liber-Danism and the Chernovs, but also of the "lefts" among the members of the PSR and the Mensheviks is wavering. But the indications that as the masses move to the left, so do the Left SRs and the Menshevik Internationalists, are of great significance. The fact that about forty percent of the Mensheviks and the SRs have gone over to the left and that of the peasants' uprising are unquestionably linked. . . .

"There is bread in Piter for only 2–3 days. Can we give bread to the participants in the insurrection? [the argument of Zinoviev and Kamenev]."

It is precisely Rodzianko and the bourgeoisie who are causing famine, and speculating on repressing the revolution through famine. Therefore, any delay in an uprising would be the equivalent of a death sentence. This is what we must say to those who have the pitiful lack of *muzhestvo* [manliness] to look to the processes of disintegration and the imminence of famine as arguments to counsel the workers *against* an uprising. . . .

"There is no mood among the masses to break out on the streets, everybody reports. Among the indications that support this pessimism is the growing popularity of the Black Hundreds [the argument of Zinoviev and Kamenev]."

People sometimes forget that, by their waverings, responsible leaders can themselves induce waverings in the mood of certain strata of the masses. Secondly—and this is most important at the present time—one must add that everyone describes the state of the mind of the masses as concentrated and as a mood of 'expectation'; that everyone agrees that the workers will come out and respond, as one man, to the call of the soviets, and in defense of the soviets; that everyone describes the mood of the masses as close to despair, and

explains the growth of anarchism on this basis; that everyone recognizes that among conscious workers, there is definitely a reluctance to go out on the streets only for demonstrations, only for the
sake of a partial struggle, because floating in the air is the expectation, not of a partial but of a general battle, and consequently [there
is a] loss of faith in individual strikes and demonstrations. . . .

The preconditions for an uprising are the determination of
conscious elements to fight to the end, and a sense of despair among
the wider masses, which are *feeling* that no half measures can now
achieve anything. It is to this combination of the degree of concentration reached by the conscious elements, and of the desperate
mood of hatred against the capitalists among the broader masses,
that the development of the revolution is now taking both the
workers and the peasants. . . . The masses can be divided between
those who are consciously waiting, and those who are unconscious-
ly sinking into despair, but the masses of the oppressed and the
hungry are not lacking in character. . . .

"A Marxist party cannot reduce the question of an uprising to
that of a conspiracy [the argument of Zinoviev and Kamenev]."

A conspiracy is *Blanquism*, if it is not organized by the party of
a definite class, if its organizers do not take account of the political
moment and of the international situation as a whole, if the support
of the party by the majority of the people is not demonstrated by
objective facts; if the development of revolutionary events has not
led already to the dissipation of the illusions of the petty bourgeoisie
about possible compromises; if among the majority of the most recognized organs of the revolutionary struggle, such as the soviets; if
in the army . . . a fully matured opposition has not already emerged
against the government, which is prolonging an unjust war against
the will of the people; if the slogan for an uprising (such as 'All Power to the Soviets,' 'Land to the Peasantry,' 'The Immediate Proposal of a Democratic Peace to All Belligerent Countries') . . . had not
already assumed the widest . . . popularity; and if the workers' vanguard is not already convinced of the desperate situation of the
masses and of the support of the countryside, as demonstrated by
the peasants' movement against the noble landowners and the government supporting them; if the economic situation did not deny
any hope for a peaceful solution of the crisis by peaceful and parliamentary means.

Enough, already!

In my pamphlet, "Will the Bolsheviks Hold onto Power?", I included a citation from Marx emphasizing the recognition of an uprising as an art. I would call on all the babblers who now denounce a military conspiracy, and distinguish in the "art" of an armed uprising a military conspiracy condemned to defeat, that they read and repeat all of the above, if they are not to expose themselves to unanimous ridicule by the workers.

Try it out, my dear pseudo-Marxists, and stop singing your little song against an 'armed conspiracy.' [100]

Thereafter, Lenin's pressure on the Central Committee and other organs of the Bolshevik party continued unabated. The ferocity of his attacks against opponents of an armed uprising prior to the Second Congress of Soviets appeared to approach a veritable state of hysteria, as the day scheduled for the convocation of the Congress approached. Yet neither Lenin's pressure nor the ferocity of his attacks had any visible effect on the strength of the opposition among Bolshevik leaders to his call for an uprising. For the most part, this opposition took the form of a silent, passive, yet seemingly indomitable resistance. Most of the representatives of this "silent majority" among Lenin's opponents appeared animated by the fear, apparently shared by many workers of the capital, that the armed insurrection on which he insisted would end in a fiasco, given the strength of the opposition to it expressed by leaders of other socialist parties (including the Bolsheviks' presumed allies, the Left SRs). This fear was obviously sustained by the bitter recollections among Petrograd workers of the fiasco of the July Days.

However, among Lenin's opponents there also had emerged a small but growing number of people who appeared animated by broader political considerations, if not by reasons of principle. By the eve of the Second Congress, this opposition was especially notable among members of the Moscow Party Committee (such as Nogin, Rozhkov, and Miliutin) and of the ex-"*Mezhraionskaia*" intelligentsia (such as Riazanov and Lunacharskii) who had joined the Bolshevik party only in June, and had so vigorously supported at the Democratic Conference the formation of an "all-democratic" government.

Within the Bolshevik Central Committee, opposition continued to be articulated most firmly by Kamenev and Zinoviev, who had so vigorously opposed Lenin in the debate on the resolution that he had submitted on October 10 "to place the conduct of an armed uprising on the order of the day."

I have already noted that Zinoviev and Kamenev had been so vehemently opposed to this resolution that they had insisted on recording their objections in the protocols of the Bolshevik Party's Central Committee. And it is from these protocols that we can draw, on the basis of their own formulations, the major theses that they had advanced for their opposition to Lenin's position.[101]

The first of these major theses rested on the proposition that the petty bourgeoisie, including the vast majority of the peasantry, constituted the key to the further development of the revolution. This proposition, as we have seen, was now shared by Martov and even Lenin. But Kamenev and Zinoviev remained far more conservative than Lenin or even Martov in their assessment of the degree to which the peasantry had in fact already liberated itself from the influence exercised on it by the bourgeoisie. From their more conservative assessment followed two conclusions about the strategy to follow at this stage of the revolution.

The first was that the further progress of the revolution would depend to a large degree on the capacity of the proletariat and its leaders for political self-restraint in their efforts to bring the peasantry over to their side. The second conclusion, which drew Kamenev's and Zinoviev's views closer to Martov's than to Lenin's, was that the prerequisite for the success of the revolution was the establishment of an "all-democratic" government distinguished by the widest participation and support on the part of representatives of the peasantry. In this connection, Kamenev dismissed Lenin's warning that the bourgeoisie would seek to prevent the Constituent Assembly from convening, arguing that if it tried to do so the peasants would be likely to vote in even greater number for candidates of the SRs.

These arguments brought out the degree of conversion between the conclusions that Kamenev and Zinoviev were drawing by this time and those drawn by Martov but also by the Left SRs—a conversion which clearly created the potential for the emergence at the Second Congress of Soviets of a majority favoring the creation of an "all-democratic" or "all-socialist" government – most delegates still did not know the difference—a government which would include representatives of a wide array of political parties and factions opposed to any form of coalition with the capitalistic bourgeoisie, and resting on the broadest possible participation of representatives of the peasantry.

Notwithstanding Lenin's growing pressure, accusations, and threats (which came to include that of resigning from the Bolshevik Central Committee and going to the sailors of the Baltic fleet to call for their support for an immediate uprising), resistance to his pressure was mounting proportionately among the members of various Bolshevik and soviet organizations.

The basic reason for this is not hard to fathom. Lenin's warnings of imminent catastrophe at home if an armed uprising was delayed, and his inflated promises of the outbreak of a European-wide revolution if it was not, steadily lost their power of conviction as the day assigned to the opening of the Congress of Soviets approached. More and more Bolshevik leaders and delegates to the Congress could ask themselves, under the circumstances, about the effects of a few weeks', and, as the Congress prepared to convene, of a few days', delay on the possibility, as Lenin catastrophically forecast, of a new *Kornilovshchina*, or of the opening to Petrograd to the German army by the Provisional Government, or on the fulfillment of his increasingly inflated forecasts of impending revolution in the West. The question was all the more pressing if such a brief delay would mean that the call for all power to the soviets and international revolution would come from a majority of the delegates to the Congress, including the Left SRs who opposed Lenin's plans for an armed insurrection.

In the face of these objections, Lenin finally felt compelled to offer a more persuasive, or at least more genuine, explanation for his position, which not only was widely resisted, but also remained beyond the comprehension of even his closest followers. This, he sought to achieve in a letter addressed to the Bolshevik Central Committee through the intermediary of Krupskaya, on the evening of October 24, 1917, i.e., on the very eve of the date that the Congress of Soviets was scheduled to be convened.

Although the text of this letter was eventually learned by heart by many Soviet schoolchildren, I shall quote it at some length since it provides the most revealing picture of Lenin's mood on the eve of the Bolshevik seizure of power:

> I am writing these lines on the evening of the 24th [at a moment when] the situation has become critical beyond measure [*donel'zia kriticheskoe*]. It could not possibly be clearer [*iasnee iasnogo*] that at this moment everything is hanging by a thread . . . that there are problems at hand which cannot be solved by conferences or congresses (including even a Congress of Soviets), but only by the people, the masses—the struggle of the armed masses. . . .
>
> The bourgeois assault of the Kornilovites, the dismissal of Verkhovskii [the popular Minister of War] show that we cannot wait any longer. This evening, this very night—whatever happens—

we must arrest this government, disarm (and if they resist, defeat) the Junkers.

We cannot wait!! Everything can be lost!! In the balance, the value of taking power immediately involves: protecting the *people* (not the congress, but in the first instance, the people, the army, and the peasants) from the Kornilovite government, which has fired Verkhovskii, and prepared a second Kornilovite conspiracy.

Who must take power?

Right now, this is not important: let the Military Revolutionary Committee or some other institution take it, and declare that it will surrender it only to true representatives of the interests of the people, the interests of the army (in an immediate peace proposal), and the interests of the peasants (to take the land immediately, and eliminate private property), the interests of the hungry.

All districts, all regiments, all forces must be mobilized at once, and immediately send delegations to the Military Revolutionary Committee, to the Central Committee of the Bolsheviks, and insistently demand: Under no circumstances, leave power in the hands of Kerensky and co. until the 25th. In no way! It is imperative that we decide the matter this evening, or tonight.

History will not forgive revolutionaries who can win today (and most surely will win today), while risking to lose much tomorrow, risking to lose everything.

By taking power today, we will take it not against the soviets, but for them. The seizure of power is the task of an uprising; its political goal will be clarified after power is seized.

It would be deadly, or a formality, to wait for a *wavering vote* [of the congress], on 25 October [my emphasis L.H.]. The people have the right and duty to decide such questions, not by voting but by force: the people have the right and duty at critical moments of revolutions to take over the lead from their representatives—even their best representatives—rather than wait for them [to lead].

The history of all revolutions has shown this, and it would be an enormous crime for revolutionaries to let the moment pass them by, knowing that on them depends the *salvation of the revolution*, the fate of the peace [process], the salvation of Piter, salvation from hunger, the transfer of the land to the peasants. The power of the government is wavering. One must *seize* it at whatever cost! [whatever the circumstances].

To delay the attack would be the equivalent of death itself (*smerti podobno*).[102]

This was a crucially important message. For the first time, Lenin explained, or at least came close to explaining, even to his closest comrades, the real underlying reason for his insistence that the Bolsheviks take power at all costs before the Second Congress convened: his fear that if left to their own devices, the delegates to the Second Congress would "waver," or to decipher the expression that Lenin used, "be inclined to support" the formation of the "all-democratic" or "all-socialist" government favored by Martov and his allies, which would include a broad representation of the socialist parties, and rest on the equally broad support of the Russian peasantry.

XIX

I suggested earlier in this discussion why this solution, and indeed the rest of the platform that Martov had outlined in *Iskra* for the representatives of the Menshevik Internationalists at the Congress of Soviets, was likely to draw wide support among the delegates, including, of course, the Left SRs, but even delegates who had been elected on the lists of the Bolshevik Party.

By the evening of the 24th, as early arrivals congregated in the halls of Smolny on the eve of the opening of the Congress, and caucused with other delegates, tangible evidence began to emerge of the breadth of the support that the proposal for the formation of an "all-democratic," or "all socialist," government was attracting among those elected on the lists of various parties and factions.

For example, at a caucus of the delegation of the RSDRP(o), *at which representatives of all the factions of the Menshevik party, including the Revolutionary Defensists, were present,* these delegates, ignoring the warning that Dan had issued to them earlier in the day to the effect that "a basic reconstruction of the [state] power would be premature," voted overwhelmingly in favor of a resolution calling such a complete reconstruction of the state power "imperative," beginning with the creation of an "all-democratic" regime. Two votes were recorded at this meeting in favor of "All Power to the Soviets" and only one in favor of preservation of coalition![103] An equally significant political development occurred at a session *attended by both the official representatives of the PSR and those of the Left SRs, which rejected by a vote of 92 to 60 the resolution submitted by the Central Committee of the PSR (presumably in support of the preservation of coalition), and voted in support of a resolution submitted by the Left SRs, proposing that contact be made with the Menshevik Internationalists in order to draw up with them a joint resolution on the issue of power* (presumably in support of the formation of an "all-democratic" government).[104]

By the end of the day, Lenin, who had been kept in strict isolation in the room to which he had been confined by the Bolshevik Central Committee, had received no response to the increasingly desperate messages that he had sent to the Central Committee through the intermediary of Krupskaya. Receiving no response and hearing no sound of the beginning of an uprising, he could not stand his isolation any longer, and in violation of the strict instructions of the Central Committee, he left his room after putting on the false beard and the cap and bandages which served as his disguise. He boarded a trolley car to take him to Smolny. (Reportedly, he spent his time on this almost deserted trolley in an animated discussion of the political situation with the conductor, a woman of equally radical political views). Upon his arrival at Smolny, Lenin was originally denied access to the building for lack of a proper pass, but after almost losing his disguise in his agitation, he finally managed to get access to the room where the Bolshevik Central Committee was in session.

What precisely Lenin told his colleagues on this occasion has not been recorded for posterity. His collected works report tactfully only that he now took in hand the leadership of the armed uprising.[105] Actually, this is something of an overstatement, for on the morning of the 25th, i.e., on the day that the Congress was scheduled to open, representatives of the Military Revolutionary Committee of the Petrograd Soviet, which had been entrusted with the direction of the armed uprising, approached Lenin with the suggestion that the uprising be postponed for a few hours, so that the Congress (which was scheduled to open at 2 p.m.) could give it its *imprimatur*.

It is not difficult to imagine the expression on Lenin's face when he received this suggestion. In an effort to avoid any further surprises, he immediately sat down at his desk and hastily drew up the text of a telegram, addressed to all organs of the press, announcing the overthrow of the Provisional Government (which, of course, had not yet taken place), as well as the transfer of power to the Revolutionary Committee of the Petrograd Soviet.

Lenin sent out this telegram at 10 a.m. on the morning of the 25th, i.e., before a single shot had been fired, and unhesitatingly signed it in the name of the Military Revolutionary Committee of the Petrograd Soviet.

This was the text of the remarkable document that Lenin hastily drew up:

> To the citizens of Russia. The Provisional Government has been
> overthrown. State power has been taken over by the Military Revo-
> lutionary Committee, the organ of the Petrograd Soviet of Workers'
> and Soldiers' Deputies which heads the Petrograd proletariat and
> [military] garrison.
>
> The cause for which the people have fought—the immediate
> proposal for a democratic peace, the elimination of the noble
> landowners' ownership of the land, workers' control of production,
> the establishment of soviet government—all of these objectives
> have been achieved.
>
> Hail to the revolution of workers, soldiers, and peasants!
>
> [signed:] The Military Revolutionary Committee of the Petro-
> grad Soviet of Workers' and Soldiers' Deputies, 25 October 1917, 10
> a.m."[106]

Lenin wired the text of this announcement, which he himself signed,
"Military Revolutionary Committee of the Petrograd Soviet" (!), to all organs of the press (*vsem, vsem*), thus seeking to foster the impression that the
issue of power had already been decided, and the program of the new state
power, drawn up.

The unfolding of Lenin's scenario was significantly derailed, however, as
the Second Congress of Soviets did not convene as scheduled at 2 p.m. While
delegates milled around the entrance to the hall, no dramatic event to signal
the overthrow of the Provisional Government occurred, and no sounds of
firing were heard to suggest that it was even under way. The opening of the
Congress was re-scheduled for 8 p.m., but even this new deadline was not
met, due to an interminable meeting of the Menshevik delegates, which finally broke up under pressure from the other, increasingly irate delegates
anxious for the Congress to begin.

XX

Upon the belated arrival of the members of the Menshevik delegation, Fedor
Dan, acting as Chair on behalf of the Central Executive Committee elected
at the First Congress of Soviets, declared the Second Congress open, at 10:45

p.m. He confined himself to the observation that he considered any political speech on his part superfluous "at a time when our comrades sitting in the Winter Palace are under fire."[107]

As soon as the session was declared open, Martov stood to raise a point of order. His voice breaking, and his body shaking from head to toe as often happened to him when he was under great stress, he demanded that the Congress give priority to a peaceful resolution of the crisis:

> The Menshevik Internationalist faction cannot assume political responsibility for the political adventure undertaken by the Bolsheviks. It is imperative that the congress assign priority to a peaceful resolution of the crisis, as this issue is serious, and a civil war has already begun.[108]

According to a fuller version of his statement, published in *Pravda*, Martov continued:

> First and foremost, the task of the Congress is to decide the question of power. The Congress has found that this question was decided in advance, and we consider it our duty to do everything in our power to resolve this crisis peacefully, through the creation of a *vlast'* recognized by all democracy. If it wants to be the voice of revolutionary democracy, the Congress must not lay down its hands in the face of a developing civil war, the result of which would be the outbreak of a counterrevolution. A peaceful way out is still possible . . . through the creation of a single, united democratic *vlast'*. It is imperative that a united democratic *vlast'* be created. . . . [To this purpose], it is imperative in the first place to elect a delegation to conduct negotiations with other socialist parties and organizations to bring to a halt the clashes that have broken out.[109]

Representatives of the Left SRs and of the United Social Democrat Internationalists supported Martov's proposal, and thereupon (*miraculus dei!*), Lunacharskii declared that the Bolshevik faction "decidedly has nothing against Martov's proposal, but on the contrary, is interested in finding a peaceful way out." As a result, Martov's proposal was adopted unanimously [!!] by the delegates.[110]

However, the miracle was to be dissipated almost as quickly as it had occurred. Following Martov, representatives of a series of Menshevik army organizations from the front came to the podium, and in the most militant language condemned the Bolsheviks for usurping the will of the Congress. Their main speaker, Kuchin, stated:

> We declare that the civil war set off by the Bolsheviks constitutes a blow in the back of the army. It is imperative to save the revolution from this insane politika, and to save the revolution, we will mobilize all conscious revolutionary forces in the army and in the country as a whole. The delegates from the front assign themselves this task, and shedding responsibility for the consequences of this adventure, announce their departure from this congress. From now on, the arena of the struggle will be transferred to the country as a whole.[111]

Following Kuchin's statement came equally belligerent declarations by other delegates from the front, and then an equally uncompromising statement delivered by L.N. Khinchuk on behalf of the majority of the Menshevik party (i.e., all but the Menshevik Internationalists). Khinchuk declared that

> the military conspiracy of the Bolsheviks has been carried behind the back of all parties and factions represented in the soviets . . . and has destroyed the significance of the Congress as an authoritative representative organ of revolutionary democracy, leading the country to civil war, threatening to destroy the Constituent Assembly, and heading toward military catastrophe and the possible triumph of counter-revolution. The only possible way out of this situation remains negotiations with the Provisional Government for the formation of a [state] power resting on all strata of democracy.[112]

Khinchuk concluded with the statement that the "fraction of the RS-DRP(o) is departing from the Congress, and proposes to all fractions, which also refuse to take responsibility for the actions of the Bolsheviks to meet with it immediately to discuss the situation." Whereupon, a similar declaration was issued by a representative of the delegation of the PSR, and the delegations of both fractions, joined by a large number of representatives from the front, left the hall.

With these statements, Khinchuk and the delegates from the front who had preceded him to the podium appeared to turn much of the resentment that delegates at the Congress felt against the Bolshevik leaders for usurping their will, against himself and other opponents of the Bolsheviks, by challenging these delegates' right to fulfill the mandate that had been assigned to them by *their* electorate to create a new *vlast'* resting on "all power to the soviets," in place of coalition with representatives of the bourgeoisie.

At this point the fluctuating sentiments reflected in this debate were further jarred by a new *coup de théâtre*, when leaders of the Bund reported that a group of representatives of the Petrograd City Duma had decided to march unarmed, but presumably under fire, to the square facing the Winter Palace in an effort to bring the shooting there to a stop. Members of the Executive Committee of the Soviets of Peasants' Deputies and of the majorities of the Menshevik party and the PSR announced their decision to join in this march:

> We have decided in this way to articulate our protest against what is going on, and to call on all those who do not want blood to be shed, to go with us. Perhaps, our departure will force the lunatics or criminals to take note.[113]

After Abramovich announced his support for this declaration in the name of the Bund, Martov, in whose hands now rested the increasingly lonely task of trying to save the situation by seeking to win a majority in favor of the formation of an "all-democratic" government among the opponents of the Bolshevik coup, read a resolution to this effect, which included in its preamble a severe condemnation of the Bolshevik uprising.

Since this was the last constructive proposal that Martov would be able to issue at the Congress, I quote the text in full. It was issued in the joint name of the Menshevik Internationalists and the Jewish Socialist Labor Party (*Paole-Tsion*):

> Taking into account: 1) that the overturn which brought power in Petrograd into the hands of the Military Committee [of the Petrograd Soviet] the day before the opening of the Congress was achieved by the Bolshevik party through a purely military conspiracy; 2) that this overturn threatens to give rise to a conflict culminating in the triumph of counter-revolution, which will drown in blood the whole movement of the proletariat, and eliminate along with it, all the conquests of the revolution; 3) that the sole way out of this situation, and to bring to a halt the outbreak of a civil war, is

the conclusion of an agreement between the part of the proletariat that has taken part in the uprising and other democratic organizations on the formation of a democratic government which would be recognized by all revolutionary democracy, and to which the Provisional Government could surrender power painlessly, the Menshevik party proposes to the Congress the adoption of a resolution stating that it is imperative to find a peaceful resolution of the crisis that has been created, through the formation of an "all-democratic" government.

To this purpose, the fraction of Menshevik Internationalists proposes to the Congress that a delegation be appointed to conduct negotiations with other organs of democracy and all socialist parties. Until the clarification of the result of these negotiations, the fraction of Menshevik Internationalists proposes the Congress suspend its work.[114]

Kamenev, who was now in the chair, noted that the delegates had voted unanimously at the beginning of this session in favor of Martov's proposal to seek an immediate halt to the conflict and of the opening of negotiations for its peaceful resolution, but that since Martov had made this proposal, any effort to implement it had been buried by the various declarations and resolutions offered by the parties and factions represented at the Congress. This effort of Kamenev at peace-making was to no avail, however, as Trotsky now came to the podium and delivered a belligerent and demagogic address loudly stating that an uprising by the people did not require any justification. He concluded his statement with a famously insulting phrase, directed at those delegates who had already left, or were planning to leave the Congress: "You are poor bankrupts who have played out your roles. Go where you should go, to the garbage pail (*v mussorskii iashchik*) of history."[115]

According to some accounts, Martov interrupted him to say: "Then we shall all leave"; but the protocols of the Congress record only that he proceeded to read the text of a resolution condemning the delegates who had already left or were planning to leave the Congress.[116] In any case, B.D. Kamkov, the leader of the Left SRs who followed Trotsky to the podium, declared that, unlike the official delegation of the PSR, the Left SRs were not leaving the Congress, and emphasized that it was imperative to tone down the sharpness of the conflict that had emerged. To this purpose, he considered it imperative to suspend any vote on Trotsky's resolution.[117]

Lunacharskii, who until the eve of the Congress, had been one of the most fervent supporters of an "all-democratic" government, was bitterly offended by Kamkov's remarks, feeling that they were directed at him, and rose to "state that he had felt the pressure of all the various organizations represented at the congress, but now felt, in the light of the events that had occurred that a peaceful resolution of the conflict was impossible. . . . After all that has been said, there is nothing left to talk about."[118]

The debate droned on into the night. It was interrupted only by the announcements of the capture of the Winter Palace and of the arrest of the Provisional Government, whose members had remained seated at their desks when Red Guards had occupied the building, with the exception of Kerensky who had departed, ostensibly to seek military help from the front.

Thus it was already early in the morning when Kapelinskii and Gutman, speaking in the name of the Menshevik Internationalists and of *Paole Zion*, rose to insist that a vote be taken on the resolution that Martov had presented, so many hours earlier, to find a way out of the conflict through the declaration of an immediate armistice and the launching of negotiations for the formation of an "all-democratic" government. Reluctantly, Kamenev agreed. Martov's resolution was then finally brought up, and rejected by an overwhelming vote. Thereupon, Lunacharskii read the text of a resolution announcing the overthrow of the Provisional Government and the decision of the Congress to take power into its own hands. This resolution was approved, equally overwhelmingly, with only two votes recorded against it and twelve abstentions.[119] By the time the session finally adjourned, on this note, it was already five o'clock in the morning of October 26, a particularly gray morning for Martov and the delegates who had supported him in his efforts to create an "all-democratic" government for an "all-democratic" state.

XXI

The next, and last, session of the Second Congress of Soviets opened on October 26 at 9 a.m., with the chair now in the firm hands of the Bolshevik *praktik*, A.M. Sverdlov. Under Sverdlov's chairmanship, this session unfolded without a hitch with a presentation of the Bolsheviks' program.

Following a few introductory words, Lenin came to the platform (greeted, by all accounts, by loud applause on the part of the delegates still present) and delivered, in succession, two addresses on the topics considered most important by his listeners at the Congress (and probably by the vast majority of the Russian people): the issue of peace and the issue of land.

As far as one is able to judge from the text of these speeches, as well as from the recollections of those who listened to them, both showed Lenin in his best form. They were written simply and delivered convincingly, bringing out Lenin's unusual capacity to impress and indeed convince a mass audience by the clarity of his theses, the logic and concreteness of their argumentation, the weight of the evidence presented in their support—and last but not least, the sense of total certainty that he exuded about the correctness of his position and the inevitability of its realization.

What Lenin had to say on this occasion on the strategy to be followed in the struggle to achieve an immediate peace did not differ significantly from the position that Martov had advocated during the sessions of the Pre-parliament (including the emphasis on the imperativeness of creating a new political *vlast'* to attain these objectives). Nonetheless, Lenin's listeners reacted to his address and to his promise of success in the struggle for peace and for socialism, as if the words were emanating from a new Messiah. The audience greeted with equal confidence and enthusiasm the speech and resolution that Lenin presented to them on the land question, even though, as he himself recognized, the decrees and the *nakaz* on this subject were taken from the platform of the PSR, and no longer corresponded to the position that Lenin had assumed earlier on the question. In the concluding paragraph of his address, Lenin stated in explanation of his turnabout: "The peasants learned something during these eight months of the revolution. They themselves want to resolve all the questions about the land in the spirit of their own lives." Lenin probably meant by this phrase the logic that appeared to dictate the peasants' redistribution of the land in the course of their Black Partition.[120] Most importantly, since the logic of this Black Partition also differed from the PSR's program of socialization of all the land, Lenin's endorsement of the SRs' land program, at this moment, was dictated first and foremost by his sense of the need to cement his political alliance with the Left SRs, which he clearly needed, at least for the time being, to hold onto the political power that he had seized.

Indeed, Lenin was reminded of the shaky character of his hold on power by a series of interventions that occurred near the conclusion of this session. The first was a brief but highly critical address by the leader of the "United Social Democrats," V. I. Avilov. Avilov reminded his listeners that the ease with which the coalition government had been overthrown was to be explained by the fact that it could not give the people either peace or bread. The left part of democracy would be able to hold onto power only if it was able to achieve progress toward the achievement of these tasks. There were great obstacles to finding such a solution; yet if the new government failed to overcome them, it too would be overthrown.

As for bread, there was little of it in the country, and most of it was in the hands of the "strong" and "middle" peasants. There were only two ways to deliver this bread to the cities, the industrial centers, and the army. One was to deliver to the countryside the consumer products it needed. But existing stocks of these goods were in short supply and to produce more would take time, as well as a more adequate supply of fuel. Besides, factories were still concentrating on military production and would continue to do so until the end of the war. An alternative was to seek to win the political support of the more well-to-do strata of the peasantry. However, this goal could be achieved only if these peasants came to view the new state power as their own, and the tasks it undertook to be in their interests. Hence it was imperative to establish a state power supported by all the peasantry, from the well-to-do to the poorest peasants, including those who had to buy bread and other necessities to feed themselves.

It would be even more difficult to achieve peace, Avilov continued in his sharp analysis. The governments of the Allied powers refused to establish contacts with Russia's new state power, and under no circumstances would they agree to its opening peace negotiations. As long as the new state power in Russia remained so completely isolated, its peace proposals would be floating in air. Neither could one count on the support of the proletariat and democratic forces in the belligerent countries, whose majority socialist parties could not even be counted upon to press for their participation in the Stockholm conference, while the left wing of the German Social Democratic Party had issued the warning that until the conclusion of the war, one could not expect a revolution in Germany.

Given the isolation in which Russia now found itself, only two outcomes were possible: the conclusion of a peace accord between the Central Powers and the Franco-English coalition at Russia's expense, or the conclusion by Russia of a separate peace with Germany. In either case, the peace terms would be most costly for Russia. Only if a majority of the Russian people combined their efforts to overcome these incredible difficulties to give the country peace and bread and to secure the gains of the revolution would they have any chance to achieve these goals. Hence if the revolution was to be saved, it was imperative to reconcile the leading groups of democracy, which were now split into two opposing camps, and to form a government resting on the support of most, if not all, of revolutionary democracy.[121]

Avilov submitted a resolution in this spirit, but it was not even brought to a vote. Instead, the delegates adopted a resolution proposed by the presidium of the Congress, calling for the formation of a new government—to be called the Council of People's Commissars—as well as for the election of a new Central Executive Committee of Soviets. This new Central Executive Committee of Soviets was to consist of 62 Bolsheviks, 29 Left SRs, 6 United Social Democratic Internationalists, 3 representatives of the Ukrainian Social Democratic Party, and 1 SR Maximalist.[122]

However, following Trotsky's concluding speech, and his proposal that the Congress adjourn, there was one more *coup de théâtre*. A representative of the Central Committee of the all-Russian Railway Union (usually identified as *Vikhzhel* by the initials of its Russian title) appeared at the entrance of the hall, and interrupting Trotsky's concluding address, demanded to be recognized. Kamenev, who was now again in the chair, originally denied his request, but precipitously reversed himself after being subjected to a wave of protests from the floor. The delegate of *Vikhzhel* then read a telegram recording the text of a resolution passed by his organization, demanding that the Congress agree immediately to the opening of negotiations under the supervision of *Vikhzhel* for the formation of a "new revolutionary socialist *vlast'*, accountable to all the authoritative organs of revolutionary democracy." If these conditions were not met, *Vikhzhel* threatened to call a general strike, paralyzing the functioning of the railways throughout the country.

The ultimatum of *Vikhzhel* could not be ignored in view of the catalytic role that this organization had played in October 1905 in setting off, through a railway strike, a truly general strike throughout the country, which had shaken the tsarist regime to its knees and induced the Tsar to issue his October Manifesto. Adding to the reality of the threat to the Bolsheviks' hold on power was the creation of an "All Russian Committee for the Salvation of the Motherland and Revolution," consisting of a whole series of democratic organizations whose aim was to organize a democratic coalition opposed to the Bolsheviks. Last but not least, was the problem posed by the persistence of armed resistance to the Bolsheviks in Petrograd, but especially in Moscow and its surrounding districts.

Under the circumstances, Lenin could not afford to boycott the negotiations demanded by *Vikhzhel*. Delegated for this purpose were Kamenev, Zinoviev, and Rykov, all of whom were members of the Bolshevik Central

Committee known for their earlier support of the formation of an "all socialist" government. These negotiations opened under the supervision of the chairman of *Vikhzhel*, Militskii, and with the participation of representatives of eight socialist parties and fractions (with the partial exception of the Popular Socialists [NS], who agreed to take part only as observers), as well as that of nine representatives of the chief state administrative organs, organs of self-administration, and public organizations.[123]

From the outset, these negotiations proved to be very difficult. Their ups and downs, as reflected in the changing behavior of the participants on all sides, appeared to shift largely in accordance with the changes in the military situation in Petrograd, and especially in Moscow and its surrounding districts. After the Bolsheviks finally achieved a military victory in Moscow, following the arrival of Red Guards dispatched from other areas of the Central Industrial Region, Lenin recalled the Bolsheviks' delegates.

The protocols of these sessions have left me with some indelible impressions. First and foremost among them, is that of Martov's consistent and undeviating pressure throughout these negotiations for the formation *without any prior conditions* of a government representative of all revolutionary democracy. Among Lenin's opponents in the course of these sessions, Martov *was the only one to be so consistent*, as even his new ally, Fedor Dan, sought to attach various unrealizable prior conditions to the formation of an "all-democratic" government. Among the delegates representing the Bolsheviks, Kamenev, Zinoviev, and Miliutin also offered support for the realization of this objective, particularly during the three days between October 29 and 31, when they were released from Lenin's shackles, as he and Trotsky were otherwise preoccupied by the grave threat that the military situation in Moscow posed for the Bolsheviks.

In the light of these events, it is hardly possible to overemphasize the plasticity of the unfolding political situation throughout the period of Lenin's efforts to conquer and consolidate his political power. Nor can one overemphasize the flexibility of the political positions that both Lenin and Martov displayed in the course of the revolution, even while remaining true to the basic precepts about the character and role of political power in the dynamics of revolutionary processes that each of them had drawn from their perceptions of the experience of Russia's Revolution of 1905.

PART II
THE WORKERS' MOVEMENT AFTER LENA

THE DYNAMICS OF LABOR UNREST IN THE WAKE OF THE LENA GOLDFIELDS MASSACRE (APRIL 1912–JULY 1914)

I

On April 6, 1912 by the old Russian calendar, a day on which the attention of Russian newspaper readers was riveted on the sinking of the *Titanic*, there appeared, often side-by-side with the latest dispatches about the *Titanic*, the first reports about another, less glamorous, catastrophe, which had occurred two days before in Eastern Siberia on the distant fields of the Lena Gold Field Company. On the afternoon of April 4, an army detachment dispatched to the fields a few days earlier had fired on a crowd of striking workers.

As yet, the newspapers could provide only the official communiqué, transmitted by the Petersburg Telegraph Agency, of the circumstances and background of the massacre. This account, which was obviously intended to exculpate the officials concerned and lay the blame for what had happened fully on the strikers, would almost immediately be torn to shreds. Yet it is worth summarizing precisely because of the cloak of legitimacy it sought to lay on the conduct of the authorities and the standards of "legitimate" conduct that it unveiled in the process.

The report noted that the strike had dragged on since the beginning of March, as the Lena Company, although prepared to compromise on certain issues, had found it impossible to accede to the workers' most radical demands: an eight-hour day, the dismissal of 35 supervisors, and a wage increase of 30 percent. The case of some of the workers involved had been laid before the local Justice of the Peace, who had decided in favor of the Lena Company and ordered that the workers concerned be expelled from the company barracks in which they were quartered. In view of the workers' "agitated" mood (*pripodniatnoe nastroenie*) an army detachment had been sent to the fields, along with the deputy procurator of the Irkutsk Circuit Court and an officer of the *gendarmerie*. All efforts to reach a peaceful settlement had proven fruitless. In the meantime, the strikers were continuing to draw supplies at the company stores and to occupy company quarters.

In addition, the authorities established that the whole movement was being directed by a strike committee headed by one of the administrative exiles (*ssylnye poselentsye*) working in the Lena fields. As the workers appeared generally inclined to return to work and were refraining from doing so only under the pressure of the strike committee, the latter resorted to "active measures" to expel non-strikers by force, as well as to prevent the deportation from the fields of the strikers sentenced by the Justice of the Peace, orders were issued on the night of 3–4 April to arrest its members. After this was done, an agitated crowd of 1,000 striking workers appeared before the Circuit Inspector demanding the immediate release of those being held, giving him until 3 p.m. to fulfill the demand, and threatening, if it wasn't granted, to assemble all the strikers to march on Bodaiko, the company headquarters, to liberate their comrades. All measures taken to calm down the workers failed, and a crowd of 3,000 workers headed for Bodaiko, where an army detachment was stationed, arriving there at 5:30 p.m. Despite warnings and signals, the crowd armed with sticks, bricks, and stones, started to move threateningly toward the army detachment, which was compelled to fire a few salvos. In the course of this, the *Okrug* inspector reported, "107 workers were killed, and 83 wounded."[1]

In this official account, the only one as yet available, there were some evident holes and inconsistencies. Opposition newspapers such as *Rech'*, *Russkiia Vedomosti*, and even *Utro Rossii*, the organ of the Young Turks of the Moscow big business and industrial community, did not hesitate to probe the most obvious ones. If an army detachment of 380 men had really been compelled to fire repeatedly in self-defense on an enraged crowd of 3,000 strikers, "armed with sticks, rocks, and bricks," how was it that, while causing so many victims among the strikers, it had not itself suffered a single casualty? More conservative newspapers refrained from raising this issue, and to the end would recoil from "besmirching the honor of the army," but they did feel compelled to raise other, almost equally embarrassing, questions: "On what grounds has the strike committee of the Lena workers been arrested?" asked the Octobrist organ *Golos Moskvy.* In what criminal activity had it actually engaged? "In and of itself, the formation of a strike committee is not a criminal act; a strike cannot take place without a committee to direct it, and strikes are now legal." The official communiqué stated that the strike committee had exercised pressure on the Lena workers to keep them from returning to work. "How can one assume that ten people can force their will on several thousands? And even assuming that the strike committee had engaged in some criminal activities, why did it take two months to order their arrest?" *Golos Moskvy* refused to criticize the behavior of the army detachment. Once it had been dispatched to the field, "it could not do anything but defend itself, when a crowd armed with rocks and stones moved to attack them." But a thorough investigation, "leaving no stone unturned" [sic], should be ordered, and the officials at fault, unhesitatingly punished. "The Lena events could have grave consequences," the editorial concluded darkly. "Everything now hinges on the government's sincerity in its efforts to overcome the complications that have to be expected."[2]

This editorial was not to be taken lightly, for on matters of labor policy, *Golos Moskvy* spoke for the more conservative elements of the Moscow big business and industrial community. But the clearest indication that the government was headed for heavy waters, even among the most "respectable" and conservative sectors of opinion, was the shifting editorial line of *Novoe Vremia,* the conservative newspaper *par excellence.* In its first few issues immediately after the news of Lena, the editorial reactions in *Novoe Vremia* had sounded markedly dissonant notes. On both April 6 and 7, M.M. Menshikov, the newspaper's most popular and unprincipled columnist, was content to depend on the director of the company, Ginzburg, as his chief source on the background and circumstances of the massacre. The company, the latter told him, had offered the workers all kinds of concessions. But it could not satisfy the demand for a 30 percent wage increase and still continue to operate. In any case, as the strike progressed, the workers' demands had assumed an increasingly political character under the influence of outside agitators. "In principle, we are ready even now to help the workers, but one must first draw the sharp distinction between legitimate desires and those demands they have advanced under the influence of the strike committee,

which, as I have told you, is led by *intelligenty*." Ginzburg still felt sufficiently secure on April 6 to criticize the local authorities for having sided with the
workers during the strike and given an open field for the activities of propa-
gandists and agitators. As far as the shootings were concerned, he was quoted approvingly on April 7 that the workers had attacked the soldiers and the
latter had had no choice but to take "decisive measures."[3]

From the outset, however, Menshikov's fellow commentators on *Novoe
Vremia* felt more uneasy. On April 7, an unsigned editorial wistfully referred
to the coal strike in Great Britain, "the largest strike in its history," which
had been settled without any blood being spilled. "Perhaps," mused the editorial, this was because "the representatives of an energetic and enlightened
administration did not identify the interests of the state with that of any single class, and acted instead as dispassionate mediators between workers and
employers, securing wage increases and a certain minimum level of labor
productivity at one and the same time." If only the Russian state had been
so active and so broadly conceived its tasks, it would have found, in the
course of two months, the basis for a just reconciliation of the two parties; it
would have protected the workers from the influence of political agitators by
conscientiously improving labor conditions, and coped with the small Lena
strike as Asquith and Lloyd George had been able to cope with "the
grandiose English coal revolution."[4]

A day later, a column written by A. A. Stolypin—with all the moral authority of a brother of the late premier—tilted the balance even further
against the Lena Company, and indeed against the local authorities, if not
the government itself: the Lena Company had used its monopoly position in
the fields to put both the workers and the local authorities completely under
its thumb. It had deprived the workers of the possibility of earning an adequate living, going so far as to reduce their wage rates and to deprive them
of the right to hold onto part of the gold they extracted which had been
theirs for almost a century. Indeed, it had deprived them of all rights—including that of redress for humiliating treatment by supervisors. It had paid
them irregularly, and contrary to law had issued part of their wages in
coupons redeemable only at company stores. Reduced to a life of collective
slavery (*krugovaia kabala*), the workers had had no other recourse but to
join in collective action. The only real solution for the indescribable conditions prevailing on the Lena fields was to break up the monopoly of the Lena
Company in the fields once and for all.

In his attack on the Lena Company, Stolypin was drawing on information that was now pouring into the newspapers, both from their own re-

porters and the letters from informed readers (including even local technical personnel and officials), about conditions in the Lena fields and the circumstances of the strike. As these reports came in, and the public reaction
to them became unmistakable, the editorial line of *Novoe Vremia* turned decisively against both the Lena Company and the conduct of local authorities.
By now, this was clearly the better part of wisdom, and after all the Lena
Company provided an easy, and narrow target: a Jewish Managing Director,
a parent company of British stockholders! Even the Tsar's confidant and fa-
vorite commentator, the arch-reactionary Prince V. P. Meshcherskii, was
now beginning to mutter in the pages of his *Grazhdanin* about the *zhidy*
[yids] and foreign capitalists sucking the blood of honest, authentic Russian
workers. Clearly, *Novoe Vremia* could do no less. "Public opinion has wait-
ed impatiently for the *zaprosy* that have now been introduced in the Duma
about the Lena events, but the interpellations (*zaprosy*) are too narrowly
conceived to dig adequately into the central issue raised by the Lena catastrophe," *Novoe Vremia* sententiously declared on April 10:

> Will the oppressive atmosphere of the Jewish rule of force under
> which oppressed people are only given the choice between slavery
> and death by bullet shot continue to reign there, a thousand *versty*
> away from the nearest civilized center? Will conditions continue to
> reign in this dark corner of Siberia, cut off 4–5 months a year from
> the rest of the world, under which all agents of the state power—all
> officials, from the justices of the peace and the representatives of the
> Inspection of Mines to the last postman and policeman—are en-
> tirely in the hands of an all powerful monopolist whom it is better
> not to question, let alone to oppose?
>
>   And if, as a result, a bloody catastrophe has taken place [the ed-
> itorial slowed down in mid-flight], what point is there in asking
> whether the local military commander was in too much of a hurry
> with his order to fire? After all, this was but the denouement, and all
> the conditions that led to it were created much earlier. [5]

With the storm now blowing, Menshikov was now ready to adjust his
sails and abandon Ginzburg. He wrote the same day:

> On that beautiful day during which we in Petersburg observed the
> eclipse of the sun, an eclipse of Russian good sense took place. Rus-
> sians fired on Russians for the glory and profit of some Jewish

barons. . . . 350 dead and wounded remained on the ground, and
from what can be made out from the reports no mutiny was involved; only the usual manifestations of worker unrest, stemming
from a strike that had drawn out for too long.[6]

To make up for his original mistake, Menshikov now meant to outdo
the other editorialists of the conservative press: "Russians support the Octobrist and even the Kadet interpellations in the Duma. The government did
not give adequate attention to the strike even though it had been going on
for over a month." Menshikov had expected a bloody outcome all along,
given a dubious company whose stock was the object of wild speculation.
And it was one of those stock companies established in Russia by Jews and
foreigners to exploit, not the riches buried under Russian soil but the small
savings of the Russian public, with the aid of the Jewish trusts and Jewish
bankers. On reflection, Menshikov felt sorriest of all for the workers who
were compelled to carry on forced labor, often without the compensation of
a modest wage, for these *aferisty* and *vdobavy* [sharpies].[7]

As I have noted, Menshikov had been forced into this sharp turnabout
by the news reports that had poured in since the announcement of the massacre, and the public storm that they set off. Indeed, even before the government braced itself to reply to the interpellations introduced in the Duma
about Lena, the public had received, in a remarkably short time, a fairly adequate picture about the massacre and its background, and would judge the
ministers' response in its light. This information would subsequently be
confirmed and amplified by the commission of investigation appointed, under public clamor, under the chairmanship of Senator Manukhin. But for
zealous readers, press editorialists, and political leaders, most of the details
needed to gauge the character of the strike and the responsibilities of the various parties were already available, as the ministers prepared for the Duma's
evening session of April 11 at which they were to face the deputies and the
public with their explanations. What did this information reveal?

Let us focus our attention on the major points that would be at issue between the company, and eventually the government and its critics.

Contrary to the first official reports, it would quickly be established that
the strike on the Lena fields had broken out spontaneously, with no previous exposure of the miners to any traceable propaganda or agitational efforts: the spark that had set off the explosion was a spoiled supply of meat
(suspected to be horse carrion) at the company store where the workers of
the Andreev field, just as all other workers of the company, were compelled

to obtain their supplies. Nor were the company or the authorities ever able to establish that there had been any organization—any group of agitators, however small—at work before the strike had actually broken out. Such an organization emerged only as the strike had progressed and spread to the other fields owned by the Lena Company, with the workers in each field electing a labor committee to represent them in their negotiations with the company, as well as *starosty* [elders] to take charge in the barracks in which they were quartered—to collect money, maintain discipline, and transmit the instructions of the local committee in their field. A central leadership had eventually emerged on the Nadezhdin field, where the administrative office of the company was located. But even in the Soviet period, when a tendency would appear to emphasize the degree of organization and planning behind such labor disturbances, the leaders of this "central bureau" would insistently recall that it had emerged spontaneously without any formal elections.

Much would be made by the officials of the Lena Company, and eventually by the government authorities, of the fact that the committee "in charge of" the Lena strike included administrative exiles with subversive political backgrounds, suggesting thereby that the strike had, in fact, been the work of outside agitators. The bureau did include a number of administrative exiles, most of them with Social Democratic backgrounds. But it is notable that these political exiles, all of them bona fide workers in the fields, sought even more zealously than their colleague to keep the goals and the conduct of the strike within strictly legal limits. Indeed, to emphasize the apolitical character of the strike, they deliberately refrained from directing any of their appeals to the Social Democratic press, addressing their letters and telegrams instead to the ministries concerned, to the deputies in the Duma, including its chairman, M.V. Rodzianko, and even to such unlikely if impeccable recipients as the Petersburg and Moscow Stock Exchange Committees. The strike leaders sought to maintain strict self-discipline among the workers, to restrain them from any act of violence, and to this end the strikers themselves undertook to refrain from drinking any spirits until their struggle was won. In all this, remarkable success was achieved, as Senator Manukhin would confirm in his official report:

> According to the unanimous testimony of all witnesses, drunkenness, which before the strike had been so widespread among the population of the fields, could no longer be observed after work came to a halt. In the four months that the strike dragged on among a labor force of close to 7,000, not a single piece of equipment was

damaged; no company property, however valueless; and there was not a single attack or act of violence directed at anyone.[8]

All this, along with the details that had now accumulated about the intolerable conditions under which the strikers had been compelled to live and work, could not help but win them public sympathy. They had been forced to labor 11 or 12 hours a day, with icy water up to their knees, in poorly ventilated shafts. Their wives and children had frequently been forced to join them in this labor, for a pitiful wage, all of fifty kopeks a day. This was often done under duress as a worker's dependents had to undertake to work whenever the company so chose in order to be allowed to rejoin him on the fields. The workers themselves earned on the average 35–50 rubles a month. Of this sum, half was paid to them in kind or in coupons redeemable only at company stores, while another quarter was withheld until the yearly contract expired. This contract ran from October to October, the beginning of the winter season in Siberia, when it was almost impossible for the workers to find any other job.

It all added up to a life of collective slavery, as even conservative commentators observed to their readers. But what probably weighed most heavily with all conservative opinion and turned it most decisively against the Lena Company was the fact, also uncovered before the opening of the Duma debates, that most of the grievances that the Lena strikers had originally voiced had been directed against company practices which violated existing legal requirements, concerning at least some of which, the company had received repeated official warnings and reprimands from the local inspector of the Bureau of Mines, and most recently from a special conference of the Irkutsk Mining Administration (the protocols of which were leaked to *Birzhevye Vedomosti*, which published them on April 8). These officials had repeatedly reprimanded the company for issuing the spoiled food supplies of which the workers complained, as well as for systematically providing different qualities of bread to workers and employees. The practice of paying workers partly in kind and in coupons was found in violation of existing legal requirements. The company had also been censured for failing to provide adequate medical facilities, and for inadequate ventilation of its shafts. All of these were among the grievances originally voiced by the Lena workers, and eventually incorporated in their strike demands.

To be sure, as the strike spread and lingered, the strikers' demands had become considerably more sweeping. But they never came to include items that could be viewed as strictly political, except by the peculiar criteria used by the company authorities. Yet, when one goes down the list of the strikers' eighteen demands, as they were finally formulated by a group elected on March 3 at a general meeting of the Lena workers—with the rank and file in the audience speaking out additional suggestions—it is easy to discern how some of them could be seen as subversive by an authoritarian *patronat* and bureaucrats of the old school—as challenges to an authority that these men were accustomed to view as peculiarly their own. This was true of the demand for the elimination of fines and especially of that for an eight-hour day, however amply the latter might seem justified, even to conservative commentators, in view of the arduous working conditions prevailing in the shafts. (The authorities automatically classified the demand for an eight-hour day as a political one, if only because it had become one of the major planks of the platform of the RSDRP.) But the point was even more obvious with respect to such items as the strikers' insistence that 26 supervisory employees—guilty of offenses against the workers' dignity—be dismissed summarily, and that "the administration not fire workers as the mood strikes them [*po lichim kaprizam*], but only with the knowledge [*s vedoma*] of a workers' commission."

However, the most notable general feature in the strikers' long list of demands, and the most novel for both the authorities involved and the Russian reading public, was their expression of a new, or at least of a more articulate, sense of the workers' autonomy and dignity and the insistence on its recognition. This assertion appeared not only with respect to such relatively tangible issues as the demands for proper bathing facilities and for separate dressing facilities for men and women and the demand that workers receive food staples as good as those provided for supervisory personnel, but also in the workers' claim to *vezhlivoe obrashchenie* (polite treatment and polite address). "Polite address by the administration," stated the workers' sixteenth demand. "Workers are to be addressed as 'you' not as 'thou.' " The assertion of their dignity and autonomy which pervaded these strike demands of the Lena workers—given the way it was perceived by those that ruled over them—necessarily brought them into conflict with the whole system of authority of which they were the object; a notable general feature, as we shall see, of the new wave of labor unrest that was in the offing.

This is not to say that all the officials immediately concerned remained impervious to the plight of the workers under their charge. Pulled by a mixture of strong, if confused, motives—a sympathy, however paternalistic, for those under their charge; antagonism for the company and its arbitrary ways; an anxious desire, which deepened as the conflict progressed, to avoid a catastrophic outcome—some of these officials repeatedly sought to get the Lena Company to abandon its illegal practices, to get satisfaction for at least some of the workers' demands, and above all to prevent the escalation of the conflict and to reach a peaceful settlement of the strike. In these efforts, two officials in particular played a notable role, Tul'chinskii, the local inspector of the Department of Mines of the Ministry of Trade and Industry, and Bantysh, the Governor of Irkutsk, the province into whose administrative jurisdiction the fields of the Lena Company at least technically fell.

As early as 1911, Tul'chinskii had sought to get the company to conform to existing legal requirements—in the quality of the staples it provided for the workers, in the medical facilities placed at their disposal, in their general working conditions, in the character of wage payments—only to be reprimanded by the authorities in Petersburg to which he reported the company's infractions for his excessive concern with the formal requirements of the law in his efforts to protect the workers' interests, while completely ignoring the interests of the enterprise. "By undermining prestige and discipline in the *taiga*," he was told in June 1911 by his superiors in the Department of Mines, "you turned against you all the senior employees as well as the doctors."[9] Nonetheless, Tul'chinskii had persisted in his efforts, and in late March 1912 as we have seen, he had succeeded in having a conference of the officials of the Irkutsk branch of the Department of Mines formally reprimand the Lena Company for the legal infractions which he had vainly reported over the previous two years.

The conduct of the Governor of Irkutsk had been equally notable. From the outset of the strike, Bantysh had pressed for a peaceful settlement and even for a wage boost for the Lena workers. Insisting on the peaceful character of the strike, he had resisted for weeks the dispatch of an army detachment to the fields for which the company's directors were pressing. But the Lena Company had powerful connections in Petersburg government circles: N. I. Boianovskii, the director of the State Bank, was a member of the board of directors; V .I. Timiriazev, the ex-Minister of Trade and Industry, was chairman of its Petersburg committee. Following the intercession of his successor, N. I. Timashev with Makarov, the Minister of Internal Affairs, Bantysh was ordered on March 19 to dispatch an army detachment to the fields (but did manage to have Tul'chinskii accompany the officer put in charge of it, Rotmistr' Treshchenkov).

When at this point the manager of the fields, Belizarov, successfully applied to the local justice of the peace to order that some of the strikers be expelled from their quarters in the company's barracks and have their supplies cut off at the company stores, Bantysh again attempted to resist these steps, which, he wired to Petersburg, were intended to put an end to the peaceful character of the strike in order to have it suppressed by armed force. He ordered the local police not to expel the strikers from their quarters, and to see to it that they continued to receive their food supplies from the company's stores. He did not intend to violate the law in order to please the Lena Company, he reported to Petersburg, "or to condemn the workers to death, or to a *bunt* under the pressure of hunger." But again he was overruled by his superiors in the capital. Bantysh then mobilized the support of the equally alarmed chief of the Irkutsk branch of the Department of Mines, who wired Petersburg on March 21 to request that the Ministry of Trade and Industry press the administration of the company to grant the strikers a wage increase. He too was overruled, the Department of Mines replying that the workers' demands were unacceptable, and insisting that its local representatives join in a "decisive rebuff" of the strikers.[10]

Meanwhile, the officer in charge of the army detachment, Treshchenkov, had been pressing, already before his arrival on the fields, for the arrest of the workers' strike committee, even if armed force should be required to effect it. Bantysh denied this request, but again, the St. Petersburg committee of the Lena Company intervened, appealing directly to Makarov and warning him (probably for the first time) of the presence of administrative exiles among the leaders of the strike. Makarov promptly telegraphed an order for the arrest of the strike committee.[11]

From this point on, the Lena events unfolded with the inevitability of a Greek tragedy. On the night of April 4, the members of the strike committee were arrested. The news spread immediately, and by 5 a.m. a crowd of 1,000 agitated workers had gathered in front of Tul'chinskii's quarters to demand the release of their comrades. Tul'chinskii promised to try, and immediately wired the Governor, warning that if the members of the strike committee were not released, the situation could become alarming. By 8 a.m. another crowd of about 2,000 workers, had gathered in front of Tul'chinskii's office. Again, he persuaded them to disperse. But by mid-afternoon, a procession of 3,000 strikers had assembled from several of the fields in order to march to the main offices of the company to submit a written petition for the release of their comrades. Forewarned of this, Rotmistr' Treshchenkov had deployed his army detachment to block their way. Trudging through the snow, the crowd approached the troops. Treshchenkov dispatched one of the *strazhniki* under his command to order them to stop and turn away. Tul'chinskii, who by this time was in a state of almost complete hysteria, ran after him to beg the workers to heed his order. As was subsequently confirmed by the report of the Manukhin Commission, the leaders of the crowd were surrounding Tul'chinskii, most of them with their backs turned to the troops, and the crowd itself had stopped while the argument went on, many of its members sitting on the curbs and smoking, when the army detachment fired its first salvo. The detachment continued firing, as members of the crowd, including Tul'chinskii, lay cowering on the ground, while the rest fled. Altogether, according to the Manukhin report, there were 170 killed and 372 wounded—the location of the injuries clearly indicating that they had indeed been inflicted while the victims lay on their stomachs, or were fleeing the soldiers' bullets.[12]

This was the climax of the tale about which the two ministers chiefly concerned, Makarov and Timashev, expected to issue their reports to the Duma on April 11. But before taking leave of its heroes and of the Lena workers, however, let us take it to its pitiful denouement. Even after the massacre, the workers continued their strike. Oblivious to the public clamor, a joint conference of the Mining Inspectorate, the local police, and the Administration of the fields ordered that all the striking workers be evacuated as soon as navigation opened. Again, Bantysh intervened, temporarily squashing the order, and instructing that the strikers be fed. The strike lingered on until the beginning of June, when, following the arrival of the Manukhin Commission, and the Senator's appeal to the strikers to go back to work pending a new contract (an appeal in which he was joined by Duma deputy Kerensky, who had arrived on the fields to represent the strikers), work temporarily resumed. But the Lena workers refused to accept the new contract that was offered to them, and on June 28 resumed their strike. In early August, 9,000 of them, together with their families, were evacuated from the Lena fields—Bantysh sending Makarov a telegram protesting the conditions under which the Lena Company carried out this evacuation.

As for those immediately responsible, the company officials charged with the administration of the fields and all the local government officials concerned were relieved of their posts in the fall of 1912. But of these local officials, only Bantysh actually suffered: he was demoted to the post of Governor of Iakutsk. Treshchenkov was congratulated on March 23 by the Department of Police for his conduct. A civil prosecution eventually initiated against him by the Manukhin Commission was squashed.[13]

The week that the Lena massacre occurred and that the first reports of it appeared in the Russian press, the State Duma was adjourned for its Easter recess (it was not scheduled to reconvene until Monday, April 9). A number of parliamentary groups had drafted inquiries to the government

in advance of this session. Three of these, submitted by the Kadets, the Social Democrats, and notably the Octobrists, were in the form of interpellations (*zaprosy*), calling for urgency in their disposition by the Duma and in
the reply demanded of the ministers concerned. A fourth draft was a parliamentary question (*vopros*), drawn up by the Nationalist faction, and did
not call for urgency.

Predictably, both the Kadets' and the Social Democrats' interpellations,
in slightly different languages, accused the government of having interfered
without any legal justification on the side of management in a peaceful economic strike, as a result of which a completely unprovoked mass shooting of
the workers had occurred. To further emphasize the peaceful and apolitical
character of the strike, the Social Democrats *zapros*, somewhat incongru-
ously, made a major point of the fact that the eight-hour day demanded by
the Lena strikers, while admittedly part of the program of the RSDRP, was a
perfectly legal demand, and indeed was already in effect a number of enterprises in Russia. Existing legislation set a legal maximum for the number of
hours worked in industry, but in no way prohibited further reductions of the
number of hours of work by mutual agreement.

Of the three interpellations, it was undoubtedly the Octobrists' which
attracted the most notice among the assembling deputies. For the Octobrists
had braced themselves to highlight in their *zapros* the most sensitive issue
that had arisen out of the Lena catastrophe, at least for respectable conservative opinion: the conduct of the troops who had been dispatched to the
fields. "Is the Minister of Internal Affairs informed that during the disturbances which arose among the workers of the Lena gold fields fire arms were
brought into use unlawfully, in view of the lack of adequate grounds?" This,
the first part of the Octobrists' interpellation (rather than the second part,
which cited the legal violations committed by the Lena Company in the
treatment of its workers) was absolutely unacceptable to the deputies sitting
on the right side of the hall in the Tauride Palace: it not only raised the issue
of the army's "honor," but prejudged it at that. Nothing was more suggestive of how much (admittedly with the approach of elections) the delicate
balance between the Duma's center and right, and between the Octobrists
and the government, had been upset.[14]

There was not the slightest hope for the Octobrists and the Nationalist
supporters of the government to reach agreement on such a text. The latter,
as I have indicated, elected instead to draft a statement of their own, in the
form of a simple parliamentary question. They asked the government whether the reports that had appeared of the persistent failure of local authorities

to intervene to satisfy the lawful demands of the labor population in the Lena fields were correct, and requested that if this was the case the ministers concerned report to the Duma what measures were being taken to establish the degree of guilt of local officials, as well as to bring them to justice.

The three interpellations and the Nationalists' more innocuous parliamentary question did not come up for discussion until late in the afternoon of the Monday session. At this hour, a very small number of deputies were still in attendance in the Tauride Palace. Indeed, even the morning session had been poorly attended, many of the deputies not having bothered to return from vacation or from early stumping of their constituencies in preparation for the fall elections. "But even of those who were present, not everyone sat until the end of the session," several newspapers indignantly reported the next day. "And the *zaprosy* about the Lena tragedy, which is agitating all of Russia, could not be voted upon for lack of a quorum."[15]

The newspapers also concurred about the flatness of the Duma debate—its failure to measure up to the dimensions of the tragedy and the public agitation to which it had given rise. Aside from the sparse attendance, itself indicative of the sense of powerlessness that already enveloped the Duma, there were, judging from the transcripts, some substantive reasons for this flatness. Both N.V. Nekrasov and A.I.Guchkov, the spokesmen for the Kadet and the Octobrist parliamentary groups, deliberately adopted in their addresses a moderate and conciliatory line, perhaps in the hope as rallying as many votes as possible for their factions' *zaprosy*. Indeed, Nekrasov sidestepped entirely in his speech the topic which roused the public's most visceral reactions—the circumstances surrounding the massacre and the behavior of the troops and the officer-in-command. He elected instead to focus attention on what he defined as the most fundamental (and least controversial) issue: the government's interference in a peaceful economic strike—an economic conflict between labor and capital—in which the government had chosen to take the side of capital. From this decision had flowed a whole series of illegal acts which had culminated in the catastrophe of April 4. The Duma deputies might differ among themselves about the proper role of government in such economic disputes, Nekrasov recognized, the Kadets for their own part holding the profound conviction that the state's proper role was to interfere on the side of the weak in the interest of social justice. But these differences of views were irrelevant in this case because the Lena strikers had not only social justice but also the letter of the law on their side.

The balance of Nekrasov's speech sought to demonstrate the point. It spelled out the legal violations committed by the Irkutsk mining office: that it was the company and not the workers that stood in violation of their contract. It also played down those of the workers' demands which might be considered at all radical by the more conservative deputies in the chamber: "We know that every strike starts with the workers demanding an eighthour day and other social demands, and ends with very minor concessions, if not the outright defeat of the strikers."

As for the conduct of the strike, all reliable data indicated that the workers had conducted themselves in an impeccably peaceful manner. Even the work of pumping the water in the shafts, necessary to keep the mines in satisfactory condition, had not been interfered with. Yet the decision had been made to send troops to the fields and, under the thinnest of pretexts, to arrest the workers' strike committee. These, even right-wing newspapers like *Grazhdanin* and *Golos Moskvy* recognized, were acts of provocation, and the reports now circulating also indicated that the decision to resort to armed force had been taken not locally, but in St. Petersburg. From the moment that the arrests had been carried out, the only possible outcome was a catastrophe. That the catastrophe had assumed such proportions—that the soldiers had ceased firing perhaps a little later than their immediate commander would have wished, and that there had been so many victims as a result—was a matter of accident. The basic outcome had been a foregone conclusion, and it would continue to be a foregone conclusion in labor conflicts as long as the existing system of administrations remained in force in Russia—as long as every chief or *gendarmerie*, every justice of the peace, every assistant procurator, continued to build their careers on blood lettings, even if more modest ones, of innocent people.[16]

This perhaps was a skillful speech, but not one calculated to arouse great passion. Only once—when he discussed the role played by Timiriazev, the ex-Minister of Trade and Industry who had become chairman of the Lena Gold Trading Co.[Lenzoto]—did Nekrasov allow his voice to rise; and even this could be attributed (at least by some of the more cynical deputies on the right side of the hall) to the speaker's embarrassment about Timiriazev's reputation as a liberal.

Guchkov's statement was shorter and even more low-keyed. He too emphasized the peaceful character of the strike and the Company's violation of the law. The text of the Octobrists' *zapros* required him to make some reference to the presence and the conduct of the army detachment responsible for the massacre. But as if he had had second thoughts about the boldness of the Octobrists' interpellation on this point, his reference could not have been more tentative and cursory: "There are no available facts about the

character of the strike or about the conduct of the strikers which at all justify—in my view—the resort to armed force." And even this mildly censoring
phrase was largely taken back as soon as it was uttered, Guchkov being quick
to absolve the army, and by implication, the government, from its stigma:

> I do not speak about the conduct of the army, which only fulfilled
> its heavy and regrettable duty. I speak of the picture that the local
> authorities—those on the spot—presented. . . . This was not the
> picture of a strong and firm *vlast'*, using with discretion the enor-
> mous powers of which it disposes. Rather, it was a picture of con-
> fusion and panic, [of local authorities] driven out of their minds by
> fear. (A disgusted voice from the left: "Nothing of the sort.")

Unperturbed, Guchkov closed: "We await a severe and dispassionate investigation of all the circumstances surrounding the regrettable events of 4
April . . . and that those persons whose guilt is established be brought to legal accounting."[17] Altogether, this had been an embarrassing performance,
and unsurprisingly it collected applause only from Guchkov's colleagues on
the Octobrist benches.

Such gingerliness was not to be expected from the next speaker on the
list, the worker and Social Democrat Kuznetsov from Ekaterinoslav, and in
this respect the audience in the galleries would not be disappointed.
Kuznetsov was quick to dissociate himself from Guchkov and from the
"hypocritical" Octobrist *zapros*:

> We, the workers, do not need a full investigation to establish who
> was truly responsible for the awful events that occurred on the
> Lena. We already know who the chief culprits are: guilty are not
> only the capitalists—the Baron Ginzburgs and the Messrs. Timiri-
> azevs—or even the government in Petersburg, but also the Duma
> itself: the deputies assembled here bear a large measure of guilt.[18]

Since the opening of the Third Duma, the Social Democratic deputies
had been introducing interpellations about the illegal actions of the Ministry
of the Interior in arresting and deporting workers for their participation in
economic strikes. But time after time the Duma majority had rejected these
zaprosy and found the government's acts lawful, thereby giving it moral support: the result had been Lena. Also to be remembered was how the Duma
majority had dealt with the Social Democrats' bill to legalize strikes. After all

it had been a very simple bill: it had provided for the right to strike, the right to organize trade unions, freedom of association. The bill had been shelved in committee.

The Social Democrats were now receiving telegrams from factory workers, demanding of the State Duma that the families of the victims be compensated, and that the guilty be punished. But he, Kuznetsov, considered it his duty to remind the workers that telegrams, petitions, were not enough. After all, they had collected 70,000 signatures for the bill for the right to strike, and the only answer had been the Lena shootings. Indeed, the working class itself bore a mantle of responsibility; it had to learn the only appropriate lesson from the Lena shootings: that words were not enough; the only answer was to organize, and to act. To act not only to replace the Third Duma and the whole existing regime, but also to elect at long last a Duma "elected by universal suffrage" which would truly serve the workers' interests.[19]

Although many of Kuznetsov's phrases were stilted, and he had had to conclude in Aesopian language, his message was clear enough. Yet his speech appeared to act only as another dampener, failing to arouse even the usual quota of interruptions from the right side of the hall. This was not simply because of the stiltedness of the phrases, but also because they could only add to the sense of the futility of the audience—majority and opposition alike. Much of his indictment could not easily be dismissed, but if Kuznetsov's conclusions were valid, what was the point of introducing a *zapros*, demanding that those truly guilty be punished, before so loaded a jury? For agitational purposes? To rouse or to at least educate the workers? But as Kuznetsov himself had noted, in the face of similar provocations in the recent past, the workers too had remained quiescent.

The debate, and the flagging attention of the audience, revived somewhat after the next speaker, Skorokhodov, a deputy from the Siberian province of Tomsk, made his way to the platform. There was a rambling quality to Skorokhodov's address, but also greater spontaneity. He tried to paint for his audience the conditions under which the Lena workers had lived and worked: isolated from all civilization; knee-deep in the icy waters of the shafts; their women and children forced to work with them ten or more hours a day; their nights, spent in overcrowded barracks. All this for coupons redeemable only at company stores, at inflated rates, for spoiled food supplies. And when the Lena workers had attempted to stand up, they had been drowned in blood: by a heartless administration and local authorities under their thumb; by colonels of gendarmes from whom even children fled in fear. One could not continue to live this way! It was hopeless! One couldn't breathe anymore. Russian citizens were being sacrificed to Moloch!

Most of the details that Skorokhodov recounted the deputies already knew by heart, but the simple if occasionally florid language of this peasant orator, the pathos (however thickly laid) especially in his denunciations of the money-changers in whose interest all this was being perpetrated, evidently reached the audience, proving especially unsettling—precisely for some of the conservative rural deputies sitting on the right benches:

> Russian citizens are being sacrificed to the power of Moloch. They are being killed for the sake of moneybags. Shame on you [*Stydites*]! (Noise and voices on the right: "[It's] the Yids!" The chairman rings the bell to ask for quiet.)
>
> The curse of Mephistopheles: People are dying! They are being killed for gold! (Voices on the right: "Correct!")[20]

Skorokhodov continued with his Populist denunciations of the money-bags and the speculators in *Lenochki*, the cursed stocks of the Lena Company, and he recited once more the long list of abuses which the Lena workers had been caused to suffer. Once again, noises broke out on the right benches: "The Yids!" Volodimerev (from his seat): "It's the Yids!" Nisselovich (a Kadet closely involved in business circles): "There are no Yids there." Volodimerev from his seat: "There are only Jews there (*tam tol'ko evrei*)!" Nisselovich: "There are only Russians there." Volodimerev: "And Ginzburg?"

Once more, the Chairman rang his bell asking for quiet, and Skorokhodov resumed his address. He compared Russia to England, where several millions of workers had struck recently without a drop of blood being spilled, while out of a few thousand workers out at the Lena fields there had been more than 300 victims. There, in England, that "country of enlightened navigators," the government knew how to approach workers, while in Russia it only knew how to squeeze them and beat them. Abroad, they knew how to look the truth in the eye. Here, in Russia, they went to Moscow to throw dust in the eyes of the truth. Only three days before V. N. Kokovtsov had told the Moscow industrialists, in the words of a French song: "Everything is going marvelously gentlemen, everything is going marvelously!" And suddenly a massacre, the like of which had not occurred even in 1905.

Who was responsible for this murderous business? Skorokhodov's list, if not his epithets, was no different from Kuznetsov's but he read it off with more murderous conviction. An inept Minister of Trade and Industry. A congenitally optimistic Premier, who from the halls of the White Stone Palace loudly declared to the whole world that all was peace, quiet, and prosperity in Russia, when in fact hunger, arbitrariness, and shootings ruled in the land. The blood spilled on the Lena fields, over 7,000 *versty* away, had indelibly stained the authorities in Petersburg. But were there no such stains on the glass roof of the Tauride Palace?

> Gentlemen of the Third State Duma, the majority of you made your way to the Tauride Palace only via the signposts of the 3 of June. For five years, most of you have done only what the government told you to do: what is your pleasure, and what are your orders (*chego izvolite i kak prikazhete*)? This, after all, is the Third Duma, which did not wish to protest against the executions and the state of sieges! It was you who gagged the people's advocates when they fought to protect its interests! And it is for your sins that, after five years of your "useful work," the chastising hand of providence has reached out in revenge to show its results, with this river of innocent blood.

The deputies on the right benches had sat remarkably quietly through most of Skorokhodov's harangue, but this was too much: Volodimerov, from his seat: "These are petty electoral tactics." Skorokhodov: "No! I don't know how to speak that way." And one last time, he soothed the deputies of the majority with his Biblical cadences:

> Your repentance comes too late! If you listen, you may hear reaching to you from out there, from the People's innards (*glubina Naroda*), from the tundra and the taiga, the avenging voice of Providence calling out: "Cain, where is your brother Abel?" (Applause from the Left.)[21]

For the first time in this already drawn-out, and largely mechanical debate, the conservative deputies, especially those sitting on the extreme right, had been audibly unsettled, even if the most genuine emotion that Skorokhodov had evoked had been one of anger. The image he had drawn of a government kowtowing to bankers and speculators—sacrificing authentic Russian people to the rule of gold—had clearly disturbed them, judging from the occasional murmurs of assent and the angry shouts about the "Yids" that his speech had provoked. The mixture of feelings that he had managed to rouse on the right side of the chamber—embarrassment, powerlessness, and eventually exploding anger—were most clearly articulated by the next speaker, Zamyslovskii, who now came forward to account for the Right's refusal to support the Lena *zaprosy*. The *zaprosy* had two sides, he hastened to explain. One—the Lena Company's treatment of its workers. "And in this area we are prepared to take account of (*usmotrit'*) a whole series of illegal incorrect actions. It may very well be that the Lena Company was engaged in the most unconscionable and illegal exploitation of workers; in this respect, of course, we would wholeheartedly support the *zapros*." But the whole thrust of the interpellations had been directed elsewhere: at the army's conduct. Here was where illegality had been found: in the fact that the army had fired, and that there had been a shooting. This was especially true of the Octobrists' *zapros*. Because of this, however reluctantly, Zamyslovskii and his friends had to oppose the substance of the interpellations, as they had been formulated, and indeed to vote against urgency. "For we affirm that in the situation that it was placed, the army had no choice but to fire; in firing, it acted perfectly correctly." The *zaprosy* should have been focused on the Lena Company, and directed only at those organs of government which had protected its actions.

"Gentlemen, it is not we, the Right, who stand prepared to defend the arbitrary actions [*zasiliia*] of the capitalists," Zamyslovskii continued, turning to the Octobrist benches with a tone of surface irritation, not unmixed with satisfaction: "On the contrary, we consider it impermissible for the government—the highest state authority—to fawn before the capitalists; to try to turn these capitalists into some kind of first estate—pushing the gentry, the clergy, and the peasantry to the side, condescendingly extending two fingers out to these estates, while overflowing with zeal in its dealings with the big industrial commercial class."[22]

By now, there could be no doubt of the earnestness of Zamyslovskii's words, or of the genuineness of the response they were evoking on the Right benches: "This situation we cannot approve! (Applause from the Right and shouts of "Bravo!") It is precisely in this [behavior] that we see the chief cause of what is happening. If we continue in the future to allow the likes of Mr. Ginzburg to reach the positions they have been granted, workers will be shot down—not by the hundreds, but by the thousands. It is impermissible to give capitalists attributes of powers which properly belong only to the state, and this is being done. It is in this that we see the chief cause of what has happened on the Lena fields," Zamyslovskii repeated with ponderous satisfaction. The opposition had spoken a great deal about Timiriazev, accusing him of the most incredible misdeeds. But this man stood closest to

Kadet and Left Octobrist circles; he was not a man of the Right. They had said much less about Mr. Ginzburg. "But, Gentlemen, as far as we are concerned, he is all yours. It is you who in every way have been trying to make it possible for the Yids to scramble their way to power, and indeed have succeeded to the point that some state institutions, like the Kiev bureau of the State Bank are turning into *zhidovakie lavochki* [nests of Yids]. Well, now you have gotten [your deserts]. You see the results. (Voice from the Right: Bravo!)."[23]

This venomous harangue had doubtlessly been delivered, and received on the right-wing benches, with considerable emotional conviction. And the chief targets who had sustained Zamyslovskii's venom as he went along, had clearly been, not the deputies of the extreme Left nor the Kadets, but the Octobrists, who had tried since the inception of their parliamentary faction to keep in the good graces of the big business and industrial class, and now had the gall to blame the state for the plight of the Lena workers. By comparison, the balance of Zamyslovskii's speech, for him as for his audience, came as an anticlimax. His genuine feelings of emotional outrage now spent, he sought as best he could to bolster the government's case.

The opposition had sought to paint the strike as purely economic. This of course was untrue. However genuine the workers' economic grievances, there had been a whole series of agitators on the Lena fields to turn these grievances into political demands. Tolmachev and Batashev, both members of the Social Democratic faction in the Second Duma, had been on the fields [this was subsequently demonstrated to have been untrue], and so had two other administrative exiles, the Yids Eduard Dumke and Rozenberg. Obviously these men had engaged in political agitation. Social Democrats did not believe in purely economic strikes; as everyone knew, they attempted to turn all economic strikes into political ones. The Social Democratic deputies in the hall should have the candor to admit it: "You, Social Democratic Gentlemen, only just called upon the Octobrists not to be hypocrites; and I call upon you in turn not to be hypocritical, and to say right out that it was your agitators who directed the Lena strike and sought to conduct it on a political basis."

The opposition had also spoken of a peaceful crowd, which allegedly had been fired upon without any justification. Even Guchkov had spoken of a peaceful crowd. This too was nonsense. After all, Zamyslovskii continued (quoting an article from *Kievskaia Mysl'*), even the opposition papers recognized that the crowd which had originally assembled to confront Tul'chinskii, early on the day of the massacre, had issued the ultimatum that unless their arrested comrades were released by 3 a.m., they would march on Bodaiko and free them by force. Could one say that this was a peaceful crowd? It might be argued that the workers in question should never have been arrested, but they had been arrested on the basis of article 125 of the Civil Code (which prohibited incitement to economic strikes), and even the opposition had to recognize that they had in fact been members of a strike committee. One could not really argue that the arrests had been illegal in any way.

And finally, what of the massacre itself? Now altogether under the spell of his legal lore, Zamyslovskii proceeded to read what the legal code had to say about the use of weapons by troops.

> I refer you to art. 30 and supplement to art. 316, of the Statute on Provincial Public Institutions. Here it says quite categorically: "A cold or fire weapon may be used by troops under the following rules: after the civil authority had turned over its powers, and warning has been issued thrice on the trumpet to enable innocent bystanders to disperse." I affirm that in this instance there was no violation whatever of the law.

Zamyslovskii was now plunging into a world of pure fantasy, although the fantasy undoubtedly rested on details that had been furnished to him by government sources (one by one they would also be charted out the next day by Makarov):

> Treshchenkov had not issued the order to fire at all. He had formally transferred his authority to the officer in charge of the army detachment, and the latter had acted precisely as the law required him to do. For him to have acted otherwise would have been to violate the law.
>
> (Voice from the Left: "So, it is all right to shoot?") "Yes, one can, and in such instances, one must. . . . " (Voice from the Right: "Correct, undoubtedly so, absolutely!") . . . because the crowd was going to free the workers under arrest by force. When it was 160 steps away, it was warned not to go any further. Engineer Tul'chinskii approached it, and began to argue with it.

One detail now followed another, all equally precise, all equally grotesque:

> A first salvo was fired, but the crowd had thrown itself to the ground before it actually reached it, and apparently the salvo didn't

cause any special harm. For after it had been fired, the crowd rose up again, and shouting "Hurrah" threw itself at the troops. (Laughter on the Left; voices: "Where did you get the 'Hurrah'?") Then, already from a distance of 100 steps, the shooting, which caused a whole series of deaths, really occurred. This is how it all happened in reality, and in all this we will not find any illegality, whether on the part of Rotmistr' Treshchenkov, or on the part of the troops. There is illegality only in the actions of those who act as patrons for Yids like Ginzburg, who promote the likes of Mr. Timiriazev, and generally kowtow before these capitalist potentates. (Applause from the Right.)[24]

A few more speakers were listed and came to the platform—most of them to repeat the arguments, and the rhetoric, that had already been used. These concluding speeches of the increasingly droning debate hardly need to be recalled in detail, for they probably made as little impression on the tiring Duma deputies as they do on the contemporary reader. But two of them at least need to be mentioned, if only because of what they suggested about the nature of the political constellation that was beginning to emerge during these waning days of the Third Duma. One of them was the address of Efremov, the leader of the *Progressisty*, the parliamentary group in which, from the outset, the spokesmen for a younger and more rebellious generation of the Moscow big business and industrial class had assumed a prominent role. Efremov's line indicated that even in this affair, which clearly involved the "image," if not the interests, of Russia's big bourgeoisie, the *Progressisty* had elected to side unequivocally with the opposition (a choice already signaled by their decision to contribute their signatures to the Kadets' interpellations). The *Progressisty* prided themselves on their directness, their bluntness, and their decisiveness—in contrast to the Kadets' abstracted and flowery *intelligentshchina*—and this was the tone that Efremov chose to adopt:

> We cannot fail to demand that the Ministry of Trade and Industry explain how it could allow on the part of the Lena Company not only abnormal, but also illegal, treatment of the workers in its employ. We cannot fail to demand an explanation of why the Ministry of Internal Affairs and the Ministry of Justice failed to take appropriate measures to see to it that the relations of the Lena Company with the local administrative and judiciary authorities be placed under the normal lawful conditions of the subordination of the company to

state authorities. We cannot fail to ask how it was that the army . . . which is charged with the defense of law and order inside the country, was turned into the blind instrument of a criminal and inhuman officer of the *gendarmerie*. Finally, we cannot fail to ask of the Minister of Justice what he plans to do to bring the whole matter up before an independent and uncompromising court of judgment to expose the whole truth . . . and [impose] a dispassionate and independent sentence . . . to ease, if not to appease, the sense of horror, the pangs of civic conscience, which must perturb all of us in the face of the horrors that has been committed on the Lena.

Therefore, the group of *Progressisty*, which has endorsed the *zapros* of the Party of Popular Freedom [the Kadets], will support not only this *zapros* but also all other *zaprosy* introduced in the Duma on this subject, and demand their urgent and immediate consideration.

This statement, which signified that the *Progressisty* would not only vote to bring the Social Democrats' *zapros* up for discussion but also support it in substance, indicated, more sharply that any rhetoric could possibly have done, how long a road the *Progressisty* had already traveled.

"I consider, I repeat, the issue so clear, so crying, so demanding of an immediate answer," Efremov concluded, "that I will not hold up your attention with any further arguments, and only call upon you to recognize this *zapros* as urgent, so that it may be raised immediately before the government. (Applause from the Left.)"[25]

The debate droned some more as additional supporters and opponents of the *zapros* explained their positions, but revealingly it was not until the very end that a spokesman for the Nationalist faction, Polovtsov, finally made his way to the platform. For a number of obvious reasons, it was more difficult for the Nationalists than for any other group in the Duma to adopt a political position in this debate. Of all the Duma factions, they stood more clearly identified with the government and were most dependent on it; by the same token, it was most difficult for them to criticize it, even on so popular an issue. In addition, the Nationalists liked to think of themselves as a modern, enlightened, and responsible group; and therefore, unlike the Right, they could not easily satisfy themselves with imprecations about the international capitalists and the *zhidy*, especially when these potential scapegoats had already been demonstrated to have had such influential official connections. Yet they, or at least their constituents, were largely agrarians—Russian landowners, especially of the Southwestern provinces, who had rallied, however precariously, around

Nationalist slogans. Under the circumstances, they could not afford to keep silent about an issue which involved the exploitation and the eventual death of so many "authentic" Russian people. But how to find a proper and measured tone? As we have seen, the Nationalists had sought to resolve their dilemma by refusing to endorse the substance of any *zaprosy* (while voting nonetheless in support of their urgent consideration), while introducing for their own part a simple parliamentary question, which did not require an immediate reply by the government and was phrased in the most cautious and conciliatory manner. In this, the last gasp of the debate, their spokesman, Polotsov, now had to justify their stand. He managed it only stumblingly:

The Nationalists were deeply disturbed by the "consternating news" of the death of 150 Russian people—a national catastrophe, which was all the more horrifying because these people had died at the hands of their brothers. Therefore, the Nationalists had decided to vote in favor of urgent consideration of *zaprosy*. But legislators did not have the right to surrender to their feelings; they had to preserve their *sang-froid*, to come to dispassionate conclusions. And so far, the only data available for their consideration were brief and unclear newspaper reports. Under the circumstances, the Nationalists did not consider it correct to pronounce themselves on the substance of the *zaprosy* that had been introduced. Therefore, they had drawn up a formulation of their own, focused on the issues of interest to them, and were offering it in the form of a simple parliamentary question, since even the government did not possess as yet sufficient information to respond with the promptness that a *zapros* required.

Besides, the Nationalists could not subscribe to the substance of the *zaprosy* offered by other parliamentary groups, since all of them included the army in their bill of indictment. On the basis of Rotmistr' Treshchenkov's report, it was clear that the army had had no choice but to fire, when—after two proper warnings had been issued—it had been threatened by a crowd armed with sticks and stones. But the available information, however inadequate, also suggested that there had been violations of legality in the conduct of local authorities before the shooting occurred. Hence the text of the *zopros* that the Nationalists had decided to introduce: "We trust that the government will not take advantage of any of the delays allotted to it by law and promptly offer its answer," Polotsov virtuously concluded. "Russian blood has been shed, and we cannot remain cold-blooded witnesses of these awful events." (Applause from the Right. Voices: "Correct!")[26]

The inglorious debate had finally drawn to its inglorious conclusion. But when the presiding officer called for a first, procedural vote on the first *zapros* to have been introduced, the Kadets', there was another anticlimax. A legal quorum was lacking, the chair had to announce after the votes were counted, and the voting would have to be held over to the next session. "There *is* a quorum," shouted an indignant voice on the Left. "There is no quorum," answered one on the Right. Kuznetsov, from his seat: "There is! There is! I ask for a count!" The presiding officer called Kuznetsov to order, and asked the deputies still in the Duma chamber to turn to the next item of business: the election of three members to a special joint commission to adjudicate the differences that had arisen between the Duma and the State Counsel over a bill regulating hunting.[27]

The delayed vote would be held the next day, Tuesday, April 10, without erasing the painful impression that the desultory character of the debate and the failure to assemble a quorum at its conclusion had produced on newspaper commentators, and presumably on the public at large. It was as if the deputies of the majority, who were most responsible for the poor attendance, had done their best to confirm—so soon before the elections—the validity of the opposition's claim of the Duma's impotence, given its existing authority. The next day's discussion was even more perfunctory. By this time, however, it was already a matter of public knowledge that the government had decided to come forward with its own explanation for the Lena events, immediately upon receiving the Duma's *zaprosy*. Under the circumstances, there was little point in holding things up. Urgency was voted for all three *zaprosy* by an almost unanimous vote, and after a brief interval to provide for discussion of their substance, each in turn was voted upon. Both the Kadets' and the Octobrists' *zaprosy* were approved, without even a formal vote count, but the Social Democrats' was narrowly defeated, 96 to 76, many of the Octobrists having joined up with the Rights and the Nationalists to reject it.

The debate was now suspended, the formula offered by a group of Siberian deputies to close it (until after the government's explanation was received) being adopted almost without discussion. After the Lena events, no deputy could afford to oppose the formula: it called upon the government to introduce legislation laying down rules for hiring, and regulating the numbers of hours of work as well as working and living conditions in the Lena gold and platinum fields.[28]

As predicted, the Duma was called into special session on the evening of Wednesday, April 11, to hear the government's reply to its *zaprosy*. The visitors' seats were packed, it was later reported, those reserved for members of the State Council "rather full," but on the floor no more deputies were in attendance than there had been at the morning session, which had been devoted to routine matters.[29] The Premier, V. N. Kokovtsev, had elected not to deliver the government's explanation himself, delegating this responsibility to the two ministers primarily concerned: A. A. Makarov, the Minister of Internal Affairs, and S. I.Timashev, the Minister of Trade and Industry. But Kokovtsov did sit in the government's box throughout the presentation, at first reportedly leafing through some documents, and eventually laying his head on his hand. It was speculated afterwards in the Duma corridors that he had done so because of the ear-shattering dissonances in the speeches of his two ministers.[30]

Makarov was the first scheduled speaker. He spoke slowly, looking frequently at his text, but whatever element of excitement may have been lacking in the delivery was more than made up by the content. Not that the content had anything like the consistency, the coherence, and especially the dramatic quality suggested by the excerpts and summaries that later appeared in the press, and that opposition commentators would naturally seek to bring out in their efforts to highlight the evilness of the authorities they were fighting. Rather, what the speech dramatized was the banality of the evil, and the degree of deterioration that higher authority, particularly in the Ministry of the Interior, had undergone since Stolypin's death. Makarov's whole presentation was imbued with officiousness and a self-contentment bordering on smugness. It was the work of a third-rate *chinovnik*, of a pedant steeped in routine, and delivered for the most part with an air of sweet reasonableness—even if the delivery slipped disastrously in the end to unveil in the *chinovnik*, in characteristic Russian fashion, the overbearing quality of a bully.

The tones of officiousness, pomp, and sweet reasonableness, were struck at the opening of the address:

Gentlemen, members of the Duma:

In public life, we often encounter phenomena which entirely absorb our attention and take a powerful grip on our feelings. When such events occur, a quite natural urge is aroused to find out the whole truth, however bitter it may be; and those who can shed light on these events do not have the right to keep silent. This is why, notwithstanding the fact that your *zapros* was adopted only yesterday, the government considers it to be its duty to come forward this very day with clarifications about the circumstances surrounding the deplorable because one cannot respond to an event which brought about the death of 163 people except with sincere grief. And believe me, in this respect the government shares the feelings that overflow in your hearts. Nevertheless, gentlemen, a feeling of grief . . . is often accompanied by an urge to identify all the circumstances that have caused it to arise, as well as the persons guilty for having brought them about. From this often flows a desire to find culprits come what may, and then begin investigation [*poiski*], which due to their impassioned character, lead to conclusions which are not always just. Permit me to ask you, first of all, to put these feelings of grief aside, if you can, and to hear my explanation out with dispassion [cold-bloodedly—*khladnokrovno*] and, if you can, attentively.[31]

His visage of judicious detachment now hopefully in place, Makarov hastened to caution his audience that the economic relations between the Lena Company and its workers did not fall within his competence. Even so, he should report that until the outbreak of the strike, the Ministry of Internal Affairs had not received any reports of abnormality in these relations: Perhaps this was because the local authorities had proven insufficiently attentive, a failure that would have compounded by the great geographical isolation of the Lena fields. Be that as it may, Makarov could assure the deputies that as soon as communications were restored, the Governor-General of Irkutsk would visit the Lena fields and conduct a thorough and severe investigation to establish if any failures of duties had occurred on the part of local officials. For his own part Makarov would now direct his attention to the two basic charges that the *zaprosy* just passed by the Duma had leveled at his ministry: 1) that of having interfered in a strike that was unfolding peacefully; and 2) as a direct consequence of this interference, of having resorted on inadequate grounds to the use of fire weapons. Makarov now gravely plunged into the heart of the matter:

"And so, first of all, did the strike on the Lena fields really unfold peacefully, and not call for interference of the administrative authorities to preserve order and security?" The strike had broken out on February 29, and the strikers already issued their demands on March 3. "Incidentally these demands included an eight-hour working day . . . " (Egorov, from his seat: "What maniacs, it makes one sick with fright [*kakaia strast', bol'no strashno*]!" Refusing to be diverted by the interruption (as he would throughout his speech), Makarov religiously continued with his prepared text:

... On 9 March, all the fields were already on strike. And about this time, the fact that the strike was being led by a strike committee was also exposed. When the Procurator of the Irkutsk Circuit Court received a report about this from the Mining Inspector, he suggested to the local Justice of the Peace that he launch a preliminary investigation on the basis of point three, article 125, of the Civil Code. This clause, gentlemen, members of the Duma, deals with participation in associations whose objective it is to incite or continue strikes, taking account of article 367....

(Kuznetsov, from his seat: "And the law 2 December [1905, ostensibly legalizing economic strikes]?" Purishkevich, from his seat: "Don't interrupt!" The Chairman: "I humbly ask for no objections from the floor.")

... while article 367 [Makarov valiantly resumed his precarious legal argument] refers only to strikes ... in enterprises which, in a strict sense, do not have state or public significance. Thus, according by existing law, if, according to the *ukaz* of 2 December 1905, participation in a strike not having state of public significance is not [legally] punishable, participation in an association which lays it as the goal of its activity incitement to strike generally remains punishable by law ... (Voice from the Left: "Pretty sharp!") ... Consequently [Makarov concluded his legal argument, if not triumphantly, at least with considerable relief] initiation of prosecution on the basis of point 3, article 125, of the Civil Code was perfectly correct.[32]

Even if anybody had cared to follow attentively the tangle of Makarov's legal argument, he would have felt, by this time, thoroughly confused. Was it the government's case that the strike committee of the Lena workers had been prosecuted and eventually arrested, on the ground that while economic strikes *per se* had been legalized by the law of December 2, incitement to such strikes continued to be a punishable offense? But if so, why bother to throw in the doubtful argument that the Lena Gold Fields Company was an enterprise of state or public significance "in the strict sense" (i.e., to be placed in the same category as means of public transport, for example, to which the law of December 2 explicitly did not apply). For if this were the case, the Lena strike was to be considered illegal *per se*; and all those who had participated in it were to be viewed as lawbreakers, not merely those who had incited them. Be that as it may, as the interruptions from the Left clearly suggested, no one was really interested in Makarov's legal niceties—all the deputies in the chamber already being aware, if only from the Social Democrats' irritating *zaprosy* of the past, that it was the Minister of Interior's fairly regular practice (whatever the actual meaning of existing legal statutes) to prosecute worker activists in economic strikes.

His difficult legal exercise out of the way, Makarov went on to explain that, in any event, the initiation of legal proceedings against the strike committee had had no immediate practical consequences, the order of the Justice of the Peace for their arrest not having been implemented due to the lack of the necessary police force on the spot. Meanwhile—and perhaps precisely because of this—the situation on the fields had become more and more threatening, giving rise "to the presumption that company property might be damaged or destroyed." When all this had been reported to the Minister of Justice on March 21, the order had been issued to send an army detachment, stationed 300 *versty* away, to the fields, and Rotmistr' Treshchenkov and Engineer Tul'chinskii were also ordered to the spot. By the time of their arrival, Makarov continued, plunging into what by this time he presumably knew just as well as his audience to be fiction, the strikers were breaking into the police station, stopping passenger trains to prevent any attempts to expel workers from the fields, refusing to allow newly hired workers to resume work, etc. Engineer Tul'chinskii had made every possible effort to mediate, warning the strikers that work would be resumed with newly hired help, unless they themselves resumed working. The situation on the fields was becoming quite impossible and the Governor of Irkutsk, who from the outset had been quite sympathetic to the strikers, was compelled on April 2 to order Treschenkov to execute the order of the Justice of the Peace for the arrest of the members of the strike committee. The order had been executed on April 4.

As most of Makarov's audience was already aware on the basis of the reports of newspaper correspondents, all the allegations he had just presented of violence and threats of violence on the fields to justify the intervention of the authorities were false. Also, what he had failed to mention—and which was already being rumored (although the details did not come out until the issuance of Senator Manukhin's report) was that the Governor of Irkutsk had originally rejected the suggestion of the arrest of the strike committee. It was only after representatives of the company had pressed the Ministry of

Trade and Industry for action, and the latter had interceded with Makarov, who in turn had issued a direct order to this effect, that Bantysh had unhappily issued the directive for the arrest of the strike committee.

At this point in his address, Makarov proceeded to recite the story of the massacre itself, but he eventually returned to this part of his case—i.e., to the argument that the strike had not been peaceful, and therefore required police intervention—as if aware that the evidence he had presented earlier (to prove the point) had not been altogether persuasive. Following a blood-curdling description of the behavior of the crowd which had confronted the army detachment, thereby forcing it to shoot, a description which clearly failed to win over most of his audience, he interjected:

> And anyway, as undoubtedly you have already perceived from my earlier presentation, the whole course of the strike can hardly be described as having been peaceful. . . . (Rosanov, from his seat: "What is the evidence for this?")
>
> . . . Besides, its underlying character anyway was not purely economic, but to a significant extent political . . . (Voice from the Left: "They wanted to establish a Lena Republic.") . . . I already had the honor to inform you [Makarov stumbled on] that the very first demands, those of 3 March, referred to the eight-hour day. . . . (Kuznetsov, from his seat: "What's political about that?")
>
> The Chair: "I implore you to observe quiet." (Makarov) . . . and at the present time . . . (Voice from the Left: "It's scandalous!" Voice from the Right: "Throw the hooligans out!" The Chair: "I implore you not to make noise.) . . . and at the present time . . . (Kuznetsov, from his seat: "It's an affront to hear this!") . . . It already established that among the ten arrested members of the strike committee who have been prosecuted on the basis of article 125 of the Civil Code are Aleksandr Sobolev, sentenced in 1908 by the Vilno Military Circuit Court for distributing illegal literature among the lower ranks, Dumke sentenced in 1907 by a provisional military court for belonging to the Latvian Social Democratic Union. . . .
>
> (Purishkevich, from his seat: "Why didn't they hang him?")
>
> . . . and Induk Rozenberg sentenced in 1906 by a military court of the Transbaikal district for belonging to a revolutionary group . . .

(Purishkevich: "He should have been hung!") (Voice from the Right: "So that's the company they keep!") (Voice from the Left: "A government provocation!")

. . . Some members of the strike committee succeeded in going into hiding, among them Batashev, a member of the Second Duma sentenced in 1907 . . . to four years of forced labor in the case of the Special Democratic [Duma] fraction . . . (Noise; the chairman rings his bell.)[33]

Aside from the fact that this last allegation was subsequently proven to be untrue (Batashev had never been anywhere near the fields), it was also a direct provocation of the Social Democratic deputies in the chamber who viewed their predecessors in the Second Duma who had been arrested as martyrs, who had been the victims of a gross government provocation, and periodically called for their amnesty. Having thus tried to even the score with the Social Democrats who had harassed him throughout his address, Makarov—now presumably in better spirits—finally drew the thread of this part of his scattered argument:

With such leaders, naturally, a strike cannot be considered purely economic, and could not have unfolded peacefully. . . . (A voice from the Right: "Bravo!") . . . If you agree with me that there was no illegal interference by administrative authority in a peacefully conducted economic strike, one cannot infer that the regrettable events of April 4 occurred as the result of this interference. . . . [34]

But Makarov was not going to confine himself to this flawless logical argument. He was prepared to give his audience a full accounting for the behavior of the troops on the day of the massacre. At this point, he picked up the second charge in the Duma that he had set out to refute: that the troops had fired without adequate justification.

Earlier in his speech, he had presented to his largely skeptical audience a version of the events on the day of the massacre which he had pieced together from excerpts of the early telegrams that had been received from Treshchenkov, the police officer who had been assigned to the fields, from the Deputy Procurator, and from Tul'chinskii who, while still in a state of shock and hysteria, had been pressed by his colleagues to go along with their general version of events. The accounts they had offered of the hours leading up to the confrontation need not detain us. They largely corresponded to the official communiqués which had been released immediately after the shooting (and which probably had been drawn up from them). In any case, they were largely irrelevant to the point immediately at issue: under precisely what circumstances, under what provocations, had the troops actually fired? In this respect, the telegram of Tul'chinskii—the only credible official witness as far as the government's critics were concerned—was of no help. It did not go into the details of the shooting, and besides Tul'chinskii was widely reported in the press to have denied in recent days that the strikers had engaged in any acts of violence. For his account of the actual shooting, Makarov had to depend on the telegram of Treshchenkov and the Assistant Procurator, both suspect sources as far as most of his audience was concerned. And the details they offered of the circumstances of the shooting not only lacked credibility, but were not wholly consistent. The two did concur that a proper warning had been issued; that the crowd had ignored it; that a first salvo had been fired; that the crowd, thereupon, had first thrown itself to the ground, and then rushed the troops, which had fired three more times in self defense. But beyond this, the graphic details which their telegram abundantly provided unfortunately clashed in every respect. Treshchenkov had it that the warning had been issued thrice on the trumpet (strictly according to regulations). The Procurator's report had the warning issued once. Treshchenkov had the crowd continuing its menacing advance after the signal; the Procurator had it surrounding Tul'chinskii, and then moving forward. Treshchenkov had the marchers yelling "Hurrah" as they rushed the troops; the procurator had them yelling "Forward." Treshchenkov reported absolute discipline among the troops when he had turned his authority over to the officer in charge and the latter had finally ordered the soldiers to fire (again, all exactly according to the rules). The Procurator's telegram strongly implied that the troops had panicked (reporting that the soldiers had "become agitated, demanding that they be allowed to fire before they were run over.")

It was unsurprising that his informants had not had the time to get the details of their stories straight, but Makarov did not appear to notice, as he read them off, or perhaps he did not even care. And adding to the ludicrousness of the occasion, he now weightily read off long excerpts from the legal code, noting after he had done so that the evidence incontrovertibly demonstrated that, under the grave immediate threat of being overpowered and disarmed by a menacing crowd, the officials concerned and the troops under their charge had in every respect followed the letter of the law.

Can one, under the circumstances, assert that fire weapons were resorted to without adequate justification [Makarov asked with a note
of triumph]? What would you say, gentlemen, if this had not been
done and a crowd of several thousand people had surrounded the
soldiers and disarmed them? (Purishkevich, from his seat: "One
would say that there is no government.") You would say, at the very
least, that the government was criminally passive (*prestupno
bezdeistvovalo*) . . . (Voices from the Right: "True! Correct!")
(Makarov) . . . And you would be right!

And then came the remarkable passage, which thereafter would be
drummed by the labor press, and become imprinted on the minds of thousands of Russian workers:

You will agree, members of the State Duma, that such actions are
completely intolerable. Troops and weapons are inseparable: the
loss of their weapons is a disgrace for the military. You don't fool
with armies [*s voiskami ne shutiat'*]. An army is guided in its actions
solely by its sworn oath, the requirements of its regulations, and the
iron discipline that binds it together . . .

(Voice from the Right: "Bravo! Correct!")

When having lost its reason, under the influence of evil agitators, a crowd therefore throws itself at troops, the troops have nothing else left to do but to fire. . . .

(Voice from the Right: "Correct!")

"So it has been, and so it will be in the future . . . "

(Kuznetsov, from his seat: "As long as you are in power.")

(Voices from the Left: "Bloodsuckers!" Applause from the Right:
Noise.)

The Chair (ringing his bell): "Duma member Kuznetsov. I ask you
to observe quiet and not to make remarks from your seat."

(Makarov) "The deeply regrettable events of April 4, I am firmly convinced must weigh oppressively, not on those who were in command of the army detachment . . .

(Voice from the Left: "[Not on them but] on you [*eshche by, na vas*].")

. . . but on those agitators who are now in jail, Sobolev, Dumke, Rozenberg, on Batashev who cowardly fled . . .

(Exclamations from the Left: "Okh!")

. . . and on all those who side with them."

(Voices from the Left: "and on Makarov!" Catcalls and hisses. Applause from the Right. Voices from the Left: "The bloodsuckers are celebrating!")[35]

In the midst of the bedlam that greeted Makarov's concluding words, the chair invited the next inscribed speaker, Minister of Trade and Industry Timashev, to the platform. But the accumulated anger and resentment that Makarov's speech had unleashed—both on the Left and on the Right—could not easily be put down:

Kuznetsov, from his seat: "Haven't you had enough blood?"

Purishkevich, from his seat: "When your term is over, you will go to the devil, Kuznetsov!"

Voices from the Left: "Hooligans!"

The Chair: "Duma member Purishkevich, I ask you to stop making noise."

As the bedlam slowly subsided, Timashev climbed the rostrum and finally began his address. His speech was immeasurably more skillful than Makarov's, more genuinely conciliatory, more tentative in tone, indeed apologetic for not being able to provide more exhaustive data. Admittedly,

Timashev's was a far easier task, for he didn't have—and didn't choose—to deal with the most embarrassing and grievous aspects of the Lena affair: the calling of the troops, the arrest of the strikers, the circumstances of the massacre. He would, he told his audience, confine himself solely to the terms of reference of the parliamentary inquiry that concerned his own ministry: "Did the Minister know that the treatment by the Lena Company of its workers did correspond to the requirements of the law?" Timashev's answer was delivered with the air of candor and directness which may have temporarily surprised his critics in the hall, for they heard him out quietly and attentively (as the subsequent debate would show).[36]

Yes, his ministry knew, was the tenor of his reply, and indeed it had energetically sought for a long time—and with only partial success—to get the Lena Company to change its ways. Timashev recounted, in this connection, how the Department of Mines had received its first reports of the Company's violations of legal requirements, and of the terms of its contract with the Lena workers, from its regional inspector, Engineer Tul'chinskii, as early as January 1911. He stated that upon receiving this report, the Department of Mines had immediately demanded an explanation from Company officials, and called upon them to fulfill Tul'chinskii's demands, while instructing him to follow the matter up. Some of the violations had subsequently been corrected by the Company, while some, as it turned out, had not, although the Department of Mines had received no further reports until after the outbreak of the strike and the reception, on March 8, of a telegram from the strikers listing their grievances and demands. Thereupon, the Department of Mines had again instructed Tul'chinskii to investigate, and to take measures to reach a peaceful settlement of the strike.

Timashev then embarked upon a detailed discussion of the workers' strike demands and of his Ministry's attitude toward them (we shall return to this), trying to demonstrate, as he went along, that his Ministry had done everything in its power to see to it that the law be respected, and the strike, settled peacefully. Indeed, on March 21, as his listeners might recall, the Mining Department in Irkutsk had reached a determination opposite to that of the local Justice of the Peace, pronounced the Company rather than the workers in violation of contract, and issued a whole series of recommendations. As late as March 23, Engineer Tul'chinskii had issued a guarantee to the strikers that many of their demands, including that for a wage increase, would be satisfied provided they went back to work. Indeed, the workers' elected representatives had appeared temporarily satisfied with this commitment (this happened to be true), but had subsequently wavered (under the pressure of the rank and file—L.H.), and the strikers had not returned to work. After this the inspector had conducted no further negotiations, and no further reports had been received prior to Tul'chinskii's dreadful telegram about the massacre.

These were all the data currently in his possession, Timashev concluded. They were in many respects inadequate and contradictory, and left much that was unclear. The most exhaustive investigation of this extraordinary affair was obviously necessary, and it would be immediately undertaken. For his own part, he could assure his listeners that the government would devote to this lamentable affair "the full attention that it deserves, and which will meet your general desire" (Applause from the Right).[37]

This was a skillful presentation of the case of the Ministry of Trade and Industry, and it rested on truths, if only half-truths. Timashev had failed to mention that after Tul'chinskii had issued his original critical report about the Lena Company, and Timiriazev had complained of his conduct to the Ministry of Trade and Industry, the Department of Mines had actually reprimanded him for placing Lenzoto "in a difficult situation." "These difficult conditions," he had been told by the Department in June 1911 had arisen chiefly because "while fulfilling those of your responsibilities that are concerned with the protection of the workers' interests, and emphasizing in this connection the purely formal requirements of the law, you have completely ignored the interests of the enterprise." The department had enjoined Tul'chinskii to take greater account of the views of the Company officer in charge of the fields, Belizerov. The latter, he was reminded, was "an experienced and widely reputed administrator, personally known to the minister, and his reputation is itself a guarantee that the enterprise is functioning properly, even in the sphere of worker-company relations." (!) It was little wonder that after the issuance of this reprimand, the Department had received no further critical reports from its field officers until after the strike had broken out.[38]

Timashev had also skipped nimbly over the fact (subsequently revealed in the Manukhin report) that the decisions to send troops in the Lena Fields and eventually to arrest the strikers' elected representatives—which had set the scene for the massacre which he had declined to discuss—had been reached only after, pursuant to company pressures, he had personally intervened with Makarov, who had overruled the recommendation of both Tul'chinskii and Bantysh, the Governor of Irkutsk.

Even though Timashev, with his speech, had achieved the objective of deflecting public criticism from the conduct of his own ministry, he did not silence it. Indeed what chiefly interested the governments' critics, both in the

Duma and in the press, about his address was not his presentation of the case for his ministry, but the ample ammunition it provided for challenging Makarov's: the evidence he had cited of the Company's legal infractions, of the genuineness of the economic grievances that had finally set off the strike; and parenthetically what his report of the strike committee's willingness to settle at the end of March—only to be overridden by the objections of the other workers—suggested about the actual relationship between these "subversives" and the rank and file among the Lena strikers. In short, as opposition commentators would point out with relish, all that Timashev really did achieve in the end was to further discredit his colleagues.

Yet, one section of his speech is deserving of closer attention because of what it revealed about the assumptions underlying the conduct of his own ministry, and government labor policy generally. Midway in his address it will be recalled, Timashev had read off the demands listed in the telegram sent to the Department of Mines on March 8 by the Lena strikers, complaining that the strikers had kept shifting their demands as the strike wore on. Despite this difficulty, he stated, one could easily divide these demands into three quite different categories; and by the same token the government's and specifically his own ministry's responses to each of these categories of demands had also been of a different order.

The first of these categories of demands consisted of grievances about what were clearly violations of existing laws and regulations, as well as of contractual terms: e.g. delays in wage payments, payments in coupons or in kind, defective food staples, inadequate housing and medical facilities, and the like. With respect to these grievances, there could be but one response on the part of the authorities: to demand of the company that it obey the law. There was a second category of demands, to which the government's response had necessarily to be more ambiguous: demands, not for redress of violations of the company's existing contract with its employees, but for changes in the terms of this contract. With respect to demands of this order, such as the workers' claims for wage increases, for example, the government could not issue orders; it could only try to give counsel and use its influence. And finally, Timashev concluded, there was a third category of demands issued by the Lena strikers: demands "which habitually come up in the course of every strike, but which are always rejected decisively by the industrialists: for example, that workers not be dismissed except with the agreement of a workers' committee; that company employees who appear unsuitable to the workers be fired; the demand for an eight-hour day; the demand that workers be compensated for the days they have struck." To these claims, Timashev freely conceded, the government could give only "a completely negative response," and had issued instructions to this effect to the local branch of the Department of Mines.[39]

Here was an admission well worthy of attention—all the more for being so freely volunteered—and indeed it would draw some if inadequate, public notice. One might well have asked what there was about the demand for an eight-hour day, or the demand that workers' representatives be consulted in hiring and firing, or even the demand that certain supervisory personnel be dismissed, which made it incumbent upon the state to reject the legitimacy of these claims so decisively and automatically—and in rejecting them, to throw its weight decisively on the side of the employers. The question was far from academic—indeed it would prove of general and burning significance—because it was precisely these kinds of claims, and the psychological urges underlying them, that would most sharply distinguish, as we shall see, the labor unrest that the Lena massacre would set off, causing the government to side—unhesitatingly, automatically, blindly—with the employers against these expressions of the workers' self-affirmation. However, in the ensuing debate, this thread of Timashev's speech was largely ignored (with the exception of some passing remarks by the Social Democrats), the government's critics generally pushing his speech aside, and electing instead to focus their fire on the final obvious target of Makarov.

The first to do so, following the brief respite of a twenty-minute adjournment, was the spokesman for the Social Democratic faction, Kuznetsov, who wasted no words before aiming with obvious relish at his chosen target:

Gentlemen, members of the Duma!

On behalf of the working class, I wish to express my profound gratitude to the Minister of Internal Affairs for the speech he delivered today from the Duma rostrum. This speech constitutes as good a proclamation as any a socialist party has ever issued, and I recommend to the working class that it print it and disseminate it as widely as any Social Democratic appeal. The essence of his speech confirmed everything that I said from the Duma rostrum at the last session: i.e., that so it has been and so it will be in the future. We assert this categorically: that the working class has been shot at and will be shot at in the future, as long as the political order headed by the likes of Mr. Makarov is allowed to stand.

(Voices from the Left: "Correct!" The Chairman rings his bell. Applause from the Left.)[40]

Having sounded this triumphant overture, Kuznetsov somewhat hap-hazardly, but not ineffectively, set out to demolish Makarov's case. The Min-ister of the Interior had insisted that the strike on the Lena fields had a po-litical character. But none of the strike demands listed by his colleague, Timashev, were in any way political. What was political even about the de-mands—which he considered so obviously subversive—that workers not be dismissed by management, except with the agreement of the workers' elec-tive representatives? After all, the workers' right to elect *starosty* was recog-nized by all, and in some factories in Russia the *starosty* already shared with management the responsibility for hiring and firing. And what was political about the eight-hour day, which was already enforced in many plants work-ing on three shifts?

To justify the intervention of the authorities, Makarov had also made a big point of the dangers, and indeed the actual instances, of violence that had occurred as the strike progressed. But all available evidence indicated that the workers, under the leadership of their committee, had actually maintained exemplary discipline, and not a single instance of violence or damage to property had in fact taken place. (As I have indicated this claim would be confirmed by the report of Senator Manukhin.) As for Makarov's allegation that the strikers had assembled on April 4 with the intention of destroying the mines, it was simply absurd. Had they wanted to destroy the mines, they could have done so far more easily and effectively by interfering with the pumping of the shafts; and this they had refrained from doing throughout the long weeks preceding the massacre. Indeed what would they have done once they had destroyed the mines, cut off as they were from Irkutsk and all civilization until the coming of spring. Starve to death?

Makarov's explanation of the shooting was equally absurd. He had quoted Treshchenkov to the effect that had the detachment not fired when it did, it would have been overthrown and disarmed within minutes. But of-ficial reports had the workers 100 feet away from the troops when the firing had actually taken place. It was now suggested that the soldiers had been panicky, and themselves impatient to fire. He preferred to think, Kuznetsov virtuously observed, that they had fired on their fathers and their brothers only because they had been ordered to do so by that *agent provocateur*, Treshchenkov. The Chairman furiously rang his bell, calling Kuznetsov to order for touching on the topic of the conduct of the army. Having made his sally, Kuznetsov happily resumed.

In the last analysis, as the protest strikes started breaking out all over Russia clearly demonstrated, all these transparent lies had been to no avail.

It knew perfectly well that the strike had originally broken out because the Lena workers refused to eat horse carrion. This had been the catalyst for the outbreak of this economic strike. The Russian workers knew equally well that whenever such an economic conflict broke out between labor and capital, the government stepped in on the side of capital on the pretext that the strike was of political character. After all, among the dozens of strikes for economic improvements that had broken out since 1910 in typographical and metallurgical works, could a single case be found in which the authorities had not stepped in to arrest ten or twenty of the participants?

No, the Russian workers knew perfectly well that the fate and the cause of the Lena workers were their own fate and their own cause. In the telegrams that they were addressing daily to the Social Democratic deputies in the Duma, they stated unmistakably that those that had fired on the Lena workers had fired at them, the whole working class. "We thank Mr. Makarov in the name of the working class," Kuznetsov insistently concluded on the theme of his overture: "one could not have expected a better speech."

> He repeated everything that we have said; that the workers are being shot, and will be shot in the future, for economic strikes, and let the working class know: in order not to be shot at in the future, it must organize, close its ranks, and march forward in a fraternal organized struggle to destroy the contemporary regime and introduce a socialist order. (Applause from the Left.)[41]

The glee which had been so unmistakably mixed with the more rhetorical notes of indignation in Kuznetsov's address doubtlessly underscored, even for the deputies on the Right, the irreparable damage that Makarov's speech had done, and the uses to which it would be put by the extreme Left. From this point on, further debate would clearly be anticlimactic: as Kuznetsov's speech reminded the assembled deputies, the chief scene of the action was now bound to be transferred from their divided, and ultimately paralyzed assembly to the court of public opinion, if not to the streets.

When discussion resumed, Count Uvarov, nominally a member of the Right but widely respected even by the moderate opposition for the independence of his views, took the stand. He launched earnestly, if somewhat listlessly, into a close analysis of Makarov's statements, carefully weighing the evidence Makarov had cited for his allegations, and finding it wanting. Why had Makarov confined himself to a reading of truncated excerpts of three telegrams, two of them obviously impeachable sources? Why had he refrained from quoting any of the reports which he must have received since the shooting from Governor Bantysh, the highest and most responsible of the local officials under his charge? Why, indeed among the three sources he had actually used, had he failed to report what Tul'chinskii, the only one of them enjoying any public trust, had had to say about the circumstances of the shooting?

All of these questions were much to the point, but the assembled deputies probably listened to them as wearily as Uvarov probably delivered them. It was late in the evening and they already knew the answers. After a deputy from the Right interrupted to remind him of the late hour (11 p.m.), Uvarov promised to stop momentarily, droning on with but one more obvious, if unanswerable question, which proved—if further proof were needed—how completely Makarov had failed to persuade his audience. Makarov had expressed the conviction that the strike had had a political character, but he had failed to present precise and incontrovertible facts to prove his point. On the flimsy grounds that he had actually laid, such an assertion appeared too "careless" and "premature," even coming from the mouth of the Minister of the Interior. "Such a question cannot be decided on the basis that it so appears to somebody or other."

With this, Count Uvarov apologetically broke off his speech, promising to resume it on the morrow (he never did). He bowed to the chair, descended the platform, and the presiding officer (by this time, the Octobrist Kapustin) called the Duma session to a close.[42]

The reaction of the Russian press to the government's presentation of its case was even more critical and more vocal than the response that had been struck in the Tauride Palace. Even the more conservative organs of opinion joined with some zest in pointing out the numerous contradictions between Makarov's and Timashev's versions of the Lena events. "Messrs. Makarov and Timashev managed to reconcile their respective tales so little," *Novoe Vremia* observed, "that one is impelled to ask oneself whether the members of the United cabinet speak at all to each other, if only on the telephone!"[43]

Although conservative commentators still steered away from any criticism of the conduct of the army detachment—some indeed continuing to argue that it had been inevitable under the circumstances—they were prepared to join in ridiculing the evidence that Makarov had brought forth to demonstrate that under the aegis of dangerous subversives, the Lena strike had assumed a political character, and therefore required police intervention. "If a demand for the introduction of an eight-hour day in the mining industry is political," commented *Russkiia Vedomosti*, "then probably the six-hour day [in force] in the Petersburg ministries is already complete socialism." *Golos Moskvy* and *Novoe Vremia* agreed, and did not find Makarov's heavy emphasis on the subversive role of the political exile on the strike committee any more persuasive.

> It was the government which was responsible for they [sic] having been deported there in the first place. And if they were able to influence the workers, it was only because the conditions that the Company created provided a veritable breeding ground for revolutionary and subversive thought. But Makarov went ahead and found a cheap culprit for the whole tragedy in a member of the Second Duma, some Rozenberg or other, and in two other people. This was as persuasive as Kuznetsov finding in his address that the Third Duma was responsible for the Lena massacre.

Novoe Vremia offered these observations with a calm bordering on contentment, for it knew the real culprits. It had already identified them in its previous issues, as we have seen, and found them easy and comfortable targets:

> British shareholders, to be sure, would not ask themselves whether they had been wrong to entrust their affairs to such expert specialists on the autochtonous (*samobytnye*) conditions of Russian life as the omniscient Mr. Timiriazev and the Jew Ginzburg. . . . But the Russian public may feel no such restraints. . . . These were the Anglicized gentlemen who, in collaboration with the Jewish Petersburg community, had stated that one must first suppress the Hindus and then agree to their demands. . . . [44]

In this fashion, *Novoe Vremia* concluded its complicated comparison, even the doubts of local authorities had been resolved; Mr. Ginzburg and his ilk had triumphed. This was the face of the real enemy, not pitiful administrative exiles deserving only of compassion. The State Duma should brand it; public opinion had already spoken out.

But while *Novoe Vremia* managed to dispose so comfortably of the problems with a xenophobic and anti-Semitic campaign, most other conservative organs could not. Even Prince Meshcherskii had felt a sense of outrage upon reading Makarov's speech, which he did not attempt to contain. "In forty years of publishing *Grazhdanin*," he exclaimed in his weekly column, "it is for the first time that I have found myself in agreement with the

Social Democrats." Meshcherskii doubted that Makarov, "who is an honest man," could have persuaded himself of the truth of the version of events he had had to present. "And no real Russian, except perhaps for a handful of slavish idiots (*gorsti dumskikh kholopov*), would be able to endorse the fateful phrase offered by the Minister: "So it will always be." For these words, which tomorrow will be carried to all Russia, will signify, not just to the workers but to 160 million Russians, that from now on unprecedented license is to be given to police chiefs and colonels of the *gendarmerie* to arrest people—not for what they had done, but for what they *may* do." As if to provide an immediate illustration of the validity of Meshcherskii's denunciations of the arbitrariness of officials, he, the Tsar's confidant, had been allowed to publish this column with impunity, while the liberal newspaper *Kievskaia Mysl'* was fined for reprinting a summary of it!

But the real underlying issue was neither the depredations of Petersburg Anglicized gentlemen and Jews, nor even the high-handedness of police officials; it was the whole texture of government labor policy. Some of the major organs of public opinion had spoken out on this broader issue even before being prodded to do so by Makarov's speech. Echoing the charges of Social Democratic deputies, a columnist for *Russkiia Vedomosti* had pointed out on April 12 that there was really nothing unusual about what had happened on the Lena fields. If one put the number of victims aside, nothing had happened there that had not occurred many times over, not in distant Siberia, but in the Moscow industrial region:

> A completely peaceful but stubborn strike breaks out, i.e., one which hits severely the pockets of interested parties. The workers raise purely economic demands; indeed some required by law. . . . The workers stick to their demands and the negotiations do not lead anywhere. In this instance, the demands include an eight-hour day and polite address; and immediately there is an outcry about socialism and political agitation—the excuse required to demand and obtain, the dispatch of troops. A reduction of hours is especially justified (in this case) given the kind and conditions of labor involved. . . . While the demand for polite address, *obrashchenie na vy* [being called "you" rather than "thou"], is now being raised by workers everywhere, and is but a manifestation of the growth of the workers' self-respect, of the growth of the very "*kultura*" which Mr. Kokovtsev is seeking. It is in no way a political demand, but it has to be treated as such to justify the dispatch of troops. But is this un-

usual? In every major strike in Russia, the dispatch of troops is called for, and they are sent. Are we not accustomed to this?

But the workers stubbornly hold on. Then it is recalled that they are living on company property, and an obliging judge is found to authorize their immediate expulsion. Again, this is the usual picture. Note that it unfolded in July 1909 during the Petersburg trolley car strike—i.e., in the capital, where it was the elected city officials who resorted to such tactics. The workers who have taken a leading part in the strike, and particularly in the presentation of demands, are arrested as "instigators," and deported. It becomes a matter of honor for their comrades to seek their release, but this time they go with their demands to the administration in a crowd. "They won't arrest everyone." [This indeed had been the reasoning of the workers on the Lena fields on April 4.] This gives the [company] office the excuse to call on the soldiers for help against the "noisy and threatening crowd" of the workers. If the workers are not yet leaderless, they are likely to withdraw peacefully. But if some youngsters throw stones at the windows, or even at someone in anger, the guns go off by themselves. A pretext to fire them has been found, and the bullets find their marks.

This was by now a familiar scenario, the columnist of *Russkiia Vedomosti* melancholically observed, even if it took a catastrophe like Lena, with many lives lost, to draw the attention of the public to it:

> Yet, if the Lena tragedy somehow succeeds in impelling the government, the Duma, and "we, the public," to look around us, to reflect and recognize the lawfulness of strikes . . . and also the lawfulness, even more the necessity in the general interest, for the workers to organize, the victims of Lena will not have fallen in vain. We shall hope.[45]

As the commentator of *Russkiia Vedomosti* pointed out in his concluding paragraph, there was only one remedy for the conditions that had brought about the Lena massacre; it was to introduce in the field of labor relations in Russia the laws and policies in effect in advanced Western countries: to genuinely accept the workers' right to organize and strike for economic improvements. In fact, *Russkiia Vedomosti* commented about Makarov's speech, the law of December 2, 1905 already recognized the workers' right to participate in economic strikes. To pretend to recognize this right, and in the same breath to declare the committee in charge of a strike a criminal enterprise was "to engage in hypocrisy, or to want that every strike assume a disorderly character." For it was imperative that strikers have leadership if they are to maintain discipline and self-restraint.[46]

That *Russkiia Vedomosti* or *Rech'* should voice such sentiments about labor relations was hardly surprising. It is more notable, however, that by this time *Utro Rossii*, the organ of the liberal Moscow industrialists Riabushinskii and Konovalov, was prepared to draw the same conclusions and to voice them with equal conviction. To enable its would-be clientele of Moscow industrialists and big businessmen to digest them more easily, it sought to place them in the broader framework of Russia's general need for the rule of law if its economy was to move forward and prosper. For *Utro Rossii* to place the need for a more enlightened labor policy in this framework was not merely a matter of expediency. Ever since its inception (in late 1909), it had sought to implant in the big business and industrial communities the conviction that the elimination of arbitrariness (*proizvol*) and the instoration of the rule of law (*zakonnost'*) in Russian life was a necessary condition for Russia's economic, as well as social and political well-being. It was only natural that its commentators could now draw their observations about Lena in the same perspective. Life had now contradicted the optimism that Kokovtsev had recently expressed in his speech to the Moscow big business community about the existence in Russia of the cultural and legal prerequisites for successful economic growth. One of the editorialists of *Utro Rossii* wrote on April 10:

> The events on the Lena fields showed that none of the preconditions for the development of Russia's economic forces are in evidence at present. There cannot be any talk of the flowering of industry when its chief moving force—man—is denied any rights, when a mass of miners assembled to conduct peaceful negotiations about its affairs do not have any assurance that they will not be the object of an unexpedited and unprovoked shooting.
>
> A whole series of dramas have been played out in the Lena events: the drama of Russian state rule (*gosudarstvennost'*), which some years ago had offered the promise of securing inviolability of person and to date has not secured even the inviolability of life; the drama of the Russian army, whose soldiers can be turned into blind instruments in the hands of the likes of Rotmistr' Treshchenkov; the drama of the Russian *vlast'*, which has shown itself incapable of perfecting the most minimal interests of the rule of law from in-

fringement by its most insignificant agents; and finally of Russian industry, which entered into negotiations with workers through the medium of soldiers' bullets.[47]

In recent days many commentators had drawn analogies between the Lena events and the sinking of the *Titanic*, the *Utro Rossii* commentator continued. As if to suggest that both had been acts of nature, accidents. The analogy was perhaps inevitable, but it was inept. In the sinking of the *Titanic*, only a ship had failed; on Lena, it had been state power itself. There, a force of nature had been the killer; on the Lena fields, the killers had been people presumably endowed with reason, conscience, a heart, a soul. On the *Titanic*, there had been a lack of safety devices. Here, there had been a lack of law.

But what was to happen now? The blood of the Lena victims had already seeped into the earth, and the Lena Company had promised to bury their bodies and compensate their families. But the political issues raised by the Lena affair could not so easily be disposed of:

> No optimistic words from higher officials can persuade us now, after the Lena events, that the required conditions exist [for the development of the country's economic forces]. For these conditions presuppose the existence of legal norms, while these graves, out there on the Lena, reek of *bespravie*—of profound and hopeless oppression.[48]

These indeed were very strong words, but their author, and the newspaper which printed them, could claim to speak, at least as yet, only for a new, younger generation of the Moscow big business and industrial class, and probably still a relatively small minority of it at that. More symptomatic, if also less dramatic, was the response of the *Golos Moskvy*. As we have seen, the early reactions of the Octobrists' official organ had been extremely cautious—deploring the massacre, to be sure; calling for a full investigation; even ready to find fault with the conduct of local officials, but shying away from blaming the army, or even the higher reaches of the bureaucracy. However, following the publication of Makarov's speech, even its editorial comments took a far more dramatic turn. On April 13, *Golos Moskvy* published, for the first time, a front page editorial on Lena, which dismissed wholesale the official version of the Lena events that Makarov had presented in the Duma chamber and sharply condemned the government's labor policy. It bluntly called Lena a crime. The strike had broken out because of the extremely difficult economic conditions suffered by the workers of the Lena

Company, and it had been peacefully conducted. There had been no shad-ow of justification for the arrest of the strike committee. The basic principle underlying labor legislation, the newspaper explained to its readers, was that workers were too weak to be left to the free play of economic forces; they had to be protected by the state to keep them from sinking into a position of eco-nomic slavery. Instead, here the state had interfered in a peaceful economic dispute on the side of the employers. The result had been disorders, and eventually the shooting of April 4. What more was needed for Social Demo-cratic theories to triumph?

This was strong medicine for some of the readers (and financial sup-porters) of *Golos Moskvy*, especially for the clientele it still managed to cul-tivate among the older and more conservative elements of the commercial-industrial class of the Central Industrial Region. And to make it more palatable the editorialist of *Golos Moskvy* sought to appeal, not so much to his readers' aspirations for a different and more enlightened political order, as to their fears of the troubles to which this kind of labor policy was bound to lead. He sought to revive in them the nightmare which had quite con-ceivably been revived in his own mind—that of another 1905:

> All peaceful citizens, all foes of revolution should be the first to de-nounce the heavy hand of arbitrariness which had again made itself felt. They should do so out of egoism, out of fear for their own com-fortable lot (*obyvatel'skaia trusost'*), if not out of more elevated feel-ings and a natural sense of grief for our brothers. . . .
>
> Look out for the workers! Like Atlas, they hold the contemporary world on their shoulders, and we have already seen what grief can come once it begins to tremble. The Social Democratic movement, that herald of social revolution, that permanent threat to our culture and our very existence, is making progress in the West. This must be a lesson for us. A [successful] struggle against Social Democracy is conceivable only if class differences are not aggravated.[49]

II

I have recorded at such length the reactions that Lena set off in the Duma and in the press because it is only if one takes them into account that the re-sponse of the public-at-large that they ultimately evoked can properly be weighed. Notwithstanding the chorus of protests sounded by the spokesmen of the moderate and radical opposition, and the range of emotions—grief, anger, fear, hope—that they expressed and sought to rouse, they seemingly did not succeed in striking a vibrant or at least enduring chord in the circles of privileged society. Even among the intelligentsia, it appears, they failed to set off any storm of public protest barely comparable to the one which, seven years earlier in 1905, had greeted the massacre of January 9. Neither the press nor the usually omniscient reports of the Department of Police record a single major demonstration, a single meeting of public protest, a single petition campaign, in the circles of educated, privileged society, even in the two capitals. Somehow, on this occasion and on this subject, the availability of the new, relatively protective, public forums—the Duma, the press—appeared to dissipate, rather than mobilize public sentiment.

In the circles of the educated and the privileged, available evidence registers but one major exception to this general rule: the student youth. The first reports of student unrest appeared in the press on April 14, barely recording the fact that appeals had been circulating in the higher educational establishments of Petersburg and in a number of factories, calling for protest demonstrations of students and workers against the Lena massacre at the Kazan Cathedral, on Sunday April 15. However, the reports of the Department of Police enable us to reconstruct more precisely the immediate background of this student unrest, as well as to gauge its mood. The first such report of the Okhrannoe Otdelenie, dated April 12, noted that the Lena events had roused the spirit (*podniali nastroenie*) of revolutionary organizations and factory workers of the two capitals, and that of the student body of St. Petersburg University. The Social Democratic and Social Revolutionary student factions at the university had decided to exploit these events to intensify their revolutionary propaganda and to recruit more members. Since the Social Democratic student faction had been greatly weakened by the police arrests carried out in February and was therefore not in a position to lead the movement, the major role was being assumed by the Socialist Revolutionaries (SR's), who had now formed two groups: an "autonomous" group and a party one. These two groups had taken the lead in agitating for a joint worker-student demonstration on April 15, and issued an appeal to this effect. A third, "nonparty," group had also emerged, which students of all progressive factions had joined. This nonparty group, which had assumed the title of Constituent Group of the Revolutionary Union (*Uchreditel'naia gruppa revoliutsionnogo soiuza*) had plastered on the walls of university buildings an appeal arguing that the temper of the workers and of the people at large was mounting, and that all students should now unite, regardless of party, to prepare a general revolutionary uprising, devoting special attention in these preparations to the army and the officer corps. The full text of this bombastic appeal (it was appended to the Okhrana's report) need not detain us, but we should take note of those of its emphases that were symptomatic of a new and growing mood among radical students.

A new revolutionary situation was developing in Russia, the manifesto declared, and it was sweeping away the melancholic apathy that had descended over the intelligentsia after 1905. The signs were multiplying of growing public unrest, and of popular resistance—if as yet spontaneous and unorganized—to the yoke of the existing regime. The struggle clearly required organization, but not in the old traditional forms. Life had outgrown them, and laid a new path for Russian revolutionaries to build a single, "practical," democratic organization. The performance of this task was substantially eased by the psychological changes that had occurred among a significant portion of the intelligentsia's youth. The old dogmatic and sectarian conflicts no longer held any meaning for them. They now realized, for example, that the "strivings for revolutionary work and more generally for the social tasks of man, rooted in the personality of the Russian *intelligent*," were not only consistent with, but implicit in "freedom of personality," if properly understood. Indeed, the manifesto insisted that the generation in the name of which it purported to speak now found the idea of *dolg*, of debt and duty to the People, which had once been so prevalent in the Russian intelligentsia—with all the denial and repudiation of self that this idea entailed—as foreign, indeed as abhorrent, as the extremes of the cult of personality and aestheticism.

Given the new attitudes toward life that were now spreading, the "old purely intellectual schemes" could no longer play the role they once had, and the psychological basis for factional disputes on a theoretical level had simply disappeared. The practical harm caused by dogmatism had become quite apparent to all those who stood close to revolutionary work, as well as to the advanced strata of the working class, which were now attempting to establish independent political organizations. A new era was opening in the history of the revolution, one of "free practical work."

All this was not to suggest, however, that any changes had occurred in the goals of the new generation of revolutionaries, the manifesto hastened to observe:

> We too consider it our task to overthrow the existing political order and establish a democratic republic, and will support all demands

for social reforms (the eight-hour day, confiscation of gentry land). We also realize the need to struggle for the elimination of all forms of the exploitation of man by man, but this is not a current and immediate task for which it would make sense to split the movement.

In implementing these goals, we will continuously keep in mind the interests of the movement as a whole, of the revolution as a movement of the whole people. Accordingly, we cannot have any enemies in the camp of the Left: we will support all organizations of the Left, and help the people in its attempts to set up independent organizations (in particular, the party of the working-class [*klassovaia rabochaia partiia*]. We do not intend to impose our tutelage over every organization which grows within the people's womb, but rather to unite them all for the sake of joint action, and to establish alliances [*soiuznye otnosheniia*] among all elements of democracy. One must raise the self-consciousness of the people, and one of our tasks must be to develop on a broad scale organizations of cultural enlightenment. It is imperative to establish a real revolutionary force. This was demonstrated by the experience of the recent revolutions (in Turkey, Portugal, China), and we consider it extraordinarily important to build a solid organization in the army, including the officer corps.

To achieve this program, the document concluded, descending closer to earth, "it is in the first place important for us to work out and disseminate our views. It is also imperative to establish an organization and a literary organ. Russian youth was always and remains in the first ranks of the revolution. We are therefore appealing to you, comrades, and calling on all our supporters to organize under our banner."[50]

Notwithstanding its insistence on the novelty of its program, it was not difficult to discern in the eclectic ideas and practical precepts of this appeal many shadows of the past: of Lavrov and the People's Will, as well as of the early PSR and the Union of Liberation. And even the mood that it sought, however clumsily, to express—the repudiation to sectarianism, the hopeful pragmatism, the tolerant and confident belief that the various organizations of the Left could be brought together, under one common intelligentsia umbrella, to fight for common, minimal, revolutionary objectives—even this mood, and the conviction that had underlain it, had pervaded once before, at the beginning of the century, the efforts to mobilize an all-nation struggle against absolutism. The differences, even in mood, with the old Union of

Liberation were subtle indeed: a more explicit repudiation of excessive the-orizing; a more emphatic emphasis on individual self-fulfillment in the re-vived commitment of the new generation to public causes.

Actually, the most dramatic contrast was not so much with the past, at least the pre-1905 past, as with the present—with the angry and rancorous squabbles dividing the ranks of the Duma opposition, and especially the ul-timate impassiveness, if not indifference, even in the wake of the Lena mas-sacre and of the publicity it had received, of the world of the adults of edu-cated privileged society. The ghost of the Union of Liberation had spoken, in however thin and shrill an adolescent voice, among a handful of St. Pe-tersburg University students. It made the continued absence of its spirit in the world-at-large even more marked.

The other appeal mentioned in the Okhrana report of April 12, the leaflet issued by an All Student Coalition Committee (dominated at this mo-ment by SRs) to all the students of Petersburg, enjoined them, it will be re-called, to participate in a student-worker demonstration on Kazan Square on April 15 in protest against the "beastliness" of Lena. Drawn up in the far more traditional cadences of radical student rhetoric in Russia, this appeal noted that the reproach had recently been extended to students that they had been so absorbed in their academic work that public causes, and in par-ticular the interests of the proletariat, had become foreign to them; that the *studenchestvo*, in short, had been "bourgeois":

> Comrades, will not this shocking, heart-rending fact pull you out
> of this bourgeois-academic state of mind, and impel you to join
> your voices to the [outburst of] public indignation, to the general
> protest? One thousand workers will be bringing their protest out
> on the street. We call on every one of you, Comrades, to join up
> with them.[51]

A report of the St. Petersburg Okhrana of April 14 indicated that this leaflet had been widely circulated in a number of institutions of higher edu-cation of the capital: the University, the Psychoneurological Institute, the Women's Courses of Higher Education, and the Polytechnical Institute. It also stated that a *skhodka*, a flying meeting, had been held at the Psychoneu-rological Institute attended by about 600 students, which had endorsed the resolution of the Coalition Committee.

Earlier reports of the Okhranoe Otdelenie had mentioned some discus-sion among workers in various factory districts about demonstrating on

Nevskii Prospekt about the Lena events. The report of April 14 stated more definitely that workers, principally from factories on the Vyborg side, were planning to participate in this demonstration on the 15th. [52] By April 14, brief reports of this agitation had broken into the press, the newspapers noting that the leaflets circulated at the institutions of higher education as well as in a number of factories of the capital called for the demonstrators to enter Kazan Cathedral to "attend a mass to be held in memory of the Lena deaths."[53]

Nonetheless, the regular Sunday service at Kazan Cathedral on April 15 was allowed to start at the usual hour. But with the ample warning of the Okhrana's reports, the authorities had taken extraordinary precautions. In the early morning, large detachments of Cossacks, mounted *gendarmerie*, and police had been deployed at Kazan Square and along Nevskii Prospekt, and to reinforce them in case of need, police with drawn bayonets had been hidden away in the courtyards of a number of houses adjacent to the cathedral. Altogether, the security forces added up to more than 1,000 men.

Despite these precautions, the Okhrana subsequently reported, a crowd of about 1,000 persons quickly assembled on Nevskii Prospekt, between Kazan Square and the cathedral, some 15 minutes after the service began. Its members took off their hats, urging bystanders and passersby to do the same, unfurled a number of red flags, and began to sing the now consecrated funeral dirge *Vechnaia Pamiat'* ("Eternal Memory") in honor of the Lena dead—"calling on innocent bystanders to do the same." At this point, the priest serving the mass inside the cathedral, who had been forewarned by the police, abruptly stopped the service and left the church, making his way through the crowd to a fiacre that had been waiting for him at the door.

Meanwhile, police on foot and on horseback were pouring into the square, and when a group of students determinedly tried to break their way into the cathedral, a thick line of police was there to meet them and push them back. The crowd on the square was quickly and easily broken into smaller groups, which fled up the avenue and the side streets leading into it. Each of these groups numbered no more than a hundred, but judging from newspaper accounts, they led the police a merry chase that afternoon: they kept reassembling for five- or ten-minute periods in different parts of the center of Petersburg to sing their revolutionary dirges up the avenue near Gostinnyi Dvor, in front of the Public Library, and at the Anichkov and Troitskii bridges—before they were finally cornered, a number of them arrested, and the rest finally dispersed.

Altogether, this had been a very visible performance, which drew considerable comment the following day even in the right-wing press—nothing like it had been seen in the streets of Petersburg for a number of years. Yet at no time had the number of demonstrators exceeded the 1,000 or so policemen deployed to meet them. And what was even more symptomatic—and portentous for the future—the crowd of demonstrators, judging from newspaper reports and police lists of those arrested, had consisted largely of students with but a handful of workers. Most of the workers who had actually responded to the appeal that they demonstrate in the center of the city—and there had been but a few hundred of them—had in fact elected not to mix with the students in front of the cathedral, but to stage a demonstration of their own in the less imposing setting of Banner Square, near Ligovka. (This demonstration too had been broken up, within 10 or 15 minutes, by police and mounted *gendarmerie*.) Thus in stark contrast to the heady days of September and October 1905, the workers on this occasion at least, had not chosen to cross the physical and psychological barriers that separated them from educated society. For the students dreaming of an all-nation movement, this evident coolness on the part of the workers—combined with the tepidness of the response of adult-educated society—constituted a poor harbinger of things to come.[54]

Some of the Okhrana's reports suggested that one of the chief instigators of the plan for the joint student-worker demonstration on April 15 had been Deputy Kuznetsov, the militant spokesman for the Social Democrats in the Duma debates on Lena. As will be recalled, Kuznetsov had predicted in his reply to Makarov that the latter's provocative speech would intensify the militance and the unity of the Russian workers' response to the Lena events. As it turned out, Russian workers did respond even more powerfully than Kuznetsov could possibly have expected, but they responded in their own way and on their own grounds.

III

On Monday, April 16, 4,000 workers of the morning shift at the St. Petersburg Metallurgical Plant dropped their work at 9 a.m., and filed out of the plant to hold a brief meeting in the factory courtyard. The report of the Department of Police offers us no details about this particular meeting, but just as at so many such meetings that were to follow, the crowd probably listened to but one or two brief addresses by fellow workers about the Lena massacre and its meaning for all Russian workers, after which, with or without a show of hands, it decided to strike in commemoration of the victims. The workers then uncovered their heads (we are told by the police report) and filed out of the factory gate onto Timofeev Street, singing *Vechnaia Pamiat'* and the *Marseillaise*. They were headed for the neighboring Rozenkrants Plant, when a police detachment arrived and broke them up without opposition. In any event, at 3 p.m. the workers at Rosenkrants themselves decided to strike, and in turn filed out of their factory singing *Vechnaia Pamiat'*. This scene was to be repeated many times in the course of the day, as one factory after another in the segregated industrial areas on the Petersburg side and in the Vyborg district of the capital had to shut their gates.

In the course of the next two days, the wave of protest strikes steadily broadened, despite the various measures taken by authorities to discourage them: searches and arrests, carried out during the night, of suspected revolutionary agitators; police deployed at the gates of most large factories and plants, and patrols in most of the industrial districts. By the evening of April 18, official reports recorded 100,000 workers on strike in Petersburg alone, most of them in the segregated industrial outskirts of the capital, while the number of arrests had passed 500, including 70 women.[55]

The lead in the protest movement, which mounted in so majestic a fashion between April 16 and 19 in Petersburg, was taken by workers in typographical and mechanical trades—generally, the most skilled, best educated, best paid, and politically most advanced workers in the capital. But very quickly, the strikes spread to less skilled and less advanced workers, in the textile and food processing industries, for example. Indeed, what was remarkable about the Lena events, and drew the notice of police observers and newspaper commentators alike, was the sense of solidarity—of their collective identity as workers—that these events so powerfully evoked among various strata of the Petersburg working class. The Petersburg workers had collectively perceived the Lena massacre as an affront to their dignity, and felt the imperious need to respond to it as a class, by a collective action of solidarity.

Apparently these feelings had been evoked even before the Duma debates, Makarov's speech, and the wide publicity that they received in the press, added fuel to the fire. A report of the Department of Police noted on April 11, that is at the very opening of the Duma debates:

> The state of mind of Petersburg workers is very interesting. One can boldly state that 90 percent of the Petersburg workers are shaken

quite sincerely. The consciousness has hardened among them that the Lena tragedy is not [just] an "episode," that the government is by no means against such a settling of accounts with the laboring masses, and that a repetition of "Lena" is possible anywhere. Among Petersburg workers, the consciousness which seemingly had been smothered that the most determined solidarity (*samaia energichnaia splochennost'*) is imperative, has unquestionably risen again. One can positively state that such a consciousness has not been present among Petersburg workers for a long time.[56]

It is important to reemphasize that this was an immediate, spontaneous response—with no evidence of any significant agitation among the workers by survivors of the badly crippled and strife-ridden revolutionary organizations of the capital. And this was also the case with respect to the wave of protest strikes which broke a few days later in the industrial districts of Petersburg. At the onset of the wave, police reports record only very rarely the appearance of outside, "unidentified," agitators at the factory gate, or even the circulation of any leaflet calling on the workers to strike. At almost every one of the striking factories, the courtyard meetings that I have described were called, and addressed, only by workers of that particular factory. Admittedly, in almost every factory, there were workers who had earlier been exposed to the appeals of Social Democracy: who had been at least occasional readers of the labor press, or who had even taken some part in the activity of a labor organization under Social Democratic influence. But this, by and large, was the extent of the outside influences which played on the initial mood of the Petersburg workers. Far more sharply than had been the case in the events of 1905, the protest against Lena arose as largely a working-class movement, and the workers' own disinclination to respond to any appeals to march out of their factory districts into the center of the capital provided dramatic evidence of their inclination to keep it that way—of the mental as well as physical distance that now separated them from even the most sympathetic, or at least the most radical, elements of society.

Yet even though we should recognize the presence at this moment of this invisible wall within Russian urban society, another observation also begs recognition. As we have noted, the actual strike wave in the capital did not mount significantly until April 16—that is after the Duma debates about Lena, and particularly Makarov's speech and Kuznetsov's response, had been drummed in the public, and particularly the labor, press. In part, these widely publicized debates undoubtedly intensified the workers' sense of moral outrage, of the necessity for them to pick up the gauntlet that had been thrown at them. But what these debates and the press reactions that they evoked also contributed to the workers' mood, I believe, was a sense of the possibility of doing so: it imparted to them a sense of power that they had not previously felt. From the defiant words of their deputies in the Duma, as well as from the editorials in their labor press, they drew the feeling that united under their own leadership, they *could* make their weight felt in the Russian body politic. But more basically, the critical reactions of the representative organs of "census" society—of its political spokesmen in the Duma and in the press—suggested to the workers a sense of movement, and therefore a sense of possibility, in national life; a sense that the unfeeling authority weighing over them was not necessarily unshakable, and the burden of their condition, therefore, not necessarily inevitable.

Outside Petersburg, and especially outside the two capitals, the character of the response of Russian workers to Lena, and its constituent elements, were of a somewhat different character. The sense of outrage and challenge immediately experienced by Petersburg workers at the news of Lena was unquestionably felt very widely among workers in these other industrial centers. Indeed, the first sympathy strikes reported, as the news of the massacre filtered out from the Siberian taiga, had broken out outside the capital: first in Irkutsk, then in Kiev (at a machine construction plant on April 9); the strike wave then spreading to many of the industrial centers of the South (Kharkov, Odessa, Ekaterinoslav), from there to the Volga (Samara, Saratov, Nizhnii Novgorod), and finally westward to Vilno and Riga. It was also the case that these sympathy strikes were largely confined to medium-sized or large urban centers, where the striking workers and the labor press which nourished their grievances were somewhat less exposed to the arbitrary repressive measures of local officials. And finally it was also true that the initiative in these protest actions outside the two capitals was largely assumed (and in these instances remained largely confined to) the "more advanced" strata of the labor force: workers in metals, metal-working and printing; and in ports like Odessa, dockers and workers in shipyards. The incidents of these protest actions substantially rose as reports of the wave of strikes in St. Petersburg spread among workers in other cities. This was true even in Moscow, where strike actions and protest demonstrations about Lena did not begin until April 23. The scenes in Russia's second capital on April 23, 24, and 25 essentially reproduced—in microcosm—those that Petersburg had witnessed the previous week. In the center of the city, there were but a couple of feeble attempts by workers to demonstrate (with apparently less student participation). For the most part, the Moscow workers, just as those of Petersburg, were content to conduct their present actions in their own factories and industrial districts. Indeed, when one pieces together the newspaper and police reports about the wave of labor protests about Lena outside Petersburg, one draws the impression that, while unquestionably more feeble in intensity, these actions were even more purely proletarian in character, even more isolated, more sharply compartmentalized from society at large. In almost no instance did the police report any agitation by revolutionary organizations, or by individual party workers in accounting for their outbreak. Nowhere, not even in Moscow, could they tangibly be related to any wider climate of public protest, even among students in the higher educational establishments. The only ties between the workers who braced themselves to launch these actions and the outside world appeared to have been the news they read, or passed on to one another (from the legal, especially the labor, newspapers which fell into their hands) of similar strike actions by workers in other industrial centers, especially those of the capital, as well as the call to rise up in protest which reached them (from the same newspaper reports) of Kuznetsov's speeches in the Duma.[57]

Under the circumstances, even though workers outside Petersburg probably contributed no more than a third of the total number of those who joined in protest strikes immediately after Lena, the sense of solidarity—of identification with their class—which they spontaneously displayed in the wake of the massacre was a remarkable phenomenon, which drew the attention of police and newspaper observers.

On May 2, the Chief of Nizhnii Novgorod's Okhrannoe Otdelenie sought to summarize his impressions of what had occurred, drawing conclusions which, to a greater or lesser degree, obtained for many other industrial centers:

> The cause of the strikes in response to the Lena events in the districts entrusted to me certainly is not the agitation of revolutionary organizations, which are being liquidated by me in good time (*svoevremenno*), but the corrupting influence of the legal press which, through its tendentious description of events, its reports of strikes in the major centers, unites these provincial workers, implants in them the consciousness of the unity of their trade (*professional'noe edinstvo*) as well as of the imperative need to consolidate [their ranks] to struggle against capital and against government, as the defender of capital.

The very way in which "Lena" strike broke out among the workers of Sormovo [metallurgical works outside Nizhnii] as well as the tailors of Nizhnii Novgorod indicated their lack of preparation by revolutionary organizations and yet also the presence of significant solidarity among the masses of the workers. This phenomenon signifies that the workers' milieu displayed so much solidarity with the workers of the capital and were so susceptible to an accidental occurrence that the initiative of a few isolated, non-party workers was enough for strikes to break out locally.

In my opinion, such a state of mind among the working masses is an extraordinarily dangerous portent for the future, for the slightest revival of revolutionary organizations, and more energetic agitation on their part, can quickly and easily arouse the masses of the workers, who will prove a beautiful fighting material in the hands of the revolutionaries.[58]

At the time he submitted this report, the chief of Nizhnii Novgorod's Okhrannoe Otdelenie could afford this candid expression of his concern because he had succeeded, temporarily at least, in restoring order among Nizhnii industrial workers. The outbreak of Lena protest strikes in the area had given him the opportunity to arrest all those who had played any leading roles in these actions, and he was therefore able to report in his concluding statement that no May Day actions of any kind had occurred either in Nizhnii Novgorod or in the neighboring Sormovo plants.

Similar precautionary measures—searches and arrests of all identified suspects conducted on April 29 and 30, plus imposing security measures on May Day to intimidate all possible unidentified troublemakers (the stationing of police forces near all large plants, patrolling of the streets by police on foot and on horseback)—enabled the authorities to prevent the outbreak of May Day demonstrations in many other provincial industrial centers. But these extraordinary precautions were not altogether successful. The Russian dailies of May 3 reported at least some May Day strike actions in a number of cities outside the capital: in Moscow, of course, but also in the industrial South (Kiev, Odessa, and Kharkov—most of whose factories were closed), and on a lesser scale even in such smaller industrial centers as Saratov, Voronezh, and Archangel. Altogether, according to unofficial reports, well over 100,000 workers struck outside of St. Petersburg on May Day 1912, a remarkable number in view of the precautions taken by the police and the almost total absence of such strikes the year before. But nowhere, not even in

Moscow (where there were more than 32,000 strikers according to the esti-
mates of the Moscow Society of Factory and Mill Owners), did the May Day
actions reach a level barely comparable to that in Petersburg.

Even in Petersburg, the pattern of the May Day demonstrations was not
markedly different from the ones that had been launched immediately in the
wake of Lena. In the center of the capital—along Nevskii and the arteries
leading into it—flying demonstrations by crowds of workers intermixed
with handfuls of students from the Polytechnical, Technological, Forestry,
and Psychoneurological Institutes (in even smaller numbers than on April
15), none of these demonstrations ever exceeding a few hundred. And whenever the demonstrators gathered to sing their revolutionary songs, occasionally unfurling their flags or even a sign reading "Down with the Autocracy!",
they were easily broken up by the police, although throughout the afternoon
and into the early evening they kept reassembling at different points in the
city's heart, more stubbornly so than they had done in their initial efforts,
two weeks earlier.

That the demonstrations in the center of Petersburg were kept to such
modest proportions was certainly due in part to the extraordinary precautions taken by the police, as well as, perhaps, to the inclement weather (according to the newspapers, it was an unusually cold and rainy day). Partly in
response to rumors that workers in several factories had decided to stage a
May Day demonstration on Nevskii, a series of searches and arrests had been
conducted the night before, both in the working-class districts of the capital
and among students of the higher educational establishments. And in the
early morning of May 1, police detachments had been posted at the bridges
and approaches leading into the center of the city, at the corners of Nevskii
and of the streets intersecting with it, as well as in the courtyards of some of
the houses on or near the avenue, with strict instructions to keep any persons wearing worker or student dress from reaching Nevskii, in groups or
even individually.

But the fact was that the masses of the workers themselves were not eager to make their way into the center of the city, and on several occasions,
according to police reports, did not respond to the appeals of unidentified
agitators to do so (they could continue to display such reluctance until late
in 1913). As had been the case in the Lena sympathy actions, the Petersburg
working-class preferred to stage their strikes and demonstrations on the familiar grounds of their own industrial districts.

In these districts, however, the strikes assumed an even broader scope
than they had in the wake of Lena. Almost every large factory and plant, and

many smaller *masterskie* and printing shops, struck in all the major industrial districts of the capital: on the Petersburg and Vyborg sides, on Vasil'evskii Ostrov, on Nevskii, Narva and Moscow approaches, on the Nikolaev Railroad. And the mood of the workers appeared different—as they gathered in the morning hour in their factory courtyards, most of them proudly wearing red buttons on their lapels—proud, exuberant, almost triumphant. But though tinged with a different mood, the ritual they observed was largely identical to the one they had followed in the wake of Lena. Occasionally, they listened to one of their fellow workers deliver an impromptu address on the significance of May Day, but usually without even such minimal prompting, they filed solemnly out of their factory gates under the drizzling rain, singing revolutionary songs. This time, however, the songs were not funeral dirges, and added to the self-assertive and exuberant mood of the occasion: the *Marseillaise*, the *Varshavianka*, *Vstavai Rabochii Narod*. Once out on the street, the crowd often unfurled a red flag or two, and marched to the nearest artery of their industrial district to join up for a few blocks with workers from other factories.

In anticipation of trouble, the Petersburg authorities had stationed significant detachments of foot and mounted police near all large plants, and ordered police patrols on all major industrial arteries. So it usually took but a few minutes for the demonstrators to run into police. However, on this occasion as before, the demonstrators, notwithstanding their high spirits, usually obeyed fairly quickly the orders of the police to disperse and with no resistance. Clearly, whatever the degree of their militance, the Petersburg workers were not as yet overcome by the anger that would later impel them to far more reckless behavior. Even the largest demonstration recorded in the course of the day, on the Vyborg side, maintained a temperate mood. Here, the workers of the St. Petersburg Metallurgical Plant had joined up with those of the Phoenix Machine Construction Works and of the Rozenkrants Rolling Mill Plant to form a crowd of many thousands, which marched triumphantly along Poliustrovskaia embankment for a long time, singing revolutionary songs—undoubtedly exhilarated by the sheer power of its numbers and its seeming impunity. But even on this occasion, the demonstrators failed to respond to the call of an unidentified orator to cross the bridges and march on Nevskii, eventually dispersing without resistance when they ran into a police detachment.[59]

It was, in part, precisely the self-discipline that the Petersburg workers displayed on this occasion, as well as their manifest psychological and physical separation from "census" society, which drew the attention, indeed often the awe, of newspaper commentators. Among liberal observers, the sense of awe was as yet quite unmixed with fear. A *Rech'* editorial commented on May 11, at a time when, as we shall see, a rising wave of economic strikes was breaking in the wake of the workers' Lena sympathy strikes and May Day demonstrations:

> The labor movement is growing. Every passing day brings the news of strikes breaking out in various places. One cannot be in any doubt about the character of this movement: it is economic, class-oriented [*klassovoe*]. The workers have taken the new economic situation [*koniunktura*] into account and are attempting to take advantage of it to increase their share of the national income. At the same time, the workers are already conscious of themselves as a separate class, and their actions are assuming a sharply defined class character. They are counter-posing themselves to the rest of society, and [those actions] which most sharply underline their class separation and opposition enjoy the greatest success.
>
> The current strike wave, in which economic elements are closely and organically tied to political-class ones, clearly shows to government people what they must do to contain this wave within legal bounds. The Lena shooting, on the one hand and the peacefully unfolding strikes on the other, should serve as sufficient proof, it would appear, that the extension to the workers of the right of assembly safeguards public life from unexpected tragedies. The extension to the workers of the right to organize has become a matter of basic necessity. Life is demanding insistently the implementation of the freedoms promised in the October Manifesto . . .
>
> The social forces must be accorded scope, and the possibility of expression, legally open to them. One must have faith in the healthy forces of the people, in its capacity to develop its own antibodies to dangerous extremes and deviations. The State power cannot act as an omnipresent and omniscient ward-keeper. On it lies the duty of safeguarding life and property, but beyond this it must extend freedom to its citizens.[60]

These truths, elementary for the statesmen of all civilized European states, were beginning to seep in even among Russia's ruling order, the editorial further observed. But there were still many signs of survival of the old psychology, of the old Okhrana habits. One of these was the current chatter in official circles about encouraging the development of Christian trade unions, a chatter reminiscent of the days of the *Zubatovshchina* and *Gaponovshchina*. "We cannot flatly assert that were will never be strong Christian trade unions in Russia," the *Rech'* editorialist concluded. "But one can say with certainty that such unions will become conceivable only when conditions are created for all citizens, in the whole country, guaranteeing freedom of conscience, speech, assembly, and association. No more than heretical Europe, will 'Holy' Russia escape this stage of social development."[61]

The confident and approving notes sounded by the *Rech'* editorialist about the rising wave of labor unrest, indeed his evident welcome of it as an additional pressure on the tsarist regime to concede the legal and political demands of Russian liberalism, had been from the outset characteristic (*at this stage*) of the private, as well as public, response of Kadet circles to the workers' strikes and demonstrations. A report of the Moscow O.O. noted on April 17:

The wave of protest strikes is being greeted with the greatest ap-proval [by the liberal circles of Moscow society]. The overwhelming majority feel that it will be a useful warning to the government, which has been acting to date in the conviction that all the active forces in the country are "dead and (or) paralyzed." The strikes are felt to be particularly valuable because of their timing, on the eve of the elections. The Kadets feel that if they assume a really massive character, the government may be forced to lower its tone in the election campaign.[62]

The warmth with which the renewed militance of the workers' move-ment was welcomed by liberal circles in this initial phase was matched by the anxiety with which it was greeted by conservatives. Predictably, the scenes of April and May revived in many of them the never-forgotten traumas of 1905. It is all the more interesting, under the circumstances, that conservative spokesmen were impressed by some of the same features in the workers' conduct as their conclusions from them. On May 3, M. Menshikov, the clever if unscrupulous editorial commentator for *Novoe Vremia*, published a long detailed column about the scenes he had witnessed on May Day un-der a title (*Samozvannaia vlast'*) which, with its obvious allusion to the So-viets of 1905, was in and of itself calculated to send a long shiver down the spines of his conservative readers. The trumpet of alarm was sounded from the very opening:

The first day of May in Petersburg went much more badly than one might have expected. . . . Despite the fact that the preparations for May Day had gone on openly and were known to everyone, and that all precautionary measures had been taken, hundreds of thousands of workers stopped work, [as if] in response to some invisible command, and came out on the street. They conducted themselves with comparative decorum [*sravnitel'naia chinnost'*], as if observing an invisible discipline. But in such cases, discipline on the part of the popular masses is much more dangerous than the noisy unrestraint of the usual crowd. Evidently, the industrial proletariat of Petersburg is already organized for some joint actions. Evidently hovering over it is some accepted secret authority, more influential than the official government. These two states of affairs are very alarming.[63]

The police were comforting themselves with their success in having prevented large-scale demonstrations on the great *paradnye* boulevards and squares of the capital. But the demonstrations conducted in the poor working-class districts and throughout Petersburg were more dangerous than any that might have unfolded on Nevskii:

Millionaires [residing] in the center are hardly likely to run out on the street, unfurling red flags and joining up in singing "Rise Up, Get Up, Narod." But for the poor [section of the] population, revolutionary celebrations become long-remembered events, which prepare the mind for new and more imposing actions. From this viewpoint, the massive May Day demonstrations in Petersburg must be considered a success. The presence in the capital of huge, revolutionary-minded masses, had to be announced; and this was done. One had to show the consolidated character [*splochennost'*], the discipline of these masses, and this too was shown. One had to demonstrate the inability of police to prevent the outbreak of strikes, or to break them up, and this was done. All of this is still not too terrifying, to the degree that it has not turned into open rebellion, but it is alarming in that [it shows that] revolutionary leaders already hold the proletariat in tow, under conditions involving the gradual gathering of forces and their economical expenditure.[64]

Menshikov's description suffered from the common tendency of reactionary observers to detect the presence of an invisible hand, where in fact none had been at work, but this qualification aside, his description of what had occurred could hardly be flawed. Menshikov, however, no more than other spokesmen of the Right, could not draw up any prescriptions for keeping the critical situation which he so clearly discerned from deteriorating even further. It was now apparent to him that the methods currently used by police—the arrests of suspects, the break-up of demonstrators, who immediately reassembled in a different spot—were completely ineffective. These methods reminded him, he said, of "an inexperienced maid who, instead of picking up dust, sweeps it from one place to another, spreading it all over." Besides, these methods were inconsistent, illogical. What was the point of expending so much energy to prevent subversive demonstrations on the streets of Petersburg when equally subversive demonstrations were legally staged by the representatives of Social Democracy in the Duma? As yet, Menshikov posed this question academically, but as the situation deteriorated in the months to follow, it would be pressed with increasing zealousness and vigor by the Ministry of Internal Affairs and the spokesmen for the extreme right, inside and outside the Duma.

For the time being, Menshikov could only conclude—pessimistically—from what he had observed:

> The government does not have the strength to prevent or to suppress the steadily growing *demonstratizm*, the spirit of opposition and discontent, which almost without obstacles is growing among the laboring masses. . . . Here lies the seriousness of the situation, which it would be dangerous to minimize: Side by side with enlightened, somewhat enfeebled government to which the cultured classes submit, a dark, self-appointed, *vlast'* is being formed in the underground, which is assuming an extremely genuine power over the dark masses. . . . [65]

The initial response of St. Petersburg and Moscow industrialists to their workers' protest strikes immediately after Lena had been unusually restrained. Indeed, concluding perhaps that caution was the better part of valor, most employers had decided not to penalize their workers for these strike actions. Even the usually hard-nosed Council of Mechanical Enterprises of the St. Petersburg Society of Factory and Mill Owners, meeting in extraordinary session on April 18, at the height of the protest actions of the Petersburg workers, reportedly recommended to its members that they restrain from fining their workers for their participation in Lena sympathy strikes, and confine themselves to the deduction from their wages of the appropriate earnings for the day they had struck.[66]

But when, in the wake of their Lena sympathy actions, their emboldened workers broke out in a rash of economic strikes, especially in the two capitals, the attitude of employers rapidly evolved. The actual confrontation came to a head when many employers, especially in St. Petersburg and Moscow, decided to fine their workers for their May Day strikes. In this decision, the employers of St. Petersburg and Moscow followed the recommendation of the councils of their respective societies. The Moscow Society of Factory and Mill Owners reached the conclusion that the original decision of their member firms not to penalize their workers for the Lena sympathy strikes had been a mistake—the workers having interpreted this restraint as "a sign of weakness," and they therefore issued circulars calling on their member firms to fine workers who had struck on May Day. The Council of the St. Petersburg Society reportedly also considered the imposition of stiffer penalties, including the firing of striking workers, but reached the conclusion that such actions would be "premature."[67]

The stiffening of the employers' stand charged even further the militant atmosphere that had emerged, especially among the workers in the two capitals. In the first two weeks of May, press and police reports recorded a proliferation of economic strikes, especially in Petersburg. In factory after factory, particularly in the mechanical and metal-pressing enterprises of the capital, the workers responded to the May Day fines imposed by their employers by striking for their cancellation, usually coupling this demand with a whole series of broad-ranging economic demands.

The Ministry of Internal Affairs was now thoroughly alarmed by the new belligerent mood displayed by the workers of the two capitals. The flurries of reports it was receiving from the Department of Police also suggested that not only were the workers plunging headlong into a wave of economic strikes, but that, also, for the first time since 1907, they were responding to the appeals of revolutionary agitators.

A report of the St. Petersburg Okhranoe Otdelenie of May 8, 1912 listed a series of mass meetings of St. Petersburg workers which had been held that day and the day before, and addressed by Social Democratic speakers. As they would continue to do until the outbreak of the war, the workers gathered outside the city limits—in most cases in one of the woods within walking distance of a suburban railroad station—in an effort to avoid police observation and interference. The first such reported meeting, which had been attended by 300 workers of a shoe factory, had nonetheless been broken up by police almost immediately after being called together. A second meeting, held the same evening, attended by 6,000 workers from the Arthur Koppel Mechanical Plant, the St. Petersburg Railroad Car Construction Factory, and a number of other industrial establishments of the Vasileostrov and Petersburg districts, had gathered near a station of the Baltic Railroad Line. This meeting, which had been undisturbed by police (although obviously under the ubiquitous eye of Okhrana agents), had been addressed by two student representatives of the Social Democrats who had discoursed about the current political situation and the forthcoming elections to the Fourth Duma. A third meeting, attended by 600 workers from the Narva District on May 8, had been quickly broken up by police. The fourth and last meeting listed in this report, attended by about 1,500 workers, chiefly from the striking trolley car lines and from the Obukhov and Putilov works, had been conducted without police interference. The attending workers had discussed the trolley car strike, and then listened to addresses by Social Democratic speakers. The latter, the Okhrana reported, had emphasized "the need for massive strikes right now, calling on the workers to raise their heads, as the Russian government has lost its prestige among all strata of the population at the present time, and is on the verge of its final destruction."[68]

A week later came an even more alarming report about the labor unrest in the capital and its organization:

> The wave of the strike movement which started after the Lena events is not calming down. Strike committees have been established in many individual factories and plants in St. Petersburg. Intensive discussions are being held about the establishment of district and all-city strike committees. (Incidentally, among the members of the various strike committees known to the Okhrannoe Otdelenie, non-party persons are predominant.)
>
> Rumors are being disseminated everywhere of forthcoming strikes in all factories and plants of Petersburg, and even of an All Russian general strike, which is being scheduled for June 3, i.e., the anniversary of the change in the electoral laws. Rumors are also circulating about strikes to be called on May 17 and 18. The dissemination of these rumors is being furthered significantly by the meetings, attended by many workers, which are taking place daily in various districts of the capital, largely outside the city limits.[69]

Under the spur of such reports, the Deputy Minister of Internal Affairs, S. I. Zolotarev, had rather timidly approached the Minister of Trade and Industry, Timashev, to intervene with Petersburg employers in an effort to dampen the situation. In his letter, Zolotarev had "allowed himself to point out"—with reference to the strikes that had broken out at Simens i Gal'ske [Siemens and Halske] and Arthur Koppel over the imposition of May Day fines—that most other Petersburg employers had not imposed such fines. Such differences of treatment had obviously contributed to the current labor unrest, and a more consistent labor policy on the part of employers was eminently desirable. Could Timashev call upon the St. Petersburg industrialists to adopt it?

Timashev apparently acted more boldly than his colleagues in Interior had dared to spell out. He reported back to Zolotarev that he had called in some representatives of Petersburg "big industry," and pointed out to them that the fines imposed by some of the major industrial enterprises for the May Day strikes had set off "a movement among the workers." Serious consideration should be given to the adoption of measures to end these strikes, and especially to the consistency in the employers' responses to May Day strikes. The representatives of St. Petersburg industry had expressed agreement with these sentiments, Timashev reported, but considered it impossible to lift the fines they had already imposed. Timashev wrote that he had told his interlocutors that the outbreak of more economic strikes, particularly in the metal processing and machine construction industries, was to be expected. Because strikes usually ended with some economic concessions by employers, was it not desirable for the latter now to take the initiative to avoid the outbreak of strikes by introducing improvements in the workers' lot, "consistent," of course, "with existing market conditions?" To this, the industrialists had replied that they would "take the suggestions under consideration." In view of the above, Timashev concluded his letter to Zolotarev, he did not consider it possible to take any further initiative.[70]

This was the extent of the government's efforts at this stage to exercise a mediating role in the economic clashes that were now breaking out on a large scale between industrial workers, especially in St. Petersburg, and their employers. Notwithstanding their evident anxiety, and the realization by at least some of their numbers that the labor conflicts were spurring the growth among industrial workers of a mood clearly dangerous to "public order," the tsarist bureaucracy and its police arm would largely confine itself to unconditional support of employers until the eve of the war. They would do so through police intervention in strikes, and the arrest and sentencing to administrative exile of strike leaders. They calculated that this policy would be more effective than any revolutionary appeals in impressing on Russian workers that the state power stood aligned with capital and rejected their grievances and aspirations.

The sense of alarm which government officials as well as employers experienced in the spring of 1912 would grow steadily in the months to follow, for the growing and increasingly explosive labor unrest that they had to confront had some of the unexpected and overwhelming quality of a natural cataclysm. In the wake of their post-Lena strike and demonstrations, culminating in the imposing spectacle of May Day, from which they had drawn a sense of self-discovery and power, workers—especially in St. Petersburg—plunged into a wave of economic strikes: spontaneously, recklessly, and with the feeling of relief that the sudden exposure and unleashing of accumulated resentments provide for persons experiencing them, especially when they are combined with the discovery of a sense of community with fellow sufferers.

At the end of May, one of the labor commentators of *Pravda* published a column deploring the disorganized character of many of the strikes—clucking his tongue with special disapproval about a strike at a rolling mill on the Petersburg side which had broken out with no explicit demands being advanced; the workers having struck, it appeared, just for the sake of striking.[71]

This is not the only example that the sources offer us of strikes breaking out during this early period without the articulation of *any* demands. The reports of the Department of Police for the month of May cite two such examples; one of them, that of a cottonprint factory whose 350 workers reported at the morning hour, but refused to start work and left without advancing any demands.[72]

But this was not the typical picture. More characteristic was the tendency of strikers to let loose a veritable flood of demands—uncovering and translating into specific grievances complaints of which at most they previously had been only dimly aware. In more advanced industries and crafts (such as machine construction and printing), strikes tended to be better organized and more prolonged, and strike demands, more focused than in more backward ones (such as textiles, or food processing).

At the Erikson telephone plant in Petersburg, for example, strikers advanced the following demands:

1. Recognize the workers' *starosty*, including their right to regulate hiring and firing.
2. The cancellation of May Day fines.
3. Wage increases [of various types].

4. Adjustments in the rate of pay [for various jobs].
5. The working day to run from 7 a.m. to 6 p.m., with a one-and-a-half hour break for lunch.
6. Work on Saturday and on the eve of holidays to be reduced to half-a-day, but to be paid in full.
7. Free medical drugs on doctors' prescriptions for workers and their families.
8. A five-minute rest allowance for workers to wash their hands.
9. Polite treatment and polite address (*vezhlivoe obrashchenie*) [we shall return to the meaning of this phrase. L. H.]
10. The right to report at the factory until 8 a.m. without suffering a fine.
11. Special rooms to be assigned for smoking.
12. Overtime work not to be compulsory.[73]

And, again taken pretty much at random, these are the demands advanced in June by strikers at the Rusvum mechanical and plumbing pipes plant, also in the capital:

1. Wage increases of 30 percent, across the board.
2. A reduction of hours, and an hour and one-half out for lunch.
3. *Vezhlivoe obrashchenie.*
4. No firing of workers without informing their comrades.
5. The right to report five minutes late for work without being fined.
6. Improvements in medical aid.
7. Work only until 2 p.m. on Saturdays and on the eve of holidays.
8. Sick pay.
9. The dismissal of two specified supervisors [described as "undesirables"].
10. No dismissals for engaging in strikes.
11. May Day to be a paid holiday.
12. The workers' wages to be paid in full for the period they were on strike.[74]

Both of these strikes, although stubbornly pursued, ended, unsurprisingly, in defeats.

But let us move to the other end of the continuum among Petersburg workers (in levels of skill, *kulturnost'*, "consciousness,") to the bakers in the Vyborg district, who went on strike in mid-summer, as the wave of economic strikes swelled to include workers in enterprises like breweries, candy-makers, restaurants, bakeries, etc. These were the demands advanced by strikers at the Kubrashev bakery: the workers were to receive (1) better meals; (2) half a pound of tea and two pounds of sugar a month; (3) clean bedsheets once a week; (4) 40 more kopecks a week to clean their personal linen and to take a bath; while workers at other bakeries demanded (along with better wages and hours) separate beds, pillows, mattresses, sheets of their own, their own personal plate and knife, towels and soap to wash their hands.[75]

Reflected in these various demands for better living and working conditions was a new, or at least a sharper and more forcefully articulated, sense of self-worth, which admittedly mirrored in part the image that workers entertained of people in privileged "society": of the way these people lived, dressed, and treated one another; of what in the eyes of these elements of society constituted *kulturnost'*. This new feeling of self-worth, and the sense that it was being debased, constitutes one of the most pervasive underlying themes of the complaints that workers address to the labor press about conditions in their enterprises. It appeared in a variety of forms in the lists of grievances and demands that they advanced during these months: in the insistence that the *obyski*, the searches to which workers were subjected at the end of the working day to prevent the pilfering of factory goods, be put to a stop, as a practice which demeaned their dignity; in the demand that they be provided with proper washing and toilet facilities, and not be harassed to shorten the amount of time that they made use of them; and in myriads of other complaints and demands about seemingly petty details of conditions of life and work in the enterprises. But the one item in which these feelings of self worth and workers' complaints about their abasement were most sharply articulated in the strike actions of the St. Petersburg workers during these months was in their demands for *vezhlivoe obrashchenie*: polite treatment and polite address.

This demand subsumed a whole range of grievances: that foremen cease molesting women workers, that they cease hitting workers, insulting them, using rude language in addressing them, that they call them by their proper names; and most interestingly (because the demand was spelled out in so many words), that they stop addressing workers as thou (*ty*), the familiar form of address used toward children and inferiors in superordinate relations (i.e., caste rather than class) relationships, and address them as you (*vy*), the polite and more appropriately distant form that members of "cultured" society used to address persons with whom they were not intimately related. To be sure, this was not the first time that this demand—and the sentiments underlying it—had been expressed by Russian workers. (One could encounter occasional expressions of it at least as far back as the 1860s, notably after the emancipation of the serfs.) But the universality and the burning insistence with which this demand was now pressed was novel, and highly symptomatic of the contemporary mood of Russian workers.

A *Pravda* editorial in early May emphasized the universality of the complaints that this demand addressed, advanced among the most variegated strata of St. Petersburg workers—from those employed in the largest and most advanced metal-processing enterprises to the smallest and most backward ones, such as sawdust factories and small ateliers. A follow-up article sought to explain:

> Readers from the workers' milieu are well aware of the rudeness that factory administrations display, from top to bottom. Not to speak of supervisors—who don't know any other form of address than "thou," including foremen and inspectors who have moved into the administration from the workers' ranks, but quickly absorbed its rude attitude toward the workers and its ways of degrading their human dignity. The treatment of women workers in the factories is even more distressing. They are treated like white slaves, to whom supervisors not only display rudeness, but advance the most indecent proposals.
>
> Generally, address as *ty* is widely used in our so-called cultured circles toward housemaids, doormen, etc. One often has to hear on the trolley car well-dressed gentlemen and ladies address the conductor as *ty*, while the latter, because of his dependent status, does not rebuff this *kulturnoe khamstvo* [cultural rudeness].
>
> All these manifestations of rudeness are survivals of serfdom, when the working man was regarded as an animal and subjected to all kinds of degradation. This heritage of serfdom—this division of people into white and black—is so ingrained in our society that the ruling classes cannot conceive that it might be possible to treat the laboring man courteously.
>
> The demand for *vezhlivoe obrashchenie* may seem amusing to the ruling classes, but the workers will continue to press it.[76]

But let us probe more deeply into the resentments and aspirations that lurked beneath this magic phrase, drawing as much as possible on the workers' own words (as they appear in the letters of worker correspondents of the contemporary labor press).[77]

Workers complain of being treated like—indeed confused with—animals, frequently criticizing fellow-workers for accepting such treatment; indeed, for acting themselves like animals.

> There is a habit in our plant, you see, to view workers as drunken animals that you can't stir without a knout. The human personality is not counted for anything (worker in a Briansk plant).

> *Tak i govoriat, rebiata* [that's what they say, lads], don't spare the whip on two-legged animals—we can harness new ones anyway (worker at the Admiralty shipyard).

> It is said that abroad they have periods of rest even for horses. But the life of our workers is worse than that of horses (clerk at the Apraxin Dvor).

> Most important, the time has come for the Russian worker to get out of his semi-animal state and to declare to capital that he is a man. If we allow any single person to be made sport of, we thereby injure everyone (worker in a printing plant).

> It is time, *prikazchiki* [sales people], to understand that you are considered to be not people but stinking animals (salesman in a meat store).

Indeed, there is an almost obsessive quality in this use of animal references to describe the way workers are being treated or allow themselves to act: the striking bakers in Petersburg complain of being worked "like horses," and fed "like dogs." Time after time, worker correspondents of the labor press condemn fellow workers at their factories for being treated, and acting, like "cattle," "beaten dogs," "sheep." A worker at the St. Petersburg metallurgical plant complains:

> The foremen treat the workers just as a herdsman does a bunch of sheep. And even herdsmen don't drive sheep all the time. The

workers are so frightened that they don't dare go to the bathroom, or to boil water for tea. The foremen check up how many times they go to the toilet and whether they read the paper [in it].[78]

Workers complain about being treated like slaves, and call on fellow workers to stop acting like slaves:

For many years, capital has told us: "You are my slaves!" Or is there something in all of us that induces the boss to spew out a stream of abuse (worker in a shoe factory).

We are not slaves of capital. We are free workers. And let the sun shine for us, as it does for other people (two workers at the Westinghouse plant in St. Petersburg).

All this is happening because a person does not want to act like a person but like a slave. Let us bring the slavery to an end (a housemaid writing to *Golos Prislugi*).

Workers complain about being treated like children, and call on other workers to stop allowing themselves to be so treated. They complain about being treated like machines, like "things": They don't count us as people. They don't recognize us as people, but see us as things which can be thrown away at any moment (worker in a printing shop).

Workers want to stop being treated like commodities that can be bought and sold. A waitress complains of having to serve people for tips:

And if you don't serve, they throw you out like a dog. And so, for tips, you have to sell your human dignity, your smiles, like an unfortunate woman whom life has forced to sell her honor.

Clearly, the ways in which the authors of these remarks now perceive themselves—or more precisely, *want* to perceive themselves and to be perceived by others—are radically at odds with the way they felt they were being treated and perceived by those in authority. They complain of being perceived and treated like animals, slaves, machines, commodities (and of fellow workers allowing themselves to be so treated), and insist on being seen and treated, instead, as persons in their own right:

> We must force the bosses to see us as people, filled with a consciousness of their work (an Astrakhan cooper).

> Most pitiful of all is to see a person who is not considered a person, who is being mocked, made sport of, and he keeps silent and can't say a word (worker in a Moscow wool factory).

> Most important is that the time has come for the Russian worker to get out of his semi-animal state and to declare to capital that he is a man: if we allow any single person (*lichnost'*) to be made sport of, we thereby injure everyone (worker in a printing plant).

> The chief thing about the excessively rude way of addressing you is that it ends up with their hitting you in the mouth. But who is at fault for this? The workers themselves! They forget their human worth and the example of other workers, who right here in Petersburg know how to defend their human rights. Little by little, workers become accustomed to anything. Sleep, comrades, sleep—what is it to you to wake up![79]

As some of these remarks suggest, there already appears—underlying the insistence of these workers on their common humanity—a considerable ambivalence. Beneath the insistence on acceptance on equal terms by privileged society, there already lurks a readiness to oppose, if not to reject; just as beneath this opposition, there continues to linger an equally insistent need for acceptance. Admittedly, this ambivalence had been implicit from the outset in the models that the Russian labor movement offered its recruits for their sense of self: the image of their *chelovechestvo*, their humanity, the sense of being persons with needs and sensibilities comparable to those of more privileged and better educated members of "society"; but also the image of being workers, locked in irreconcilable conflict with capital, with the bourgeoisie. But there is little question that this ambivalence had now become far more genuinely and deeply ingrained in the attitudes of many workers—so much so as to evoke the comments of labor commentators of all shades of opinion. This ambivalence was continuously reinforced by the situations that workers encountered, day in and day out, inside and outside the enterprise. Two examples may suffice to illustrate the point.

A plasterer complains of being forced off the sidewalk when he walks on Nevskii Prospekt wearing his spotted working clothes:

> Whom does the well-dressed public turn away from? Plasterers, bricklayers. Everyone has the right to walk on the sidewalk: a *Barin*, a prostitute, a good-for-nothing in fashionable dress; but for a worker, an honest worker, there is no room. If you walk on the sidewalk, you will dirty up the "clean public." And who will be forced by the policeman on the bridge to get down from the steps of the trolley? Always the same worker, held in contempt.

If a plasterer feels his self-image attacked because of his spotted working clothes, other workers may feel attacked for dressing properly, like gentlemen, *gospoda*. A *samovarshchik* recounts that in Tula, factory owners regard workers who dress well as "enemies who are insulting them by [asserting] their human dignity."

> It is as if the worker was saying to them: "*Obrashchaite so mnoi lushche* [treat me, address me, better]." And however shameful it is, when workers to go a factory owner to apply for a job, they dress so as to look like peasants, forgotten by life.

I have deliberately used these two illustrations, because in this, as in so many other revolutions of consciousness, dress becomes the most tangible, the most visible way in which a new sense of identity is established and proclaimed. "*Davaite*, let us remember that we are people too," writes a worker in a shoe factory. "And throw away our *oporky* [cheap slippers], and put on shoes. It is shameful that we make shoes for other people, and ourselves wear *oporky*."

In early May, an article in *Russkiia Vedomosti* about the new strike wave, after taking note of the demand for *vezhlivoe obrashchenie*, comments perceptively how the workers' new sense of self-worth, and the insistence on the recognition of their civil equality which is conjoined with it, are now being reflected, especially among young workers in the way they dress.

> The administrations of most factories do not notice, or wish to notice, that the workers have changed. They want to keep up the old

habits in their ways of addressing and administering them, and then complain that the workers have become sharp and rude, and that discipline in the factories is falling off.

Yes! The workers have changed. There is a great difference from a generation ago. A large percentage of them have become literate; the young ones are almost all literate. They are more mature and efficient, as shown by their greater labor productivity, their ability to handle more complex machines, etc. But the greatest difference I see is in the growth of feelings of self worth, which incidentally is expressed in dress.

As Spencer pointed out long ago, strivings for equality are reflected first externally, in the way people dress. And a worker when he goes out for a promenade puts on a *"troiku"* [slang for a suit of clothes] and a *"krakhmal'nyi vorotnik"* [a stiff collar]; and a working girl, an inexpensive hat, and under no circumstances a kerchief, as in the past. They say "you" to each other, and they are insulted, of course, when they come up against the use of "thou" and rudeness of tone on the part of their *nachal'stvo* [supervisors]. In my opinion, this is the basic source of all the complaints about the fall off in [labor] discipline.[80]

Occasionally we can already find in the labor press an opposite motif, reflecting the ambivalence of which we have taken note (and the alternative models of identity in which it is expressed): letters of worker correspondents denouncing the emptiness and the sham of "bourgeois culture," and enjoining the workers not to imitate it since they can and indeed are developing a different and better "proletarian" culture of their own. Such notes of pride also appear in the verse that worker amateur poets painfully composed for publication in the labor press. Frequently these poems seek to express the authors' sense of oppressiveness about their factory environment, their revulsion—indeed their hatred—for the factory regimen to which they are bound, and the machines to which they feel chained. The factory appears an impersonal world, a world of things, a gigantic mechanism in which the worker feels caught and reduced to nothing, and he cries out his hatred for those who are responsible for having entrapped him in it.

This sense of *nichtozhestvo*, of being diminished, shriveled, by the machines and the regimen of factory life, the feeling that for the few pennies he receives, the worker is condemned to a life of slavery in a world which crushes his personality, denies his rights as a person—are the themes most frequently expressed in the poems. With less frequency, a contrary theme also emerges in this verse, expressing the worker's pride about his capacity to handle his monstrous labor, his sense of power about his ability to harness the machines of the industrial age, and even articulating the faith that the industrial age and its factories is giving birth to a new race of new and stronger men, and offering the promise of a better and happier future.

Admittedly, this image of the proud proletarian—steeled by the experience of the factory and by the struggle with capital in which he is joined with his fellow workers is being fostered by Social Democratic, especially Bolshevik, appeals. But there is little doubt that a genuine sense of identity as workers, a genuine sense of class distinctiveness, and a concomitant sense of the need for solidarity have now become implanted among many members of the working class, modulating their assertion of their common humanity.

This sense of class identity and class solidarity is most tangibly reflected in the *sbory*, the financial contributions that workers collect in support of *their* own labor press and of strikers in other factories and plants—in their refusal to take the place of striking workers, or even to handle orders diverted from striking enterprises to their own, and especially in the sympathy strikes which they occasionally call in support of strikers in other enterprises, particularly in the capital, but also in other cities.

Most strikingly, this growing sense of solidarity among workers is reflected in the pressures that build up against those who fail to display it, above all strikebreakers. The latter often succumb under the pressure of the boycotts to which they are subjected by fellow workers, and of the general atmosphere of shame and contempt with which they are surrounded. The strikebreakers begin to feel like cripples "without legs"; they become ashamed of looking at other workers in the eyes, and under this combination of outer and inner pressures, we witness the appearance in the labor press of letters in which they plead for the forgiveness of their comrades. Here are a few examples:

> Comrades of Vasileostrov, carpenters, and everyone in general. We are former strikebreakers. We worked when you were striking to improve your lot. Now we are conscious of the unworthy conduct of those like ourselves, who break the strikes of their comrades. We implore you, comrades: take us back into your powerful family; our conscience does not allow us to look at you calmly in the eye. We give our honest word that we shall be exemplary comrades.
>
> Riaban and Iv. Bogdanov[81]

I, the undersigned, was a strikebreaker at the Weisberg and the Gushuni printing shop. I ask, comrades, and particularly the press, to forgive me for my thoughtless behavior. I ask most humbly the comrade printers to take me back into their midst. I say, and give my word of honor, that I will never again commit such an act as strikebreaking.

ex-strikebreaker, Master S. Urvichev[82]

And one last such letter, striking for its liturgical quality:

I, the undersigned,, printer Pavlov, bring my repentance to you, comrades, for having violated, *po svoemu malosoznaniiu* [because of my inadequate consciousness] the workers' interests by acting as a strikebreaker at the time of the strike at Schvarz. Conscious of my guilt, I ask you to forgive my behavior. I sincerely promise that it will not happen again in the future.[83]

There is a pervasive quality about the feeling of shame so clearly expressed in these letters of repentant strikebreakers. In one form or another, it appears in almost all of the reports of worker correspondents of the labor press concerning strikes or conditions in their enterprises—underlying and bolstering their appeal to their fellow workers' sense of pride and honor. In these reports about the horrors of factory life and the self-abasement that they so often induced among its victims, there is usually little trace of the traditional forgiveness for—and ultimate acceptance of—human frailty usually emphasized in our stereotypes of Russian, especially peasant, culture. Shame, rather than a sense of sinfulness (and the ultimate acceptance of sin) is the dominant feeling expressed: shame—and shaming—acts of commission or omission for which individuals are held accountable to the group, and the group to Russia's working class as a whole.

Shame and shaming for workers who allow themselves to be mistreated by their foremen, for their passive submission to insults and humiliation—to the denial of their human dignity—or even worse, for their bowing and scraping before superiors in an effort to buy their favor:

A correspondent from the Nevskii paper mill in Petersburg complains that workers in his factory are treated and viewed like animals. The helpless unskilled workers (*chernye rabochie*), suffer most. One of the foremen, while drunk, hit a worker in the mouth, for no reason: "Shame, comrades,

for acting like lackeys in the face of brute force. Register faster. Join a union.
Shame on those workers who continue to believe that they can improve
their situation by abasing themselves (worker in Elizavetgrad)."

> Think yourselves: for the right to your work, you give even your
> soul away to be insulted (*Podumaete sami, za pravo na svoi trud vy
> otdaete i dushu na poruganie.*) For workers who are conscious of
> their worth, all forms of abasement (*vsiaiia podnosheniia*) are im-
> permissible (worker at the Langenzipen plant in St. Petersburg).

> Keep it up, keep it up, comrades, and they will sit on us, walk all
> over us (worker at the Voronin factory in Petersburg).[84]

Shame and shaming of those girls in the factory who sell themselves into
prostitution, or who allow their foremen cheap liberties for the sake of better treatment. Shame and shaming of the workers who are searched when
they leave the factory at the end of the working day, as well as for the petty
thievery, the *vorostvo* which encourages this humiliating treatment. Shame
and shaming of the workers who put up with the intolerable working conditions and the endless hours, and then seek escape at the end of the working day in gambling and drunkenness:

"We shall continue to be spat upon as long as we continue to spend our
leisure time in drunkenness," a worker correspondent complains. "The tav-
erns and the beer joints should not be the places where we share our joys and
our sorrows. The more we seek to find in vodka solace and a feeling of joy,
the deeper, the more unbounded, is the sea of our degradation, of our humiliation." ("*Chem bol'she zhelaem v vodke naiti uteshenie i radostnoe chu-
vstvo, chem sil'nee, bezpredel'nee, i more unizheniia.*") (worker at the Sorokin
sausage factory.)

But the deepest sense of shame is expressed by those who have sought to
rebel by striking, sometimes for many months, and then are forced to return
to find working conditions in the enterprise essentially unchanged, foremen
as imperious as ever, and have to mingle with ex-strikebreakers, while those
of their fellow strikers who have been fired for their militance, stand helplessly outside the factory gate, or even worse (even though they are not physically present to shame them) have been the victims of arrest and administrative exile.

A worker correspondent writes in from the Erikson plant, where a strike
has been broken, after many weeks:

Everyone is back at work, except for sixty comrades who have been thrown out to the street, and twelve who have received sentences of administrative exile. When we leave the factory, we run continuously into comrades who have been thrown out, and in whose faces we read reproach for our indifference, our insensitiveness. We have no truck with them. We are working today and have eaten our fill, so why should their suffering be our concern!

The administration is happy about the split [among the workers]. One more time, it has been persuaded of its strength and of our helplessness. The administration views its minor concessions—like smoking on the stairs, washing one's hands—as toys which they have handed over to a child so that it won't start crying. And what are we workers doing? We are throwing dirt on our advanced comrades; we are joking and shaking hands in a friendly manner with strikebreakers; we are scraping low before the foremen, smiling cautiously.

What are we to do now? It is imperative to conduct a review of what has happened, and to collect among ourselves at least a half-day's wage for the benefit of our unemployed comrades.[85]

And a similar report, after a strike has been broken at a cable manufacturing plant in St. Petersburg:

A group of workers, let them be ashamed (*pust' im budet stydno*), asked the engineer to let them come back to work after they had been laid off, because they were dying of hunger—and this after they lay dead drunk near the gate. Within a week, the majority went back to work, the [class] conscious ones as well as those who were not (*malosoznatel'nye i soznatel'nye*). For what could the group of truly conscious [workers] do under the circumstances?

When we resumed work, we were ashamed to look not only at the engineers, but also at the foremen in the eyes, and the latter went about looking at us contemptuously, as if we were not people but a bunch of sheep. Some of the workers left, not being able to bear such a *skandal*! Are we really not fed up with these slaps at our self-respect? Has the strike taught us nothing? To conduct a successful struggle, we need to unite. "Join a union; to do so will make us strong."[86]

Which strata of the Russian working class are most deeply affected by the various attitudes, and psychological pressures, that we have been describing:

the ambivalence—the sense of attraction as well as hostility to the mores of polite "society"—the assertion of pride and of a sense of honor, bolstered by shame; and ultimately the new sense of class identity and class opposition into which these various whirling, sometimes conflicting, feelings may ultimately be ultimately channeled, if not fulfilled? The available statistical data can tell us a great deal about the relative intensity of the new strike wave among workers employed in various geographical areas and industries of the Empire.[87] But certain observations can also be drawn from more impressionistic data: the letters of correspondents of the labor press that we have been quoting, the observations of newspaper commentators of the labor scene, the reports of the Department of Police, and in particular its records of arrests of militants of the strike movement, including the slowly reviving revolutionary organizations, particularly those of the Bolshevik and Menshevik factions of Russian Social Democracy, but to a lesser degree, also the PSR.

From these various sources, one draws the clear impression that it is workers in more, rather than less, advanced industries and crafts, workers who are more skilled and better educated, rather than the most exploited and most downtrodden ones, those for whom the opportunities for economic, social, and cultural advancement have been partly fulfilled (or at least, more clearly beckon) rather than those to whom they are fully denied, who tend to be the most agitated, the most perturbed, the most dissatisfied. Thus, it is in enterprises located in large urban centers, and especially in the capital, rather than in those in isolated industrial settlements—and among workers in the capital and other large urban centers workers employed in metal-processing, and especially mechanical plants and printing shops, rather than those employed in cotton mills and food processing enterprises, who lead the strike wave and most consistently advance the demand for *vezhlivoe obrashchenie*— for polite treatment and polite address. It is those workers who at this moment give the movement so much of its specific flavor. This is hardly surprising, for it is always a sense of movement rather than a sense of doom, some sense of hope rather than of hope entirely denied, feelings of discontent rather than ones of inexorable necessity—as well as the ability to translate this discontent into specific grievances—which usually drive men to affirm themselves, and when they encounter resistance, to revolt.

A second impression, less easily confirmed by statistics, is that in addition to workers in more advanced industries and crafts, the most discontented—although not necessarily those most capable of translating their discontent into effective strike actions—are those elements of the *nizi*—the lower strata—of the big cities who come into closest and most frequent contact with "society": trolley car conductors, clerks in retail stores, waitresses, doormen, and even housemaids. For they, too, in a different way, feel most sharply the magnetic attraction of the life of the privileged and, even more sharply and more consistently, a sense of being rebuffed by them.

The third, and by far the most striking impression that one draws concerning the major concentrations of dissatisfaction and militance in the new labor unrest is that they also reflect a generational phenomenon. The records of arrests of the Department of Police, the letters of worker correspondents, the observations of commentators of the labor scene all indicate that it is primarily the younger generation of urban workers who provide the most militant recruits of the new wave of labor unrest, as well as most of its specific political coloration. It is they who provide the most active participants in the increasingly militant political strikes and demonstrations, as well as most of the new recruits drawn through this spontaneous movement into the reviving centers (in the open and in the underground) of Social Democracy.[88]

To what factors can the militance of these young workers and their prominence in the prewar labor movement be attributed? When, within a few months, Menshevik commentators on the labor scene, who originally greeted the explosion of Lena and its aftermath with such joy and relief, begin to develop second thoughts about what they come to describe as the *stat-echnyi azart*—the foolhardiness and recklessness of the strike movement—and become even more alarmed, as the militance of the new generation turns against their own, older, Menshevik oriented labor intelligentsia, they will find an obvious and easy explanation for all this recklessness in the "greenness" of those who display it: the natural "hotheadedness" of youths who have not experienced the sobering defeats of 1905, and the travails of the labor movement during the years of reaction.

And indeed it would be hard to deny that there is a quality of impulsiveness about the behavior that many of these recruits to the labor movement display: their quickness to explode in anger, to rise to the heights of joy and unbounded sense of power, and then, as often as not, to succumb just as vertiginously to the depths of depression and despair. Yet, whatever the measure of truth in this stereotype, we should take note of other factors to account for the attitudes and behavior of this rebellious new generation of young workers.

The vast majority of them are urban bred, if not urban born, having grown up during the years of industrial stagnation and recession, in which the industrial labor force remained relatively stable, and indeed occasionally declined. It is undoubtedly among many of these young workers that the countryside and its traditions have become psychologically as well as physically most remote, contrary to the stereotypes drawn by Menshevik commentators on the labor scene. It is undoubtedly within this age group that one would find the smallest percentage of workers who have maintained any physical connection with the countryside, including the practice of returning to the village in times of hardship, or to help with the gathering of the crop in the summer season.

More broadly, of all elements of the Russian working class, it is these young urban born and/or urban bred young workers who have left the traditional culture of the countryside furthest behind: the memory of its more circular, stagnant, and ultimately resigned, tempo of existence, in which the seasons succeed one another, and periods of famine follow periods of bountifulness, under the seemingly imperious dictates of a divine and/or natural necessity, and of the rigidly binding traditions, of patriarchal and communal ways; of the many surviving shreds in economic, social, and psychological interrelationships and relations with authority of *krepostnichestvo*—of the heritage of serfdom and the implicit acceptance of those marked by it of superordinate relationships between masters and serfs, but also between parents and children.

By the same token, for this new generation of young urban workers, the city and its pavements have ceased to represent a strange forbidding world. Since childhood, they have become familiar with its ways, and learned to decipher them, if not wholly to master them. Indeed, they have been caught up in, and uplifted by the sense of movement, the breezes of change—the sense of possibility—that the city's bustling rhythm, and just as dramatically the character and tempo of industrial life, can communicate to those who are not stunned by them—as so many of their elders still feel because of this very sense of constant motion and the absence of familiar or stable landmarks.

Last, but not least, we should take note of one more characteristic feature of this new generation, this one, statistically verifiable, and intercorrelated with their urban upbringing: their high degree of literacy. As both census figures and the findings of our quantitative analyses clearly suggest, almost all of these young workers are literate, far more generally than their elders.[89] And what is more specifically at issue is not simply the basic fact of literacy, but the kind of literacy—the frequency and ease with which one actually reads, and the role that reading plays in shaping one's outlook. Most suggestive in this respect is the fact that one of the frequent criticisms that

worker correspondents of the labor press, particularly in Petersburg, offer of
fellow workers as telling evidence of their backwardness—of their lack of
consciousness and *kulturnost'*—is not that they do not read, but of what they
read: cheap tabloids like *Kopeika* and especially the installments of cheap fiction that daily appear in them—instead of properly instructing and elevat-
ing themselves by reading the labor press:

> And so they remain oblivious to how people live and struggle for a
> better future. It is no longer a mark of distinction to read *Kopeika*
> because in Petersburg, at least, everyone reads it. The *izvozchik*, the
> prostitute, the doorman. Besides, he who does not want to poison
> himself spiritually must read the workers' papers. Books, the work-
> ers' papers, the workers' courses—these are the means by which we
> will substitute a human outlook (*oblik*) for an animal one. Only a
> conscious worker can truly respect the human personality, woman-
> hood; cherish the tender soul of a child (*nezhnuiu detskuiu dushu*).
> This we will learn from no one except ourselves. We are conscious
> working people; we don't have the right to be like the bourgeois.[90]

Literacy is so important in accounting for the attitudes of this new generation of the young partly because it subjects them so much more fully to
the attraction of privileged society—and to the new image of human dignity, of *kulturnost'* in human conduct and human relations which the mores
of this society seem to provide—at the same time as it exposes them, when
they feel rebuffed by the world of the privileged, to the message of radical appeals. This double exposure steadily and powerfully reinforces the feeling of
ambivalence to which these workers are subject, and the new sense of militant class-consciousness into which these feelings of ambivalence are ultimately translated, and partially resolved. To this we should add a perhaps
less obvious observation: literacy also plays a major role in steadying, as well
as focusing, the feelings of antagonism and rebellion which it so clearly in-
tensifies. The elaboration of a radical world view—the translation of vague
dissatisfactions into specific grievances, and the elaboration of these into a
polarized image of the world, a Manichean world divided between capital
and labor, workers and bourgeois—this whole process of intellectualization
makes it easier for these young workers' feelings of antagonism to rule more
firmly over the feelings of attraction to which they are the counterpoint, at
the same time as it directs their antagonism at more specific and more
sharply focused targets. It tends, in substance, to reduce, if not eliminate, the

great swings in mood that I have described: between exhilaration and de-spair, between a sense of unbounded power and one of complete powerless-ness. Thus it is that, even in adversity, many of these young workers will re-main more steadfast in their militant radicalism than their youthfulness, their "greenness," might otherwise lead us to expect.

From the very outset of the new labor unrest, these rebellious young ur-ban workers—and more generally the activists of the strike movement—come most sharply into conflict with two groups of workers in the factory. The first of these consists of the older, more senior workers, especially the more established and privileged ones. These older workers denounce the young as irresponsible firebrands and consistently try to *put them down*, while the young respond to them rebelliously, and sometimes with genuine hatred, denouncing their elders as pliant tools of managements, "hangers-on," "outlived tails," "dark old men" (*chernye stariki*).

There is a universal and inevitable quality to this conflict. The older and more senior workers may have ten to fifteen years invested in their jobs and bear the scars of long periods of hardship and unemployment; they are usual-ly loaded with family responsibilities and dreaming of the day when they may be able to afford their own homes and a life of somewhat greater comfort and ease. Naturally, they *are* reluctant to relinquish all—the relative security that they have gained in their jobs, the higher pay, the tangible and intangible fa-vors of the *nachal'stvo*—to join precipitously in strike actions which appear to them, usually quite correctly, to be headed for inevitable defeat. To ease their lot, they are far more likely to court the favors of the *nachal'stvo*, and the lat-ter in turn, to reward their docility and zeal by discriminating in their favor, and against the younger and more rebellious hands. Young workers frequent-ly complain to the labor press that older workers are rewarded by the foreman for their servility, receive higher pay for the same jobs, get preference in over-time work and the like, while the young are discriminated against.

But however natural and inevitable the conflict, we should not lose sight of its distinctive features. Many of the older workers still have rooted in them, largely unshaken, the traditions of the superordinate and patriarchi-cal relationships of the old society of *sosloviia*: they find such relationships—and the patterns of behavior and forms of address in which they are reflect-ed—quite natural, "customary"; all the more, since, in their own cases, these relationships are usually contained, however thinly, in some semblance of the traditional patterns of mutual responsibility between superior and infe-rior. Thus they tend to accept their imposition without tremor, and in turn seek to impose them on others, especially on the young.

This is the distinctive psychological element which infuses the conflicts between older and younger workers with their peculiar quality of bitterness and even hatred noted by the shrewder observers of the labor scene, as the struggle between them turns into veritable patricidal conflicts. And indeed these conflicts in the factory often spill over into the home, inducing the sons to revolt against their fathers' attempts to assert "rudely," "arbitrarily," his traditional patriarchical authority. Many of these young workers will no longer allow themselves to be beaten in the home, anymore than in the factory.

A worker at the Langenzipen metallurgical plant, one of the hotbeds of strike activity in Petersburg, complains in a letter to the labor press:

> Father, an old worker, has felt the blows of fists on his skin his whole life. And he has translated his paternal rights into a law of fists—*kulachnoe pravo*. He has never known any other. . . . Is it right for a father to dispose of his children as if they were things, property? No! Nothing is more precious than the dignity of the human person, and workers must protect this dignity in themselves and in others. Workers must loudly complain: down with beatings and the use of force by the bosses and their hangers-on, and at home, in family life.[91]

This equation of treatment in the factory and in the home is not atypical, and what is reflected in the complaints about both by young workers is nothing less than the erosion of the legitimacy of an old system of authority, and the assertion by the young of a new conception of personal rights and autonomy.

As of the summer and fall of 1912, the self-assertiveness, the impatience, and the anger of the activists of the new labor unrest had not yet turned, at least massively, against the older, largely Menshevik-oriented, labor intelligentsia, which had sought to keep some semblance of an open labor movement alive through the years of reaction. But some of the young workers are already beginning to flock to the trade unions, the peoples' universities, and the societies of enlightenment administered by these more experienced and more cautious veterans. And all too quickly, conflicts will break out between them, as is inevitably the case between men of such different ages, temperaments, and experience. To be sure, different issues, and to some degree, different attitudes, are involved, but it is not a matter of accident that these ostensibly ideological and political conflicts quickly become infused with some of the bitter and ruthless quality that the conflicts of generations within the working class have already begun to assume. Writing about this later stage, when the conflict between Bolsheviks and Mensheviks spread to all the open organizations of labor, a Menshevik observer of the labor scene comments in the spring of 1914:

> Here, the representatives of two different periods, [men] of different habits, different practical schools—two forces of workers, "young" and "old"—encountered one another for the first time. . . . The take-over [by the young] which occurred extremely quickly, for many almost unexpectedly, took place in an atmosphere of patricidal conflict.[92]

Besides the older generation of the more senior and privileged workers, we can distinguish a second stratum of the labor force about which militant young workers most often complain, and at which they most often direct their ire during this period. These are unskilled workers, the *chernye rabochie*—especially those who are now pouring in great numbers into the industrial labor force from the countryside. These recruits from the countryside originally settle quietly in the city and in the factory. Naturally, they are quite disoriented at first, as they register the shock of new, strange, and frightening environment. Besides, as some of them put it, they have embarked on their new life in the city "not to cause any scandals, but to make some money (*My priekhali ne grubit', a den'gi zashibit'*)." Thus, initially, they do not provide recruits for strike actions, and are much more likely instead to submit passively, "slavishly," "like a herd of cattle," to conditions that young urban workers now consider so intolerable a denial of their human dignity and of their proud new sense of identity as industrial workers.

But the tone of the militant young workers' complaints about the passivity and self-abasement of the unskilled is different from that of their denunciation of their elders. There is less hostility, less aggressiveness, and more "shaming," a contempt usually tempered by at least some drops of pity.

The illiterate unskilled workers are denounced—and especially "shamed"—for their slavishness, for "bowing low before their masters," and "behaving like drunken cattle": They fail to react when the foreman addresses them rudely, or hits them in the mouth. They do not seem humiliated when they are searched, or "contemptuously" handed out a few coins "for vodka" at the end of the working day. After all, these newcomers from the dark countryside don't know any better. And, the young urban workers' attitudes toward them consequently waver between a contempt, reflecting the old attitudes of superordination inherited from the old caste, and the effort to "shame" these new unskilled workers also to perceive and insist upon the recognition of their humanity and of their proud identity as workers.

Under the stimulus of the new wave of labor disorders, and the catalytic influence of the younger, urban-bred workers, this recognition, for many of the unskilled, including those who have arrived from the countryside, appears remarkably quickly, among the young. As the strike statistics show us, these new workers shake themselves out of their passivity, and by the eve of the war are flocking in great numbers to the strike movement.

Some years ago, I sought to account for the rapidity of this process of radicalization—so markedly different from the far more persistent apathy displayed by the *chernye* during the previous major period of industrial expansion and rural immigration of the 1890s—by emphasizing the barely submerged discontents that this generation of recruits to the labor force brought with them to the city from the countryside, under the impact of the Stolypin land reforms. They were resentful, because of the severing of their ties to the land and to the peasant community, as a result of the process of separation and consolidation of landstrips, which were achieved, as often as not, under irresistible economic and administrative pressures. In addition, they also felt an even more brutal sense of dispossession, which was probably created, for many of the younger rural immigrants, by the transfer of the title to the land to the head of the household as a whole. The shocks that were caused by this process, as well as the sense of disorientation originally felt by the new immigrants from the village in the city and factory were maximized by the changes that had been taking place in the pattern of immigration from the countryside to the big cities, especially Petersburg, since the turn of the century. As the labor supply available in Petersburg and nearby provinces of the lake region declined, a modest but growing proportion of the recruits into the Petersburg metropolitan labor force probably had to be drawn from the more distant and over-populated Central Agricultural Region of European Russia.[93] This, of course, was a purely agricultural region, with few or no traditions of manufacturing or, indeed, handicraft work; it was also the area in European Russia in which the repartitional commune had sunk its deepest roots. By the same token, it was the region whose recruits to the industrial labor market were likely to experience most deeply and painfully the shocks administered by the Stolypin land legislation, as well as the impact of their new industrial and urban experience.[94]

In an effort to account for the growing explosiveness of the prewar labor unrest, Menshevik commentators eventually emphasized the significance of the scars and memories of village life. Indeed, the factors just discussed may have accounted, in part, for the attitudes increasingly displayed by rural immigrants into the labor force during this period, and cannot be dismissed any more than their numerical weight in the process of expansion of the industrial labor force during these years. By early 1914, even Lenin recognized the social and political significance of their presence; in commenting on the labor scene, he consistently cited the revival among Russian workers (as reflected in the leadership of trade unions, the leadership of labor newspapers, etc.) of Left Populist tendencies.

In a series of articles published in the spring of 1914, Martov also commented on this revival of Left Populism, which threatened to overtake Menshevism as the chief rival to Bolshevism in the Russian labor movement by the eve of the war. "A swilling mixture of anarchist and syndicalist tendencies with remnants of peasant urges and utopias" appeared to him to animate the Left Populists' supporters. "These workers might have physically left the village, but they had by no means broken their psychological ties with it. As they face the hardships, the darkness of city life, they hold onto their dream of returning to a patch of land with their own cow and chickens . . . and they respond to the slogans of those who promise them the fulfillment of their dream."[95]

Given the massive influx from country to city that characterized these years of rapid industrial expansion, Martov's explanation can hardly be dismissed out of hand. But it is *not* the whole story, even in accounting for the attitudes of peasant recruits into the labor force, and especially for the *evolution* of their attitudes within a few years, indeed a few months, after these recruits had moved to the city and the factory. For what is remarkable, I think, is how rapidly these peasant recruits proceeded during these immediate prewar years to absorb a working-class psychology; more precisely, *how quickly* they registered the lessons provided by being shamed by their younger worker counterparts; how quickly they began to absorb the new model of consciousness, the new attitudes toward self and toward others, especially those in authority, recorded in the message of the urbanized young. As a result, by the outbreak of war, the conflict between young urbanized workers and the unskilled recruits from the village was greatly attenuated, as many of the *chernye* learned their lessons in class solidarity—they joined the strikes and demonstrations in growing numbers and with growing zeal—and acquired remarkably quickly an image of themselves as industrial workers.

The rapid pace of this process, and the consolidation of the working class in the major metropolitan centers, and especially in the capital, to which it led, were partially obscured by the fact that each passing week, each passing day, during this period of industrial upsurge was marked by a new influx of peasant recruits into the industrial working class. Their clothes, their mores, their attitudes, which they brought from the countryside to the city, would remain highly visible right up to the outbreak of the war, and indeed right up to the revolution.

Admittedly, the scope and rapidity of the process we are examining—that of the transformation of ex-peasants into workers, and of the emergence among them (to use the political jargon of the time) of a working-class consciousness—is extraordinarily hard to pin down analytically. For the reasons already suggested, the improved fortunes of Left Populism on the eve of the war do not provide an accurate gauge for it. And neither do the terms that the increasingly alarmed and disillusioned Menshevik observers of the labor scene used to describe the evolution of working-class attitudes and behavior on the eve of the war. The problem is not merely that words like *buntarstvo* [rebelliousness], and the like were politically loaded, and that the Menshevik commentators who used them viewed working-class behavior through the prism of their own political preconceptions. It is also that these capsules, which admittedly reflect, however distortedly, a genuine phenomenon—the growing explosiveness, the increasingly angry and indeed reckless mood that come to characterize the workers' strikes and demonstrations, especially in the capital, as war approached—can be applied not only to the behavior of peasant recruits, but to other strata of the working-class as well, and indeed in Petersburg (as strike data glaringly demonstrate) to practically the working-class as a whole. Specifically, they can be as validly used to describe the mood and behavior of urban-born and urban-bred industrial workers, especially among the young, as to describe the more recent recruits to the labor force to whom by 1914 these urbanized workers imparted their spirit of revolt.

By 1912, and early 1913, that is to say, *before* the prewar labor unrest became completely intertwined with the respective changes in the fortunes of Bolshevism and Menshevism, various observers of the Russian labor scene freely recognized, with mixtures of awe, admiration, and alarm, how wide and rapid the crystallization of working-class consciousness had become. Of all contemporary observers of the labor scene, the Social Democrats were obviously the most enthusiastic about this phenomenon, but they were by no means the only ones to take note of it.

The already cited editorial reactions of *Rech'* and *Novoe Vremia* to the May Day demonstrations and economic strikes of 1912 illustrate the perceptions that these so different organs of political opinion drew about the atti-

tudes that Russian workers in these collective actions: above all, of the workers' increasing consciousness of themselves as a separate class, and of the
sense of opposition to the rest of urban society that was conjoined with this
consciousness. A year later, the Kadet commentator Izgoev, in an article
seeking to explain the sway of Social Democracy over the workers, emphasized that the processes underlying Russia's social crisis had now given rise
to an extremely significant "process of social crystallization." Izgoev recognized that the process was still in an early stage and that a strong external
blow could upset it before it matured. But one could already observe, he asserted, the impressive sight of the collection of the "human dust" in Russia's
national life, and of the shaping of this dust into organized social bodies.
One of the most impressive and significant manifestations of this process of
social development, he observed, was the current "transformation of the
chaotic Russian laboring masses into a working class . . . under the ideology
of Social Democracy."[96]

If the admittedly impressionistic conclusions that I have drawn are correct, the process of social crystallization of the working class noted by Izgoev was already beginning to encompass even the masses of the unskilled,
notwithstanding the rapidly changing composition of the labor force resulting from massive influx of immigrants from the village to the city. How is
this fact to be explained? Some Soviet historians sought to account for it by
denying, or at least minimizing, the importance of the countryside as a
source of labor recruitment, even during these years of rapid industrial expansion. Instead, they emphasized the steady growth of the proportion in
the industrial labor force of a hereditary urban proletariat, and its capacity
by the eve of the war to provide most of the necessary recruits for the ex-
panding labor force through the natural reproduction of its own ranks. The
demographic data necessary to prove the point—one way or the other—are
unavailable for this period, but I am convinced, nonetheless, that this line of
interpretation is belied by the fragmentary evidence we do have: by the many
contemporary reports of the influx of these *derevenshchiki*, as well as the admittedly fragmentary statistical data that are available about the geographical origins of the labor force in a number of industrial centers.

In the last analysis, the scope and tempo of the expansion of the industrial labor force could hardly have been assured, exclusively or even predominantly, by the natural expansion of a purely urban labor market. The
period from January 1910 to July 1914 would see the Russian industrial labor
force expand from 1,793,000 to 2,400,000, a rise of over 30 percent. The same
years would see even sharper rises in particular geographical and industrial

sectors: in the Petersburg industrial labor force, for example, and in the met-al and metal-working industry for the country as a whole, the increase would be over 50 percent. Even if we dismiss the observations of contemporary observers, it is simply implausible, in my view, that such rapid and dramatic increases could possibly have occurred without massive movements of immigrant workers to the capital.

But among the evidence advanced by Soviet spokesmen for their view, there is one highly suggestive additional set of data. I have in mind the annual statistics on the number of passports issued to urban workers to go to the countryside, usually in the summertime to help with the crop. Strumilin, Raskin, and other Soviet labor historians have shown, quite conclusively, I believe, that the number of such passports issued actually declined, even during these years of the new industrial upsurge, and have inferred from this evidence that the relative proportion of workers of rural origin likewise declined in those sectors of the industrial labor force that they surveyed. I believe that the evidence cited is conclusive, but that the inference drawn from it, is faulty, and that it suggests a different and more useful line of thought. Even though the relative percentage of recruits to the industrial labor force from the country-side undoubtedly rose during the years 1910–1914, these rural immigrants to the city and its industrial enterprises no longer bore the same connections, the same ties to the village, as did their predecessors. This, as I suggested earlier, was because, in many cases at least, the impact of the Stolypin land reforms loosened dramatically the ties to the land, to the commune, and to the extended families from which these rural immigrants came.

It matters little in this context whether, after the separation of titles, these peasants sold their land eagerly (for the cash it brought them) or reluctantly, under irresistible administrative and/or economic pressures. Neither does it matter whether they lost it as a result of the arbitrary, legal act of the state's transfer of it—from the family as a whole to the head of the household. For even those, usually the peasant poor who had originally received the land in private title and decided to sell it, managed through these two actions to loosen, if not to sever their legal, economic, social and psychological ties to the land, the village commune, and indeed to the peasant *soslovie*. They loosened their ties to the peasant community, separating themselves from it and from nature more fully, and more suddenly than the vast majority of previous rural immigrants to the city had ever done.

As a result, many of them came to, and settled in, the city and the factory without anchor in their earlier existences. This probably resulted in a sharper initial sense of disorientation than their predecessors. By the same

token, however, it facilitated and accelerated, especially among young immigrant workers, the absorption of the values, the ethos, the self-image of themselves as industrial workers which the urbanized young workers with whom
they came into contact imparted to them along with their spirit of revolt.

Here, I think, lies the real explanation for the rapid evolution and consolidation of the sense of class consciousness and class solidarity that many
contemporary observers of the labor scene recorded with such awe.

To this image of the growing class unity among Russian workers, especially in the large urban centers, one important qualification has to be registered. While the conflicts between young urban workers and young labor recruits from the countryside could be defused fairly quickly, the generational
conflicts between the urban young and older, more established urban workers could not. Unlike the rural immigrants, the older generation of urban
workers had a vested pattern of existence and sense of identity—economic
interests, possessions, personal values—an entire mode of life, which it had
taken them a lifetime to build. It was natural that they should defend it
fiercely when it came under attack, and all the more so when it was attacked
by those who, symbolically or even literally, were their own sons.

Thus it was, as the months passed, that the conflict between the older
generation of urban workers and the new, became more bitter and enven-
omed. Indeed, as I suggested earlier, it would soon assume new, political dimensions, as the more militant young urban workers poured into the trade
unions, the clubs of enlightenment, the peoples' universities, and began to
fight with the older, more moderate, leadership of these organs of the open
labor movement over the conduct of their affairs, and eventually over their
control. This would be one of the major springboards for the struggle between Bolsheviks and Mensheviks in the Russian labor movement.[97]

I have so far discussed the changes in consciousness that came to the
surface in the Russian working class in the wake of Lena, and the conflicts of
attitudes, of values, of individual and group self-image, which they precipitated by identifying them with distinctive strata and age groups of Russian
workers. This group differentiation between older and younger Russian
workers, as significant as it was, constituted only one aspect of these conflicts
of attitudes—toward authority, toward self, toward other workers—which
obtained, with different degrees of intensity, for all Russian workers, however militant or politically conscious they might be.

The process of shaming and the experience of the shame in which these
new attitudes were so powerfully expressed were ultimately addressed to all
workers. For within them, including the young urban rebels, there remained,

however deeply buried, an inclination—or the fear of an inclination—to surrender, to lapse back into the old ways. Each feared that he would submit, in the factory or in the home, to the foreman or to the father, to the old patterns of superordination, to the old servile and patriarchial ways—only to gain or regain the temporary peace, the temporary sense of security and superficial intimacy which however briefly such a surrender might bring. Each carried that desire for escape, if only for the spell of a drunken evening, from the tedium, the oppressiveness, the humiliations of their factory environment and from the *burden* of accountability to self and to others, that the new models of identity demanded of them in their struggle to resist and overcome the old ways. Were this not so, the ambivalence we have noted—and the need to shame and to be shamed—would not have been as sharp or as universal.

One of the important and relatively neglected insights that the study of personality and culture can bring is the elucidation of the distinction between a sense of sinfulness, shame, and guilt. Just as all other analytical distinctions, this one is partially artificial. Yet however crudely this stereotype is occasionally advanced, it is valid to state, I believe, that underlying the moral and religious values of traditional Russian culture, and especially of the traditional peasant community—underlying its acceptance and/or reconciliation with suffering, human weakness, and the arbitrary and yet always seemingly inexorable, dictates of nature, of custom, of authority—was a sense of sin. One was born a sinner, and had to be reconciled with the burden of one's sins and of the sins of others. As an integral member of a tight, interwoven community, which was necessarily sinful, since it was of this earth, one bore the sins of others as one bore one's own. One was, in a sense, responsible for all actions, and indeed for all thoughts and feelings—for thoughts and feelings were the moral equivalent of actions, even when they were not acted out. And yet ultimately, by being involved in all acts, all feelings, all thoughts, one was left personally accountable for none. (To be sure, one had to repent for one's sins, but by the same token, the more numerous and greater the sins, the greater the capacity for redemption.) Hence, the relative ease with which any *specific* violation of moral standards, whether one's own or those of others, could be, and were ultimately forgiven, at least if one repented for them. After all, each of them counted for little in the ultimate balance of judgment.

These, I believe, however stereotyped my rendition of them, were some of the underlying attitudes that Russian workers, especially the recruits from the countryside, originally brought with them to their new factory and urban environment, and never completely left behind. The sense of shame and shaming which emerged, and was so cultivated, especially in the wake of Lena, constituted an effort to resist and oppose the inclination to surrender to human frailty, or more precisely to what was now considered especially by the young, to be intolerable weakness in the light of the new image of human dignity that had emerged among them. It meant, as well, the necessity of resisting the former easy toleration of human frailty, the tendency to pity and to forgive, provided the old sense of sin and sinfulness. *An individualized sense of guilt was not as yet sufficiently deeply and firmly internalized* to provide an adequate defense against the old ways. Hence, the necessity to support this defense, externally, by the shaming I have described: shaming by one's own self, but also by other workers tied by the new bonds of solidarity that had been established in the shop, in the enterprise, and in the working class as a whole.

Only if one bears in mind how precarious the new ideals of human dignity and new models of self and of other still were, how difficult they were to uphold, day in and day out, in one's conduct at home, in the factory, and in the street; and how thin a reef shame and shaming provided to the ever-present inclination to revert to the old ways, can one properly understand the attitudes that Russian workers, especially the young urban militants, displayed at this moment, and would continue to display through the revolution of 1917. Much of the belligerence that workers, especially the more militant young workers, now displayed in word and action, much of the intensity of their shaming of other, less militant, workers, was precisely a function of their *own residual inclinations* to bow *themselves* before authority, to surrender to their *own* weaknesses and to the traditional ways of the past, which, in even the most militant, were still so deeply ingrained.

The internal tension that this conflict produced, especially in the course of the increasingly stressful struggle against authority that was to follow, would further intensify the sources of their ambivalence: the simultaneous sense of attraction and opposition to the culture of privileged educated society, the desire to rejoin it and the rejection of this desire fed by the fear, and the actual experience of its rebuffs.

In the wake of Lena, and for a long time to come, this ambivalence and the internal conflicts to which it gave rise, found its expression and partial resolution in a phenomenon which would assume growing social and political significance with the passage of time: an insistence on both equality and separateness.

Underlying the new sense of human dignity which Russian workers, especially the young urban militants, felt that they were being denied, and which they so stubbornly pressed, was an insistence that they be recognized as human beings with needs and aspirations, and therefore *rights*, equal to those in superior positions to them with whom they came into contact in the enterprise, in the street, in the shop, in political life. But as we have also seen, the statements in which these demands for equality were expressed were almost invariably coupled with assertions of their authors' distinctive identity and solidarity as workers—who could rely only on their own strength—by independently organizing their own unions, their own workers' papers, their own workers' party.

To be sure, in the records of workers' statements during this period, we can find expressions of their social and political attitudes that seem to reach—in one direction or the other—beyond the ambivalence of which we have spoken.

On one hand, in the texts of resolutions and petitions sent by workers' groups to their Social Democratic deputies in the State Duma as well as to the labor press, is expressed the conviction that the cruelty and gross injustices of which Lena stood as a symbol would persist as long as the "bloodthirsty" existing political regime and the rule of capitalism that it supported was allowed to survive. Juxtaposed with these statements were the frequent references to the "brighter future," or more explicitly to the socialist society, in which workers would finally determine their own fate, and fully realize their ideal of human dignity.

On the other hand, in these very same resolutions and letters to the workers' press, and of course in the lists of demands issued in the course of economic strikes, are statements which suggest that what the workers really wanted was that those who currently held authority over them concede to them a better material existence as well as the right to live as free and equals: freedom of speech, of association, freedom to organize trade unions, to strike, and the like.

These statements lent themselves to conflicting conclusions as to the state of political consciousness that the working class had reached at this point. Bolshevik and Menshevik spokesmen were already doing so. Yet I would suggest that—especially as of this moment—both of the warring factions of Social Democracy were drawing conclusions about the workers' state of mind which oversimplified the attitudes of even the more militant and/or more "conscious" workers.

While workers might invoke a brighter future, when the whole structure of existing authority would have been overturned, and the sun of socialism shine in its full glory, it is difficult to escape the conclusion that this day as yet existed for them only in the realm of fantasy—a fantasy from which they could draw considerable comfort, to be sure, especially at times of disappointment or defeat. At the other end of the scale, the seemingly more "realistic," more specific statements of the workers' grievances and aspirations—those that appeared to be addressed to a contemporary reality—and at a present authority—also suggested by the scope and multiplicity of the workers' grievances and demands, and by the militance and intransigence of their tone, that they provided merely an opportunity to express a need for self-affirmation and revolt, which could not have been easily appeased, even if the workers' demands had been even partly satisfied.

In this respect, the behavior of most of the workers' Duma deputies toward their potential liberal allies, whose support they needed if they were to achieve their objectives, at least on certain issues (the intolerance, the frequent insistence on "going it alone," which the Bolsheviks, and even some of the Menshevik deputies, frequently displayed in their dealings with the Kadets and *Progressisty*) were as symptomatic as the "reckless" conduct of the workers' strikes of which the Menshevik labor press already complained.

The workers and their spokesmen ostensibly demanded equal rights from existing society, but they did not really trust even the most liberal spokesmen of this society to support them in pressing for these aspirations. This, I would argue, resulted not merely because they feared betrayal, but also because of a fear of being *disarmed* and thereby depriving themselves of the militant new image of themselves and of their class which kept them, however precariously, from surrendering to their own weakness as well as to superordinate authority. Hence, their fervor on the need to organize independently, to trust only their own strength, their own class, their own party. Hence, the vehemence and the intransigence of their demand for the recognition of their separateness as well as equality.

These, it seems to me, are some of the distinctive psychological underpinnings of the emerging phenomena of class consciousness which commentators of such different political persuasion widely recognized at this moment in the attitudes and behavior of Russian workers. It explains as well the various, seemingly conflicting facets of these phenomena—the insistence on equality but also the assertion of difference and opposition; the demand for acceptance, together with the readiness to reject; and the ultimate resolution of these ambivalences in the insistence on both equality and separateness.

These notes should not surprise us because of their obvious contemporary references. For we should recognize that they are characteristic of the psychology of hitherto dependent, or inferior, groups in societies undergoing the painful transition from caste to class—from relations of superordination to subordinate, if not equal, relationships. Above all, they are characteristic of those groups at the bottom of modern or modernizing societies, which finally rise up in rebellion against dependent relations and dependent status, which have become anachronistic, even according to some of the ostensible values that are now emerging in these societies.

In this perspective the insistence on equality *and* separateness should be viewed as a basic feature by the eve of the war, of the psychology and social and political behavior of Russia's working class. During the war years, it would mark the behavior of even the more moderate spokesmen for the workers' interests, such as leaders of the Labor Groups of the War Industrial Committees, in their dealings with their would-be allies in society. And in 1917 it would find its ultimate expression in the dealings of the Soviets with the Provisional Government, and more broadly, in the precarious and ultimately unsuccessful experiment of the *dvoevlastie*—dual power.

In the immediate aftermath of Lena the workers' demand for equality and separateness in their dealings with authority would be more modestly expressed, not only in the political process but also in their day-to-day struggle with their employers. Its most symptomatic manifestation would be the demand, advanced particularly by urban workers, especially those employed in advanced industries, that the employers recognize and agree to deal with their elected representatives, their own *starosti* or *upolnomochennye*, and that these workers' representatives be allowed to take part in the negotiations of disputes about working conditions, and even in decisions about such issues as wage rates, hiring, and firing.

These new claims were already voiced with a frequency comparable to that of the workers' demand for *vezhlivoe obrashchenie* (and indeed bore an intrinsic psychological relationship to it) during the strikes of the spring and summer of 1912, particularly among the printers and metal-processing workers of the capital. Possibly, the striking workers who advanced them were not always fully conscious of their implications, but they contributed to the bitter and ultimately irreconcilable character of labor disputes, locking workers and employers into a direct confrontation, and a head-on struggle over power and authority.

Most employers, especially the members of the St. Petersburg Society of Factory and Mill Owners, perceived demands that they agree to deal on a continuous basis with their workers' elected representatives and that they recognize these representatives' right to participate in decisions concerning wages and working conditions, let alone the demand for the dismissal of supervisory personnel accused of rude treatment or impolite address, as intolerable challenges to *their* God-given rights to run their enterprises, *their* property, as they saw fit.

Pravda, which was always quick to discern the new sources of conflict in the labor disputes of the period and their potential significance for its agitational efforts, already reported at the end of May 1912 that the St. Petersburg Society had called upon its member firms to do all they could to prevent the election of *starosty* [factory elders]. "What do Messrs. Capitalists have against *starosty*?," it rhetorically asked in one of its lead editorials:

> The Russian industrialist, who is accustomed to exercise unlimited authority in his enterprise, views himself as the "fatherly benefactor" and "wet nurse" of his workers. Such "patriarchical," i.e., "fatherly" relations between the boss and the worker, in which the employer and the worker face each other in a one-to-one [relationship], are very convenient for the capitalist.
>
> It is another matter when a *starosta* comes in on behalf of the workers who have elected him. Drawing on their strength and trust, he [can hold] a different kind of conversation; he is not so easy to scare off. Besides, the election of *starosty* provides a nucleus for labor organization, and that is what the employers, who prefer to deal with an unorganized crowd, hold against it.[98]

Pravda took note, in this connection, of another resolution recently adopted by the Council of Mechanical Enterprises of the St. Petersburg Society; this one recommending that its member firms list the names of all those of their workers who were enrolled in trade unions, for the ostensible purpose of "studying the effect exercised by trade unions on labor relations, and particularly on strikes." "As if the effect of trade unions on strikes were such a mystery," *Pravda* wryly observed. The editorial concluded:

> The Russian industrialists want to be regarded [in the same light] as their European confrères. [But] for this, it is necessary for them to absorb European habits, *perestat' byt' "chumozym" i men'she nadet'sia na uchastok* [to stop being a grub and long less for your little piece of land.][99]

In this last, virtually untranslatable phrase, reeking of the countryside and its traditions of patriarchical relations, the *Pravda* editorialist was suggesting (as did many other contemporary observers of the Russian labor scene) that the employers' response to the workers' demands bore the psychological imprint of the Russian past—that indeed it bore the indelible mark of the traditions of *krepostnichestvo*, of master-serf relations still so deeply embedded in the countryside. Given the strikers' use of such terms as *starosty*, it is equally tempting to view the strikers' demands largely in such traditional terms, as an attempt to restore some of the patterns of mutual accountability in which superordinate relations had usually been contained in the old rural society of *sosloviia*. But however traditional the mold in which the conflict between workers and employers over authority was still occasionally cast, the point should not be pressed too hard. For as I already indicated, the strikers who most universally and most forcefully pressed the claim for the participation of their own elected representatives in the administration that governed their lives *were not* workers in the more backward and traditional occupations and trades, but those in the most advanced enterprises, particularly in the capital. And by the same token, the employers at whom their challenge was not directed and who responded most uncompromisingly, should be categorized among the most, rather than the least, advanced representatives of the Russian industrial management of the period. Indeed, the challenge was first largely issued by workers in St. Petersburg metal-processing plants (as well as workers in Petersburg printing shops) and the most militant response came from employers in these industries. To be sure, the enterprises involved included a large percentage of state firms, especially in armaments, munitions, and shipbuilding. This factor only contributed to the rapid escalation of the conflict, as it necessarily turned into a struggle against all authority—the authority of the state as well as that of private management. Nevertheless, the initiative in triggering and mobilizing employer resistance, at least within the St. Petersburg Society of Factory and Mill Owners, largely came from representatives of private corporate firms, which in many cases were filial enterprises of foreign firms, and staffed by a large percentage of administrators of foreign origin.

This last factor further exacerbated the labor conflicts of the period (frequently noted by worker correspondents of the labor press), as the workers perceived themselves to be locked in their struggle for self-affirmation with men who were foreign to them in language and culture as well as spirit. By the same token, the symbolism of foreign management, and of corporate affiliation of the firms at the forefront of the labor conflict of the period, imprinted a far more modern and ultimately intractable character to the struggle than was suggested by liberal observers of the labor scene.

I have already mentioned in this connection the prominence of the role of the St. Petersburg Society of Factory and Mill Owners. Even this society, however, whose policy stands on labor issues were largely set by representatives of its Council of Mechanical Enterprises, did not find it easy at first to adopt a united front in the face of the new wave of labor unrest. To be sure, unlike its counterpart in the Central Industrial Region, the Moscow Society, (which was dominated by textile firms organized along more traditional family and partnership lines) the St. Petersburg Society was inclined from the outset to respond to the workers' new militance with an iron hand. Thus, whereas the Moscow Society came to the decision not to fine workers who engaged in protest strikes after Lena, the automatic response of the Chairman of the St. Petersburg Society, Glezmer, was to recommend that the Society apply the rules of the convention it had enforced since 1905, and fine the participants in the Lena protest strikes. As we have seen, however, alarmed by the scope and intensity of the Lena protests, the St. Petersburg Society recoiled from taking this step, deciding instead to confine itself to the recommendation that member firms not pay their workers for the period of their strike actions.[100]

A few weeks later, the St. Petersburg Society had to consider whether to impose fines for the strikes expected on May Day. As before, there were voices raised in opposition to the imposition of fines, led by the representative of the state-owned St. Petersburg Metal Plant. The latter explained that his plant, similar to other metal-processing plants in the capital, was loaded with orders, and suffering from a shortage of qualified workers to fill them. Good workers had to be wooed; and enterprises were competing to hire them. Under such circumstances, it was plainly inexpedient to rouse labor dissatisfaction through the imposition of fines. Although the spokesman for the Petersburg Metal Plant was supported in his stand by four other members of the council, the latter finally decided, by a vote of 25 to 5, "to maintain the existing system of fines and undeviatingly to impose fines for strikes like the May Day ones."[101]

On this occasion, even the Moscow Society of Industrialists, now alarmed by the rash of economic strikes that had broken out in the wake of the Lena protest action, and feeling that the workers had interpreted their original policy of leniency as a sign of weakness or indifference, also passed a resolution recommending that participants in May Day strikes be fined.[102] Most member firms of the Moscow Society did not in fact heed this recommendation. And even in the more intransigent St. Petersburg Society, only 19 member firms actually imposed May Day fines, while 76 members did not.

But however haphazardly it was implemented, the policy of imposing fines for the May Day strikes helped set off the wave of economic strikes in which the new unprecedented demands for the participation of workers' elected representatives in the settlement of labor disputes were voiced. And it was these strikes which, notwithstanding the difficulties of which employers complained (the orders to be filled, the shortages of and competition for qualified labor, etc), finally galvanized the members of the St. Petersburg Society to adopt a united and adamant stand. On June 28, the St. Petersburg Society adopted a new "secret" convention, codifying the rules to be followed by all member firms in their handling of labor disorders (its text was soon to be leaked to the newspapers). This convention generally sought to insure that all members of the Society follow a consistent policy in regard to all major issues that might arise in labor disputes, for example, to refuse to agree to any reduction in hours, or to any increase in the number of holidays, without the preliminary agreement of other plants of the St. Petersburg Society. The convention also called on member firms not to accede to any demands for a minimum wage, or to demands for wage compensation for days struck. But its most stringent, most detailed, and most novel provisions concerned the strikers' demands for labor representation. Three of the convention's eleven points called for the categorical rejection of all such claims. The participants in the convention undertook:

5. Not to tolerate permanent representation of the workers in the form of deputies, *starosty*, etc.

6. Not to tolerate interference, and the participation as intermediaries [in labor disputes] by trade unions, societies, and, generally, any organization extraneous (*postoronnye*) to the plant.

Note: In instances when this proves to be imperative, to allow oneself to enter into negotiations only with one's own workers.

7. In particular, interference is not to be tolerated: (a) in hiring and firing of workers; (b) in decisions concerning wages and conditions of hiring; (c) in questions of internal arrangements (i.e., factory regulations).[103]

To enforce these rules, point 9 of the convention provided that member firms issue lists of striking workers at their plants, and that other firms undertake not to hire these workers until notified that the lists had been recalled. If a worker was hired before the blacklist on which his name appeared was received, he was immediately to be given a two-weeks notice. And even after work was resumed at a striking plant, its administration was to turn over to the Council of the Society a list of those strikers whom it had considered necessary not to rehire. These workers were to be put on a permanent blacklist.

A note appended to this article of the convention suggested to member firms that they draw up lists of their workers in advance, so as to be able to provide the requested blacklists to other members of the Society immediately in the event of a strike. Finally, in an effort to ensure the effective observance of the convention by its signatories, detailed "rules to guarantee the fulfillment of the convention" were appended to the text, which specified fines to be paid by member firms in the cases of violations of its various articles.

In substance, this convention of June 1912 was considerably more stringent and sweeping than the one concluded at the onset of the previous major wave of labor unrest, on March 15, 1905. It rejected even workers' representation by factory elders (*starosty*) (sanctioned by the now dormant statute of 1903); it prohibited contacts of any kind with trade unions, called upon member firms to make no concessions whatever to their labor force "under duress of the threat of the use of force" (Article 10); and it codified, in a fashion never before attempted, the blacklisting of strikers.

By the end of June—the date of the conclusion of the new convention—most of the major strikes that had originally broken out, chiefly in mechanical and other metal-processing enterprises, over the imposition of the May Day fines had already been defeated, some of them after a long, painful, heartbreaking struggle by the strikers concerned. Unable to resist the various pressures to which they were subjected—mass firings and lockouts, the arrest and deportation of elected representatives and other strike leaders, the specter or actual experience of hunger by their families, even the more militant of the striking workers had to resume work, or were replaced by strikebreakers. The Rozenkrants and the Kreiton plants had resumed production in the last week in June; so had the Erikson telephone workers who had been on strike since the beginning of May, and now resumed work on the old terms—all their strike demands having been denied.

At many of these plants, a number of the more militant workers had not been taken back, and of those who did, many returned, as we have seen, with a profound sense of shame: shame about having to work in the plant along with strikebreakers; shame about having to exchange heavy pleasantries with foremen and supervisors; shame before their blacklisted comrades, often standing helplessly before the factory gates, and above all, shame about abandoning those of their strike leaders—especially the representatives they had elected in the course of their strike to present their demands to management—who had been arrested, and then, more often than not, sentenced to administrative exile. At Erikson, for example, 200 workers had not been taken back, 10 had been sentenced to administrative exile, and 7 were still under arrest as of the end of June.[104]

Notwithstanding all the pressures to which their workers had been subjected—the dismissals, the arrests, the experience of hunger and of eviction from their quarters—a number of metallurgical plants were still holding out at the end of June, most notably the workers at Pastor, at the St. Petersburg Metallurgical plant, and at the two plants of Simens i Gal'ske (all of which had been on strike since early May). The conclusion of the convention, and the publicity given it by the labor press, not only infused these labor conflicts with additional stubbornness and bitterness (if any more was needed), but they also contributed to the accentuation of their symbolic significance for both sides—to the transformation of ostensibly "economic" disputes into veritable conflicts of will not only between the workers in these enterprises and their employers, but also between the industrialists of the capital and the Petersburg working class as a whole.

Of all the labor conflicts of this period, the one charged with the greatest symbolic significance was the strike at Simens i Gal'ske [Siemens and Halske], an enterprise making electro-technical equipment, a branch of a German firm of the same name. The two Simens Petersburg plants, which would come to occupy so prominent a place in the hagiography of the Petersburg labor movement, were substantial, but not especially large. Combined they employed a working force of 1,200: 800 skilled, and 200 unskilled men; 100 women and 100 apprentices. The wages of the skilled workers ranged between 1.40 rubles to 4 rubles a day, averaging at about 2.80 rubles, substantially higher than the average wage even in this better-paid industry. The average wage for unskilled workers was only 1.10 ruble a day, and that of apprentices, 50 kopeks a day; but even this was probably above the average. The workers worked a ten-hour day. The Simens i Gal'ske workers were therefore among the better paid, even in their relatively privileged industry. Nonetheless, they proved to be among the most militant of Petersburg workers. They were among the first to strike in response to Lena; they played a prominent role in the May Day demonstration in their district; and when the management of their plants—one of the stalwarts of the Mechanical Council of the Petersburg Society—sought to impose on them a symbolic fine (of 25 kopeks) for their strike on May Day, they struck again, the very next day (May 3).

As was the case in so many other strikes during the heady spring of 1912, this protest action against the May Day fines opened the floodgates for a host of other grievances and demands. Some two weeks after the outbreak of the strike, a mass meeting of 500 workers at one of the two Simens plants (the one on Moscow *chaussée*) assembled upon learning that the administration adamantly refused to cancel their May Day fines, and then proceeded to draw up a long list of additional demands to be transmitted to management by their elected representatives. The demands included: a 25 percent wage increase for skilled workers, and a 50 percent increase for the unskilled; a full-day's pay for the half-day of work on Saturdays; the public display of wage rates on lists confirmed by the Factory Inspector; hot water and better ventilation in the toilets; and last but not least, *vezhlivoe obraschenie* on the part of supervisors, and the recognition by management on a permanent basis of an elected council of workers' representatives (*sovet starost*). At the conclusion of their meeting, the strikers at Simens i Gal'ske drew up an appeal to other St. Petersburg workers not to take their jobs, as well as one to the workers of the German plants of the firm not to fill any orders from Russia until their strike demands were met.[105]

By the time of the conclusion of the convention, the strike at Simens i Gal'ske was already in its eighth week. During this period, the management of the two plants had made determined but unsuccessful efforts to break the strike and to resume operations: they had managed to hire but a few strikebreakers, most of these, lacking in the necessary skills for the plants' highly technical operations; they made these strikebreakers file in and out of the factories' gates repeatedly, and kept the factory whistles blowing in a futile effort to create the impression that the plants were actually running; they induced the police to arrest some of the striking workers, and indeed, innocent bystanders idling by the factory gate, but all of this failed to break the strikers' spirits. They sought to divert their orders, far behind schedule, to other firms, but the workers of these other firms were passing resolutions not to fill these orders. Finally, they attempted to hire some of these other workers (primarily from the Zissel and Arthur Koppel plants) to come and work at Simens i Gal'ske on an overtime basis, but only a few agreed to do so; and their fellow workers agreed not to take them back, and even beat them up upon their return.

On July 4, a worker correspondent reported some of these details to *Pravda*, noting that only 20 strikebreakers had reported for work at Simens i Gal'ske. "And an interesting spectacle can be observed: the siren blows endlessly, but the machines stand idle. And workers walk nearby looking contentedly at the scene."[106]

On July 1, three days after the conclusion of the convention, another correspondent from Simens i Gal'ske published a lengthier, more sober, but equally militant report about the situation and the mood of the strikers. At this time, in the two plants combined, only 48 workers were on the job, and of these only 7 had worked at Simens i Gal'ske before.

Such a lengthy strike did not come into the calculations of the administration at all: it didn't consider workers as people; it was accustomed to view them as machine parts, as joints, as wheels. The administration thought that it could break a strike in a few days: *golod, mol, ne tetka*! [Hunger, as they say, is not your auntie!] It forgot that these are no longer the days of old, that class self-consciousness and brotherly solidarity have developed among the workers. [The latter] have come to understand that the strike at each individual enterprise is the common cause of the whole working class, that victory and defeat affect [even] workers who are furthest away.[107]

Obviously, this report was intended to give heart to the Simens strikers, and much of the language used was that of Social Democratic agitation. But the references to workers' solidarity were not, for all of that, idle talk. By the beginning of July, the strike at Simens i Gal'ske was arousing an extraordinary outpouring of sympathy and support among St. Petersburg workers. And the fact that the management of this firm was so sharply identified with the St. Petersburg Society of Factory and Mill Owners, whose convention had just received such wide, if unexpected, publicity, only reinforced the sense among other workers of the capital that the cause of the strikers at these two plants was indeed their own.

I have already referred to the beatings that strikebreakers from Zissel and Arthur Koppel suffered at the hands of fellow workers for working overtime at the striking plant. The labor press also reported that the workers at Glebov and Arthur Koppel were refusing to handle orders diverted to their plants from Simens i Gal'ske. In a further gesture of solidarity, the workers at Arthur Koppel decided to contribute a day's wages to those at Simens i Gal'ske for the duration of their strike. Indeed, a few rubles at a time, contributions were now pouring in from workers at a great many Petersburg enterprises. By the end of the strike, more than 3,000 rubles 'would be collected in support of the Simens i Gal'ske strikers, a modest, but unprecedented token of such workers' support in the previous history of the St. Petersburg labor movement.

On July 11, with the strike in its tenth week, one of *Pravda's* worker correspondents reported, probably in only slightly inflated terms:

> Over the past week, the attention of all Petersburg workers has been focused on the strike. In various districts [workers'] meetings have passed resolutions praising the determination of the *Simentsy*, and declaring that the strike has become a matter of principle—that the victory of the *Simentsy* will be the victory of the whole Russian working class, and even of the international proletariat.
>
> The mood of the Simens strikers was reported to be astoundingly stalwart (*udivitel'noe bodroe*). At a recent meeting attended by 1,000 strikers—many of them accompanied by their wives and children—they reiterated their decision not to compromise and to continue the strike until complete victory has been achieved.[108]

Such mass meetings of the Simens i Gal'ske strikers, usually held at the *Moskovskaia zastava*, had become a regular affair since early May. From the labor press here is a brief description of one of them:

> A factory meeting of 500–600 [workers], 15–20 local workers speak. One speaks better than the other. One feels that people are not blindly following the leader who speaks, but rather [that there is] a veritable fusion, so that it is the words and the cause of the mass of the workers themselves that are given expression.[109]

These electric mass gatherings, consecrating the common struggle and common suffering of the strikes at Simens i Gal'ske, as well as the example that they were offering to other Petersburg workers, uplifted many of the strikers by the beginning of July to a veritable state of exultation:

> The talks about solidarity, about our common class, economic and other, interests, have so infused our souls as to push our personal interests aside. We have become so imbued with this state of mind that we have decided to strike—a month, two, or more—as long as our strength holds out. . . . Some of the workers have sent their families home [presumably to the countryside]; others, one must say the majority, have put all their personal possessions in hock, so that everyone carries 3–4 pawn tickets in his pocket. And nonetheless,

even though the majority have families of several mouths to feed, who are going hungry, even though many of them have been frightened, received threatening letters, thrown out of their apartments, arrested; even though strikebreakers have been hired, the workers have remained unbeaten (*nepobedimy*); steadfast. It is this steadfastness which deserves attention. Here, everything has been put at stake (*postavleno na kartu*) and notwithstanding all the conceivable [hardships] characteristic of Russian conditions, the workers have continued to hold fast.[110]

But in this now open contest of wills, the militance and steadfastness of the strikers reinforced—by an inexorable dialectic—the stubbornness of their employers. Just as the will of the Simens strikers was now bolstered by their sense of the example they were offering to other Petersburg workers and by the warmth of their support, so the stand of management of Simens i Gal'ske was hardened by the significance that the strike had come to assume in the eyes of other member firms of the Petersburg Society, and in particular of those of its Council of Mechanical Enterprises.

In addition to the moral support offered by other employers, and their blacklisting of the Simens i Gal'ske strikers, harsher police repressions soon added to the pressure on the strikers. At one of the sessions of the Mechanical Council of the St. Petersburg Society in early July, the representative of Simens i Gal'ske complained that the authorities had taken no action even though the leaders of the strike had been identified, and their names submitted first to the local police department, and then to the St. Petersburg Chief of Police, with a request that these strike leaders be arrested and deported from the capital. The names had then been forwarded to the Governor of St. Petersburg, but two weeks passed and there were still no results.

Actually, at this time, according to the labor press, more than sixty of the Simens workers were already under arrest, and twenty of them had been deported from the capital. But in response to the appeal of the Simens i Gal'ske representative, the Petersburg Society decided to send a delegation to make representations to the Minister of Internal Affairs. Its delegates were received on July 28. According to the Society's protocols, they told the Minister (N.A. Maklakov, who had recently succeeded Makarov, discredited by the Lena affair) at the helm of the MVD that "it would be extremely regrettable if loyal industry were left at the present moment to its own devices. The fact is that the leaders and inciters (of the strike) are going completely unpunished." Although their names had been presented to police officials, the strike leaders were not being arrested or deported, but were now walking about in the capital free and in perfect tranquility. A list of the names was then turned over to the Minister who promised to take the necessary measures. The deputation then raised the question of having the strikers expelled from their factory-owned barracks. To this, Maklakov replied that the industrialists should appeal for this purpose to the competent Justice of the Peace. But he also advised them to turn for assistance in all such matters to the police, expressing a certainty that the industrialists would not "be dissatisfied with its actions." As the meeting came to an end, Maklakov, according to the Society's record, invited the delegation "to call him directly over the telephone" in the event that any critical problems arose.[111]

Maklakov kept his word. Within a few weeks, the number of arrested strikers rose to 120, including all those members of the strike committee and other strike leaders at Simens i Gal'ske whom the police were able to identify.[112]

Under this kind of pressure, the desperate Simens i Gal'ske strikers could not hold out much longer. The report of the worker correspondent of Simens i Gal'ske in the *Pravda* of July 18 was already much darker in tone than the previous one. The strikers had nothing to eat. They were being put out of their living quarters for lack of rent money. If it had not been for the financial support of workers in other plants, they would long since have been forced to go back to work. As for the administration, it remained adamant about what had been the workers' most insistent, if symbolic demand: the cancellation of the May Day fines over which they had originally struck, and the inclusion of May Day on the list of recognized holidays. Still, intent on the strikers' unconditional surrender, the administration had finally succeeded in hiring a substantial number of strikebreakers, 299 by the date of this report. The strikebreakers were still "good-for-nothings (*oni ne kuda ne godiatsia*)," the Simens worker correspondent insisted, and the firm's customers were complaining about the failure to deliver their orders. While the strikebreakers' appearance had caused waverings among the strikers, a meeting attended by 800 of the strikers resolved to hold on, and not to send representatives to negotiate, until officially invited to do so by management. Only 18 of the workers attending reportedly voted against this resolution.[113]

The next few weeks witnessed the appearance in the labor press of reports of various desperate, but ultimately successful, attempts by the administration of Simens i Gal'ske to recruit strikebreakers to break finally the resistance of its workers; 20 locksmiths hired from the Moscow trolley park, who earlier reportedly had helped break the Moscow trolley strike (*Pravda*,

as was often its practice, listed the names of the evildoers); railroad techni-
cians from 500 *versty* around, who were offered jobs as trainees but turned
them down once they found out about the strike; even more students who
were otherwise unspecified.[114] There were also reports of strikebreakers re-
penting, quitting their jobs, and even asking for the strikers' forgiveness; as
well as more reports—right up to the very end—of mass meetings at which
the strikers, by overwhelming majorities, passed resolutions to continue
striking until all their demands were met. But what with the ever-growing
pressure of need, with as many as 600 strikebreakers at work in the two
plants of Simens i Gal'ske by the time the strike ended, and with the toll of
arrests of strikers by the more-than-ever zealous police mounting above
120—the morale of the remaining strikers undoubtedly began to waver even
before the strike was finally broken.[115]

In the files of the Department of Police, there is a report about one of the
last mass meetings of the Simens i Gal'ske strikers, held on July 27 (it is the
only one I have been able to find in its files), which reflects, probably far more
accurately than the articles in *Pravda*, the mood of these gatherings during
the last gasps of the strike. The Okhrana reported that this meeting, attended
by almost 1,000 of the workers in the two plants, gathered to escape (vainly)
the attention of the police. The first speaker, the worker Berezin, was still in
a militant mood, or at least sounded the appropriate militant notes. Reporting that a group of *mastery* (skilled workers) intended to open negotiations
with the administration in an effort to come to an agreement and resume
work, he insisted that the workers at Simens i Gal'ske should consider their
strike not simply as their own affair, but as a struggle of principle (*printsi-
pal'naia bor'ba*) between the workers of the capital and the St. Petersburg Society of Factory and Mill Owners. The other workers of the capital, to whom
leaflets were being sent out calling for collections in support of the Simens
strikers, would surely help them in their struggle. But the next speaker, the
worker Demin, was reportedly more skeptical. Berezin, he said, was living on
illusions, when he promised this financial assistance to his comrades; it was
not in evidence even though the Simens workers were now starving. It was
imperative to put an end to the strike and get back to work. A few more workers spoke, in support of the strike, the Okhrana agent reported, before the
chairman of the meeting put the issue to a vote. This time, only 12 raised their
hand in favor of continuing the strike; 2, against; while the rest of the huge
number attending abstained, thereby keeping the issue open. It was then decided, by a majority vote, to wait until the following Tuesday, and if no money was collected by then in support of the strike, to go back to work.

At this point, the Okhrana report stated, the strike leaders who had convoked the meeting, wanting to keep the workers present from reaching an
agreement to end the strike, gave the signal that the police were approaching. The workers in attendance started to flee, but then realizing that no police were there, gathered again, sought out their leaders, and demanded an
accounting of the strike fund currently in hand. It turned out that the strike
finance committee still had about 300 rubles, which were distributed on the
spot to the families of workers under arrest.

A small number of mimeographed leaflets, appealing to workers in all
the factories in St. Petersburg to come to the aid of the strikers of Simens i
Gal'ske were been distributed at the meeting. And the Okhrana report also
noted that the chairman of the strike finance committee had asked the representatives of local organizations of the PSR for some bombs that could be
disarmed, but would "make a big noise" when they exploded without doing
any harm (SD organizations were generally opposed to such tactics).

The Okhrana report concluded with the standard remark that the leaders and members of the strike committee still at large were to be arrested as
soon as they were identified.[116]

The end was not long in coming. The issue of *Pravda* of August 10 (23),
1912 carried a report of the strike's conclusion, "after three long months of
struggle." The report duly listed the pressures to which the strikers had finally succumbed—their desperate need, the strikebreakers, the arrests. It also
listed the terms for which they had finally settled. In contrast to most similar
strikes of the period, even the ones most arduously fought, these terms did
not add up, on paper at least, to complete, or at least abject, defeat.[117]

To the last, the administration had refused to lift the workers' May Day
fines, but it did agree in future to recognize May Day as a holiday "if the factory inspectors do not object." It refused to compensate the workers for the
wages they had lost during the strike, but agreed to give them an additional
three rubles at Christmas time (one ruble for each month of the strike!). Finally, and most important, the company agreed to take back all the striking
workers, without a medical examination, "to try to get arrested strikers released, and those deported from the capital, returned." This was not much
to show for three months of trials and suffering, but by comparison with the
outcome of the strikes at Pastor, at Rozenkrants, at Nobel, at the St. Petersburg Metallurgical Plant, and at Erikson, it was almost a moral victory.

"So ended the strike of three months, which taught the workers a great
deal, and which they will long remember," concluded *Pravda's* Simen i
Gal'ske's correspondent. "And now, all, as one, join a union, which will trace

for us the path to a rightful existence. (*A teper' vse, kak odin v soiuz, kotoryi nam ukazhet put' pravil'noi zhizni*)."[118]

Indeed, at least from the reports of their worker correspondents, it appears that in sharp contrast to the workers at Erikson, for example, the strikers of Simens i Gal'ske went back to work, their spirit remarkably intact. In their contest of will with their employer, they had gained some concessions, if mainly of a symbolic nature, and above all, they had won the respect, the admiration, of their fellow Petersburg workers, not to speak of their own. Judging from these same reports, their employers and supervisors were well aware of this. We have two descriptions in the labor press of the atmosphere at the Simens i Gal'ske plant immediately after the strike. They suggest the continued prevalence among the returning strikers of an extraordinary sense of independence, indeed of a continued sense of their own power. The Simens workers displayed this spirit in their dealings with strikebreakers and the latter responded in turn with remarkable circumspection in their contacts with the returning workers. I should note that the displays of these attitudes stood in glaring contrast to most contemporary descriptions in the labor press of the treatment and state of mind of returning strikers, even in other militant plants of the St. Petersburg metal-working industry, following the conclusion of unsuccessful strikes. For this reason, a second, more detailed, report of the situation at Simens i Gal'ske, three weeks following the conclusion of the strike, is worth rendering in full:

Three weeks have passed since the strike ended. On the surface, things have gone back to normal, but this is not really so. Strikebreakers, who are no longer of any significance to the administration, are being fired at any pretext [*na vse*]. The *malorazvitye rabochie* [the less advanced, and also probably most recently hired, unskilled workers] who became strikebreakers begged the *starye rabochie* [the workers of longer standing at the plant] for their forgiveness, and they are prepared to pay indemnities in support of repressed workers at the plant [those arrested, and sometimes deported]. But another group of strikebreakers, those who have engaged in such dirty deeds (*nizkoe delo*) before, are resisting, knowing full well that they will eventually have to fly out of the plant in dishonor, like a cork pops out of a bottle of sour cabbage soup.

Some foremen are doing everything they can to make peace between the *starye rabochie* and the strikebreakers. But everyone refuses to take on any strikebreaker as a helper. The friction is accentuated by the fact that the strikebreakers were hired at higher wages than the ex-strikers. How, under the circumstances, can the latter take them on as helpers?[119]

The reporter concluded on a darker note, observing that the returned strikers were upset over the fate of those of their fellow-workers who had been sentenced to administrative exile in the course of the strike. Despite its promises, the administration at Simens i Gal'ske had not lifted a finger to help bring them back.[120]

Notwithstanding this concluding note, it is evident that the returned Simens i Gal'ske workers did not feel—or act—like victims, left at the mercy of their employers and supervisors after the failure of their strike. As the *Pravda* report clearly indicated, their continued sense of autonomy stemmed in part from an economic reality: given their skills, no strikebreakers could be easily found to take their place, and they and their supervisors knew it. But as I suggested earlier, an equally important psychological reality was also involved: the Simens strikers did not feel morally beaten; their spirits were still whole; and of this too, both they and those who stood over them appeared almost tangibly aware.

V

On the Russian labor scene at this moment—the summer of 1912—the spirit of proud independence, and even self-affirmation, that many of the workers of Simens i Gal'ske continued to display after the conclusion of their unsuccessful three-month strike, was admittedly the exception rather than the rule. The beaten spirit reported among so many of the workers at Erikson, at Rozenkrants, at the St. Petersburg Metallurgical Plant, after the defeat of their strikes, their beaten spirit tinged with shame, according to their own workers' correspondents, was undoubtedly far more typical.

But to this cautionary observation, one should add a qualification. It is characteristic of this period, that even when in the wake of the defeat of their strike actions the workers' spirits appeared dampened or even broken, they often emerged, in a remarkably short time, miraculously mended. Indeed, already by the fall of 1912, a psychological mechanism—not uncommon in movements and periods of genuine revolt—was becoming manifest. The more a group of workers appeared crushed, humiliated, under the immedi-

ate burden of defeat, the more subsequently they would feel driven, impelled—precisely under the whip of their shame and resentment—to rebel
and affirm themselves, again and again, in a mood of steadily rising anger.

The phenomenon is discernible, even in the impersonal language of statistics. In the wake of their defeats of the spring and early summer of 1912 the
wave of the workers' economic strikes, which had risen so suddenly and dramatically in the wake of Lena, now abated equally dramatically, even among
workers in the stormy metal-working industry. But the slack was entirely
taken up in early fall by a new series of strikes and demonstrations, most of
them ostensibly directed at more specific political targets and more "offensive" in spirit than before. In early October, protest actions were launched
against the government annulment of the first stage (the elections of workers' *upolnomochennye*) of the elections to the State Duma in twenty-two of
the largest plants in St. Petersburg. Later that month, protest strikes broke
out against the sentences imposed on 142 sailors convicted by a court-
martial in Sebastapol of having plotted a mutiny of the Black Sea fleet; in
mid-November on the opening day of the Fourth Duma, another wave of
protest actions took place against the "Black Hundred," reactionary, composition of the Duma, and the inequity of the "System of the Third of June."
Finally, in December new strikes broke out in protest against the appoint-
ment (rather than the election) of worker representatives to the St. Petersburg Insurance Council, as well as against the government's persecution of
the labor press. Among the stratum of the workers of the capital class who
were at the center of this new storm of protest actions—the workers of St.
Petersburg's mechanical and metal-processing enterprises—these political
strikes and demonstrations also set off in early November a new if more
modest wave of ostensibly economic strikes.[121]

There were a number of notable features about this new flurry of economic strikes. First of all, it was clearly counter-seasonal in its timing in the
late fall, usually a period of slack rather than upsurge in both economic activity and labor unrest. Secondly, the "economic" strikes in the Petersburg
metal-processing industry, although marked as usual by demands for wage
increases, also provided the occasion for a new contest of wills and even
more naked conflict over authority. In part, its occasion was the extension
of demands that had already appeared in the strikes of the spring and early
summer for *vezhlivoe obrashchenie* (and specifically for the firing of supervisors accused of rude conduct or rude address), as well as for the recognition by management of the workers' elected representatives. But in some of
the strikes, the contest was now joined over an additional, equally explosive,

issue: the strikers' demand for the general elimination of the system of industrial fines in effect in their enterprises. Predictably, employers responded to this sweeping demand even more adamantly than to the workers' earlier claims—viewing it as a yet more glaring attempt to infringe on their
legitimate authority, on *their* right to operate their enterprises, *their* property, as they saw fit.

By this time, even the members of the Moscow Society of Manufacturers
who had responded with circumspection, if not approval, to their workers'
sympathy strikes in the wake of Lena, and who later in the spring had considered the possible advantages of dealing on a continuous basis with some
regularly elected representatives of their working force, now felt themselves
confronted by an intolerable assault. Notwithstanding the political liberalism
of some of their more prominent representatives (Riabushinskii, Konavalov)
and their earlier readiness to blame the labor disorders on the government
and the "abnormal conditions of public life," most of them began to view
their workers' political strikes as an unconscionable interference with the op-
eration of their enterprises, and as a factor contributing to the bitterness—
and ultimate insolubility—of economic disputes. In late November, therefore, a meeting of the Council of the Moscow Society of Manufacturers, after
receiving the latest statistical reports on the toll that political strikes had inflicted on the Moscow industrial district during the year, reportedly decided
to participate in a joint conference with representatives of the Societies of St.
Petersburg, the Baltic region, Poland, the Urals, and the industrial South to
work out effective joint measures against these strikes, which were inflicting
such heavy losses on the industrial enterprises of the Empire.[122]

In the fall of 1912, employers were not alone in expressing their concern
over the rash of workers' political strikes and demonstrations and the infu-
sion of ostensibly economic strikes with obviously noneconomic motifs. So,
by this time, did commentators in the Menshevik labor press. These commentators had originally responded to the explosion of the workers after
Lena with a joy and sense of hope comparable to that of their Bolshevik
counterparts. Writing shortly after the "grandiose political strikes" of April
and May, Fedor Dan had assessed them as not only "a turning point for the
Russian labor movement," but also "the beginning of the liquidation of the
Regime of the Third of June." Dan had even quoted gloatingly the observation of a *Rech'* editorial to the effect that the workers were now opposing
themselves to the rest of society, and that the working-class movement generally was assuming "a much more sharply defined class character" than it
had done in 1905. This, Dan argued, was indicative of the growing maturity

and capacity of the proletariat, and a testimonial to the successful work that
the Mensheviks had conducted, even during the years of reaction. Besides,
Rech' was being expediently silent about the other half of the picture. If the
workers were now opposing themselves to society, so society—including its
bourgeois intelligentsia—was now opposing itself to the workers:

> To the growing class maturity of the proletariat corresponds a
> growing class maturity of the bourgeoisie. And the "support" that
> now surrounds the labor movement has little in common with the
> foggy romantic support which in 1905 impelled *Osvobozhdenie* to
> exclaim: "How enchanting the workers are"; and Mr. Struve to de-
> clare triumphantly: "We have no enemies to the left . . . " The pro-
> letariat has ceased to appear "enchanting" in the eyes of bourgeois
> society, and the "support" of this society is confined to those min-
> utes when the proletarian movement constitutes a necessary factor
> in its own emancipation.[123]

Whatever the merits of this observation—delivered in the heady days
after Lena, by late fall, Menshevik commentators were already beginning to
express second thoughts about the *statechnyi azart*—the reckless, in their
view suicidal, character and tempo of the movement. "The masses cannot
strike 10–20 times a year," *Luch'* commented about the new outburst of
strikes, in early November. "This weakens them too much and deprives the
strike [weapon] of its significance as a very powerful tool." The recent strikes
had demonstrated, according to *Luch'*, that the masses had not yet "found
and mastered a perfected weapon for the political struggle."[124] To this "reckless" resort to political strikes and demonstrations, the Mensheviks already
opposed more "economical" and "rational" methods of mobilizing and organizing the workers, such as the "petition campaign" they conducted in
support of the Social-Democratic deputies' bills for the legalization of trade
unions and for the reform of the new system of labor insurance.

The Bolsheviks' response to this line of argument (even in the legal press
it was presented in only slightly disguised Aesopian language) was that by
their current criticism of political strikes and the emphasis they now laid as
a substitute for them on such slogans as *svoboda koalitsii* (freedom to form
alliances) and the petition campaign to be conducted on its behalf, the Mensheviks were sapping the process of revolutionary mobilization of the workers and fostering among them "constitutionalist illusions." After all, no legislation giving the workers genuine freedom to organize could conceivably

be passed under the existing political system, and to suggest that it could served only to "confuse" and "disarm" the working class. This was not to say that campaigns could not be launched in conjunction with the parliamentary activities of the Social Democrats' Duma faction, but they should be so conducted as to expose the hopeless paralysis of the regime of the Third of June, and not to foster any hopes of reform as long as this system was allowed to survive.

Underlying these differences about specific tactics, certain basic issues already clearly emerged in the conceptions that Bolsheviks and Mensheviks were advancing in their disputes about the new labor unrest. The Bolsheviks expressed delight about the ways in which, since early April, the waves of political and economic strikes had succeeded, overtaken, and ultimately reinforced one another, and indeed about the intermixture of economic and noneconomic motifs that both they and their Menshevik opponents discerned in the workers' individual strike actions. All this represented in their view a brilliant confirmation of the inextricable link between politics and economics which had characterized the development of the Russian labor movement ever since the inception of Russia's first revolution in 1905. And it was precisely the fusion of these two elements which, in turn, infused the workers' movement with its dynamic revolutionary potential. "Nothing so insures the life quality, the power, the massive character of the movement," Zinoviev editorialized in November 1912, "as the fact that economics goes side-by-side with politics, each reinforcing and strengthening the other."[125]

But it was precisely this intermixture of political and economic motifs in the strike movement that now openly alarmed some of the Menshevik commentators. Martov's older brother Ezhov, for many years a *praktik* of the open labor movement, worriedly observed but a few weeks before the publication of Zinoviev's editorial:

It is not sensible to complicate one's [political] protests with economic demands, any more than it is sensible to complicate a normal strike with demands of principle [i.e., political demands of a basically revolutionary character, L.H.]. A streak of economic strikes is now in front of us. It would be an irreparable error for the workers to bound them up with political actions. Such a mixture would affect harmfully both the workers' economic and political struggles.[126]

In these lines—triumphantly picked up by Zinoviev a few weeks later— Ezhov was expressing the concerns, understandable for a veteran *praktik* of the open labor movement, that the headlong course of the new labor unrest might set back the now barely reviving trade union movement for years to come. Zinoviev discerned a broader ideological and political meaning in these remarks, as well as in the Mensheviks' advocacy of such "perfected" weapons as the petition campaigns, in place of a continuous resort to political strikes:

> Two lines emerge from this vivid example. One leads to the substitution for general demands of exclusively constitutional reforms on the basis of the existing [political framework] [*na pochve dannogo*]. The other leads to a struggle for new foundations [*novaia pochva*— in Aesopian language, revolutionary change]. For a worker, for a consistent Social Democrat, the choice is not a difficult one.[127]

These concluding strokes of Zinoviev's editorial repeated, in barely disguised Aesopian language, the indictment that the Bolsheviks were directing at the Menshevik "Liquidators": that the latter had really ceased to be true revolutionaries; that the tactics they advocated were really "reformist" tactics—an indictment which fitted neatly with the earlier, now standard, accusation that the Mensheviks really favored the "liquidation" of the party's underground revolutionary organizations. In the case of Ezhov, who for almost two years had been taking a prominent part in the effort to revive the Menshevik underground through the establishment of *initsiativnye gruppy* in Russia's major cities, the indictment was, to say the least, unkindly. But implicit in the argument between the two men, there was indeed a genuine difference of basic viewpoints, even if this difference was still covered up by the corset of language and dogma.

The Bolsheviks had emerged from the experience of 1905 hardened in the conviction that the revolution for which they thirsted would have to be directed against *both* the state power and *all* the *tsensovye elementy* of existing, privileged, society—as Lenin put it, from "Pureshkevich to Miliukov." To be successful, it would need to mobilize the *nizi*—the workers and peasants—against the *verkhi,* the strata of "census" society intertwined with the state structure, and it would have to induce the *nizi* to overturn this whole structure, this whole edifice—and, as Zinoviev put it, establish a new framework—new foundations—in its place. To be sure, Lenin and the Bolsheviks still insisted on calling this cataclysmic overturn a bourgeois revolution— largely on the grounds that it would not immediately bring about the elimination of capitalism and the establishment of a socialist economic order,

especially in the countryside. But there was no doubt whatever that the issue of the peasantry and its economy aside, this "bourgeois" revolution
would have to be won over the opposition of the "bourgeoisie." Every word
and action of Lenin and his followers—including the fervent campaign that
they would conduct primarily against the Kadets in the elections to the
Fourth Duma—clearly suggested that under the nomenclature of "counter-
revolutionary bourgeoisie" the Bolsheviks were now prepared to include *all*
the political and social formations, however "liberal," of Russia's privileged
"census" society.

Almost all the Mensheviks, on the other hand, including those who in
1905 had indulged in the "youthful folly" of dreaming of a permanent revolution, had emerged from the crucible of Russia's first revolution, hardened
in the opposite conviction. They might now differ among themselves, and
indeed individually waver from month-to-month, as to whether a "revolutionary situation" was or was not at hand—and adjust their sights and their
tactics accordingly. They might even differ among themselves about precisely which elements of the "bourgeoisie" were now potentially revolutionary, and which were not; and a heretical few (such as Potresov) might even
question the validity of this term. But there was *one point* which few, if any
of them, dared to question ever since their hopes had come crashing down
on their heads in 1905: *to be successful,* to achieve any useful results, the next
revolutionary round would have to be fought by the Russian proletariat in
alliance with some significant elements of established "census" society, in
some combination—however pragmatic or even tenuous—with the political factions and parties representing the more "liberal" elements of society.
In the absence of such a condition, *there could not be* any genuinely "revolutionary situation" for there could not be any successful revolution. Once
again, the proletariat would find itself alone, and in its isolation, it would be
driven to exhaustion, and eventual defeat. Many considerations, conscious
and unconscious, entered into this conviction, which for most members of
the Menshevik faction had now become a conviction of instinct and of the
heart as well as of the head: a persistent, ingrained distrust of the Russian
peasantry, and of its potential as a revolutionary ally; an equally ineradica-
ble, if usually suppressed, sense of identification with the Russian intelligentsia—including its more established liberal elements; a profound dread
of the dark, savage, Russian past, as well as of the "uncultured" peasant
masses identified with it; an equally irrepressible sense that the Euro-
peanized society and culture that the Mensheviks—*praktiki* and ideologues
alike—were so anxious to build could not be successfully erected, at least at

first, without the collaboration, of precisely some of the more "cultured," privileged elements of Russian society on whose political elimination the Bolsheviks were now so intently set.

This is not the place for us to weigh the political and moral validity of these attitudes and of the conclusions to which they led. But we should take note of a crucial historical *fact* which was now discernible. It is that by the fall of 1912, it was already becoming evident even to the Mensheviks, that at least in Russia's major urban centers, and particularly in the capital, the Bolsheviks' conceptions, the tactics they advocated and the emotional notes they struck were now more in tune than were the Mensheviks' with the attitudes, the mood, the conduct that the industrial workers themselves were increasingly displaying in the still largely spontaneous expressions of their labor unrest.

And it could not be otherwise. The Mensheviks still insisted upon drawing distinctions between the political and economic struggles, between liberal allies in the political struggle (including, in the eyes of some Mensheviks at least, the "potentially revolutionary" bourgeoisie) and economic antagonists in the factory or plant—and ultimately their underlying distinction between the "bourgeois" and socialist revolutions. While perhaps such distinctions still bore some connection to current political realities, they no longer found—if indeed they ever had—any genuine correlatives in the workers' own psychological reality, in the reality of the workers' day-to-day experience and of the feelings that they drew from it.

For the reasons I have already described, practically every day, every hour, every minute of this experience confirmed the Russian workers in the instinct, and ultimately in the conviction, that they were locked in an irreconcilable conflict with all authority—with all those who stood politically, socially, or economically over them in the factory, on the streets of their industrial slums, and on the broad and elegant sidewalks of Nevskii Prospekt.

NOTES

PART 1. LENIN, MARTOV, AND THE ISSUE OF POWER

1   Z. Galili, A. Nenarokov and L. Haimson, eds., *Men'sheviki v 1917 godu*, 3 vols. (Moscow, 1994–96).

2.   See *Iskra*, no. 111, October 1905.

3.   Akselrod, in fact, had wanted to conclude a genuine alliance between the Mensheviks and the Kadets, notwithstanding what he described as the "politically backward" attitudes of Russia's working class. This political defeat of the Mensheviks was the inevitable result of his advocacy of this course. Generally, it became an invariable pattern during the prewar period, as well as subsequently, that the Bolsheviks suffered political defeat when they failed to exploit legal opportunities to improve the lot of the St. Petersburg working class, while the Mensheviks suffered equally predictable defeats when they sought to use these legal opportunities to conclude alliances with the Kadets.

4.   This article was written on November 2–4 (15–17), 1905, but was not found, according to the editors of Lenin's works, until the fall of 1940. See V.I. Lenin, *Polnoe Sobranie Sochinenii*, 5th ed., (Moscow, 1959–66) [henceforth *PSS*], vol. 12, note 42, pp. 443–44. For the text of the article itself, see pp. 59–70.

5.   Ibid., pp. 63–64, 66–67.

6.   *Proletariat*, no. 25, November 16 (3),1905, in *PSS*, vol. 12, p. 80.

7.   "O reorganizatsii partii," *Novaia Zhizn'*, nos. 9, 13, 14, published on November 10, 15, and 16,1905. In *PSS*, vol. 12, pp. 83–93.

8.   Ibid., p. 87.

9.   Ibid., pp. 92–93.

10. *Novaia Zhizn'*, no. 11, November 12, 1905, in *PSS* vol. 12, pp. 94–98.

11. Petr A. Garvi, *Zapiski Sotsial Demokrata (1906–1921)*, Russian Archival Series, Russian Institute, Columbia University (Newton, MA: Oriental Research Partners, 1982), pp. 23–24.

12. As was his wont, Lenin attributed his statement to "a group of leading figures of the RSDRP" who had convened to discuss the tasks of revolutionary Social Democracy, and particularly those of Russian Social Democracy, in response to the war.

13. See "Mertvyi shovinizm i zhivoi sotsializm," *PSS*, vol. 26, pp. 98–105.

14. "Sotsializm i voina (Otnoshenie RSDRP k voine)," *PSS*, vol. 26, pp. 307–50.

15. It was already common knowledge among the leaders of the Menshevik party that, with Lenin's blessings, Stalin had been involved in some of these "expropriations" of private banks. In addition to the controversy over the Schmidt inheritance, which the Bolsheviks stubbornly held onto in toto although it was supposed to be divided equally between them and the Mensheviks, this caused Martov to break his personal relations with Lenin, and indeed to cease speaking to him. In this connection, my late friend Alexander Erlich, the son of G.M. Erlich, the leader of the Bund, described to me the following episode, which had been recounted to him by his father. G.. M. Erlich had sat at a table between Lenin and Martov on the eve of the war. Since Martov refused to speak with Lenin at that time, Erlich had to play the role of an intermediary. Thus, Lenin would lean over to Erlich and ask him to say to Martov, "Please tell comrade Martov . . . " and in turn, Martov would lean over to Erlich and ask him, "Please tell comrade Lenin . . . " (The Bund was the leading political organization in the Jewish "pale," the territories of western European Russia and eastern Poland, to which, with the exception of the educational and property requirements that it spelled out, the vast majority of the Jewish population was confined up to the fall of the tsarist regime. G. M. Erlich continued to be the leader of the Bund during the period of Poland's independence after the First World War. Following the invasion and occupation of Poland by German and Soviet troops in 1939, Erlich became a member of the Polish government-in-exile in London. In 1942, he was lured to the Soviet Union at the invitation of Stalin, promptly arrested, and executed.)

16. See Israel Getzler, *Martov* (Cambridge: Cambridge University Press, 1967), pp. 145–46. Getzler refers to the text of the resolution adopted at the conference in Kienthal, published in English translation in I. H. Gankin and H. H. Fisher, *The Bolsheviks in the World War: The Origins of the Third International* (Stanford: Stanford University Press, 1940), as well as to the unpublished report on the morning session of the third day of the conference reported in the papers of Robert Grimm, deposited in the archives of the International Institute for Social History in Amsterdam.

17. The citation of Martov by Getzler is also drawn from the papers of Robert Grimm in the archives of the International Institute for Social History, Amsterdam. Indeed, these papers suggest that the third section of the resolution, on the preservation of the international socialist bureau adopted at the conference in Kienthal, was drawn up by Lapinskii, who would emerge in 1917 as one of the major figures of the group of Menshevik Internationalists led by Martov. See Getzler, *loc. cit.*

18. On Martov's writings on the subject, see *inter alia*, the article "Bor'ba s imperializmom i russkie zadachi," published in *Izvestiia* (Geneva), no. 6, 12 September 1916.

19. RGASPI (formerly the Central Archives of the CPSU in Moscow), f. 366, op. 1, del. 51, ll.43–44.
20. RGASPI, f. 362, op. 1, del. 19, l. 51, cited in the very estimable biography of Martov published by I. Kh. Urilov, *Iu. O. Martov, politik i istorik* (Moscow: Nauka, 1997), p. 231. I must note, to his credit, that Urilov is an amateur historian who has conducted his historical studies while pursuing a very successful career as a businessman.
21. RGASPI, f. 362, op. 1, d. 19, ll. 53, 64, as cited by Urilov, *Martov*, pp. 200–01.
22. See *Sotsialisticheskii Vestnik*, nos. 6, 7, and 8, 1961.
23. The Russian-language edition was published in a pamphlet entitled, "Imperializm kak vysshaia stadiia kapitalizma," (Petrograd, 1917). See *PSS*, vol. 27, pp. 299–426.
24. According to the preface Lenin had engaged in the research for this work in the libraries of Bern and Zurich from late 1915 through late 1916. Upon the completion of the manuscript, Lenin sent it to M. N. Pokrovskii in Paris, in order to have it submitted to a series put out by the editors of the French publishing firm Parvus on western European states during the First World War. The pamphlet finally appeared as a book in Russia, with a foreword written by Lenin, on April 25, 1917, i.e., barely a week and a half after his arrival in Petrograd.
25. *PSS*, vol. 27, pp. 420–26.
26. This was also the meaning of Lenin's statement in his "Farewell Address to the Swiss Workers," that he would not live to see the day of the triumph of socialism. This statement has been incorrectly interpreted by many Western commentators to mean that Lenin thought that he would not live to see the Bolshevik seizure of power in Russia.
27. RGASPI, f. 362, op. 1, d. 51, ll. 129–1300b.
28. Ibid., ll. 131–330b.
29. Headed Lenin's April Theses (as recorded in his article, "O zadachikh proletariata v dannoi revoliutsii," published in *Pravda*, April 7, 1917.) See *PSS*, vol. 31, pp. 113–116, and Appendix I, below.
30. See *PSS*, vol. 31, pp. 9–59.
31. "Pis'ma o taktike," in *PSS*, vol. 31, pp. 131–44.
32. Lenin's speech on the political situation ("O tekushchem momente") at the Bolsheviks' April Conference also included the curious observation that the English capitalists had supported the overthrow of the tsarist regime, and indeed, conspired to this purpose with Guchkov, Miliukov, and the Army's High Command. See *PSS*, vol. 31, pp. 257–58.
33. Ibid., p. 258.
34. Ibid., pp. 251–52.
35. Ibid., pp. 344–45.
36. Ibid., p. 363.
37. Ibid., pp. 427–28.
38. Ibid., p. 451.
39. "Nabroski k tezisam rezoliutsii o sovetakh," *PSS*, vol. 31, pp. 382–86.
40. "Vvedenie k rezoliutsii sed'moi (aprel' skoi) vserossiskoi konferentsii RSDRP (o)," in *PSS*, vol. 31, pp. 454–57.

41. This telegram, dated April 27, stated: "Cable to Chkheidze our view that any participation in the coalition government is impossible." See *Men'sheviki v 1917*, vol. 1, p. 250.

42. *Men'sheviki v 1917*, vol. 1, pp. 357–58.

43. Letter to N.S. Kristi dated May 22, 1917. See *Men'sheviki v 1917*, *vol.* 1, pp. 456–59. The first issue of the Internationalists' journal, *Letuchii Listok*, to which Martov referred in this letter, appeared in late May 1917.

44. Ibid.

45. It is notable that one of the arguments that Tsereteli had voiced in support of military offensive in the debates on this issue in the Menshevik O.K. was the need to give a positive response to the pressure of the British government, given Russia's dependence on Britain's financial support for the Russian economy! See the O.K. protocols "Zasedanie O.K. 28 May, 1917," in *Men'sheviki v 1917*, vol. 1, pp. 487–93. To be sure, Tsereteli continued to emphasize in these debates the need to press Russia's Western allies for a review of the secret treaties negotiated with them by the tsarist government. But he did not make this review a precondition for the military offensive to be launched by the Russian army. Rather, he reversed the order of these preconditions: i.e., he argued that the launching of a military offensive by the Russian army was a precondition for a serious consideration by the Western allies of Russia's request for the publication of the secret treaties , and by the same token for a review of the terms for the conclusion of a peace agreement with the Central Powers.

46. See "Deklaratsiia men'shevikov internatsionalistov," *Letuchii Listok Men'shevikov Internatsionalistov*, no. 1, Petrograd, May 1917, in *Men'sheviki v 1917*, vol. 1, pp. 508–13.

47. *Izvestiia Soveta Rabochikh i Soldatskikh Deputatov*, no. 82, June 3, 1917, as cited in *Men'sheviki v 1917*, vol. 1, p. 527.

48. Martov to Kristi, dated 17 (30) June, in *Men'sheviki v 1917*, vol. 1, pp. 590–91.

49. Ibid.

50. Ibid.

51. *PSS*, vol. 32, p. 267.

52. Ibid., p. 268.

53. Ibid., p. 266.

54. Ibid., p. 275.

55. *PSS*, vol. 32, pp. 275–76. Text originally printed in *Pravda*, nos. 82 and 83, June 15 (28) and 16 (29), 1917.

56. *Pravda*, no. 81, June 13 (26), 1917.

57. Alexander Rabinowitch, *Prelude to Revolution: The Petrograd Bolsheviks and the July 1917 Uprising* (Bloomington: Indiana University Press, 1968).

58. For the complaint of the Petrograd Committee, and Lenin's clumsy reply in lieu of an apology, see the protocols of the Petrograd Committee of June 11 (24), 1917. Notably, this text was published for the first time only in 1923, in the journal *Krasnaia Letopis'*, no. 9.

59. See Rabinowitch, *Prelude to Revoltution,* p. 95.

60. It is notable that this proposal had been originally advocated by Chernov's predecessor as Minister of Agriculture, the Kadet Shingarev.

61 GARF, f. 6978, op.1, del. 138, ll.13–24.

62. Ibid., ll.10–11.

63. This article, drafted by Lenin under the title, "Na chto mogli rasschitivat' Kadety, ukhodia iz ministerstva," was published in *Proletarskoe Delo*, 102, July 28 (15), 1917. See *PSS*, vol. 32, pp. 406–07.

64. It is ironic, of course, that throughout this period, Lenin was in fact receiving money from Parvus in Stockholm, whose funding could unquestionably be traced to German sources, a fact of which Lenin was undoubtedly aware. Yet Lenin would have dismissed any criticism of the support provided by Parvus to the Bolsheviks as a symptom of "petty bourgeois morality." The difference, from Lenin's point of view, was that Parvus was a genuine revolutionary, whose acquaintance with Lenin (and Trotsky) dated back to 1905. Under the circumstances, Lenin undoubtedly considered that the funding he received from Parvus, while obtained indirectly from German sources, would also contribute eventually to the success of a socialist revolution in Germany.

65. "K lozungam," written in mid–July 1917, was originally published in pamphlet form by the Kronstadt Committee of the RSDRP(b). See *PSS*, vol. 34, pp. 10–17.

66. Ibid., p. 16.

67. A stenographic copy of the protocols of the Menshevik "Unification Congress," including Martov's speech, is in RGASPI, f. 275, op. 1, del.2. A summary version was published in *Rabochaia Gazeta*, no. 139, August 22, 1917.

68. Ibid.

69. Written on September 3 (16), 1917 and published on September 6 (19), 1917, in *Rabochii Put'*, no. 3.

70. See *PSS*, vol. 34, pp. 138–39.

71. In this, as in so many other cases prior to the Bolshevik seizure of power, the divisions that emerged in the representative organs of "revolutionary democracy," and even the relative closeness of the vote, had been prefigured by those that had previously appeared on the same issues within the Menshevik party's Central Committee, and in this instance, as well, at a two-day meeting of the Menshevik delegation to the Democratic Conference held on the eve of its opening. In the course of this two-day meeting, the Menshevik delegates had originally voted in support of a resolution in favor of coalition by a vote of 81–77, but following its adoption had endorsed a compromise resolution introduced by Dan, rejecting coalition with representatives of the Kadet party by a more substantial vote of 86–51, with five abstentions. To the best of my knowledge, no precise breakdown of the votes of the Menshevik delegates at the Democratic Conference on the issue of power was ever recorded. But it appears likely that they reflected roughly the same voting patterns as those that were subsequently recorded on this issue, but a few weeks later, by the delegates to the Pre-parliament, for which a breakdown was provided. In this breakdown of the vote in the Pre-parliament, the delegates representing local Soviets of Workers' Deputies were recorded as voting overwhelmingly in support for the

formation of an "all democratic" government, while those representing organizations in the countryside, including local Soviets of Peasants' Deputies and rural cooperatives, were recorded as continuing to vote substantially in support of coalition. See also *PSS*, vol. 34, pp. 133–39.

72. For a description of these negotiations, see my introduction to *Men'sheviki v 1917*, vol. 3, pt. 2, pp. 17–58.

73. Dan's article appeared in *Izvestiia*, no. 184, September 29, 1917; Martov's editorial was published in *Iskra*, no. 2, October 3, 1917.

74. A full text of the platform presented by Martov in this number of *Iskra* is to be found in *Men'sheviki v 1917*, vol. 3, pt. 1, pp. 381–84.

75. Ibid., pp. 382–83.

76 Ibid., p. 383.

77. See GARF, f. 8978, op. 1, del. 129, ll. 4–14, for the original corrected copy of this resolution. Its text was published in *Iskra*, no. 3, October 4, 1917.

78. GARF, f. 1244, op.. 2, del. 24, ll.. 156–57, contains the stenographic record of Martov's speech. A copy of it appeared in *Izvestiia*, no. 192, October 8, 1917.

79. The comments of various Menshevik leaders are recorded in "Neskol'ko Inter-v'iu po povovu ukhoda bol'shevikov iz Predparliamenta. Zapiski G. Likhten-shteina. 7 October." In GARF, f. 1244, op. 2, del. 24, ll. 156–57.

80. In his public statements, Martov chose to consider this outcome less dramatically than his opponents, electing to view it as a temporary development. He was probably following the tactics, outlined earlier in his letter to Kristi, of refraining from precipitating an open split in the Menshevik party until he had won a majority of its members over to his side.

81. The full text of the resolution proposed by the Menshevik Internationalists on the issue of the country's defense capability was published in *Iskra*, no. 4, October 17, 1917.

82. *Izvestiia*, no. 198, October 16, 1917.

83. The text of this joint resolution was published in *Izvestiia* and *Rabochaiia Gazeta* on October 25, 1917.

84. In an article that he published in Berlin well after his emigration to Germany, entitled "Poslednie dni Vremennogo Pravitel'stva," (*Letopis' Revoliutsii*, no. 1, 1923), Fedor Dan recounted a visit to Kerensky's headquarters to which he induced the chairman of the Pre-parliament, Avksentiev, to join him, to explain to the embittered premier why he and the majority of the other members of the Pre-parliament had voted against his request that they endorse his demand for full powers to suppress the Bolshevik uprising. When Kerensky finally received them after a long delay, and while he demonstratively continued to pore over maps of the capital to draw up his battle plan, Dan sought to explain to him that any endorsement of his demand by the Pre-parliament would have been worthless in the absence of tangible signs, such as the immediate posting of announcements on the walls of the capital of the decision of the Provisional Government to take immediate action to satisfy the demands of the population on such burning issues as the land question and the struggle for peace. Acting as if he were taking no notice of Dan's explanation,

Kerensky continued to pore over the maps, drawing up his plans for the defense of the capital.

85. It is notable that the text of this resolution was published for the first time only in 1922, in *Proletarskaia Revoliutsiia*, no. 10. See *PSS*, vol. 34, pp. 391–93.

86. Sections 1–3, and 5 of this article were published in *Rabochii Put'*, no. 30, October 20 (7), 1917. The restricted sixth section was first published only in 1924. See *PSS*, vol. 34, pp. 272–83.

87. Ibid., p. 277.

88. Ibid., pp. 279–80.

89. Ibid., p. 281.

90. Ibid., pp. 281–82. Emphases in original.

91. Ibid., pp. 282–83.

92. A note to Lenin's works explains that by "the proposal from Minsk," Lenin meant the proposal made by Sverdlov at the previous meeting of the Central Committee to send a revolutionary corps to Petrograd to support the uprising. We should note that the text of Lenin's speech was published for the first time only in 1922, in *Proletarskaia Revoliutsiia*, no. 10, as was the text of the resolution itself. See *PSS*, vol. 34, pp. 391–93.

93. Kamenev and Zinoviev's remarks were recorded in *Protokoly Tsentral'nogo Komiteta RSDRP(b), Avgust 1917-Fevral' 1918* (Moscow, 1958) pp. 83–86.

94. *PSS*, vol. 34, p. 394.

95. Ibid.

96. Ibid., p. 395.

97. Ibid., p. 396.

98. Ibid.

99. Lenin's thinly disguised account of this meeting, including his exchanges with his critics, is presented in an account titled, "Letter to Comrades," written on 18 October 1917, but published for the first time only on 1 November 1927, in *Pravda*, no. 250. See *PSS*, vol. 34, pp. 398–416.

100. Ibid.

101. *Protokoly Tsentral'nogo Komiteta*, pp. 83–92.

102. Written on October 24, 1917 but published for the first time only in 1924. Lenin's note containing these words was formally addressed to the party's Central Committee, but his instructions to Krupskaia indicated that it was to be distributed to a wider readership, including the members of the Petrograd City Committee. See *PSS*, vol. 34, pp. 435–36.

103. The third and fourth clauses of the resolutions were equally indicative of the mood of the Menshevik delegates. They stated: "3. While responding negatively to the Bolsheviks' action we must also condemn the policies of the government that provoked it. 4. Any attempt by the government to repress the Bolsheviks' action by force of arms must be rebuffed." An additional resolution, against the use of force was tabled by 39 votes to 6, with 12 abstentions. See *Men'sheviki v 1917*, vol. 3, pt. 2, p. 227.

104. See *Novaia Zhizn'*, October 26, 1917.

105. See *PSS*, vol. 34, p. 504, note 131.

106. A photocopy of this cable is to be found in Rabinowitch, *Bolsheviks Come to Power,* p. 175.

107. The shots to which Dan referred were fired by the cruiser *Aurora* which, in the course of the day, had cruised down the Neva to face the Winter Palace. These shots were likely blanks (which sounded louder than real shots) and if so, only added to the dramatic effect.

108. *Izvestiia*, no. 207, October 26, 1917.

109. *Vtoroi Vserossiiskii s"ezd sovetov* (Moscow-Leningrad, 1928), p. 4.

110. *Pravda*, no. 170, October 27, 1917; *Izvestiia*, no. 208, October 27, 1917.

111. *Izvestiia*, no. 207, October 26, 1917; *Vtoroi Vserossiiskii s"ezd sovetov*, pp. 36–37.

112. *Izvestiia*, no. 208, October 27, 1917; *Vtoroi Vserossviskii s"ezd sovetov*, p. 37.

113. *Men'sheviki v 1917*, vol. 3, pt. 2, p. 241; *Vtoroi Vserossiiskii s"ezd sovetov*, pp. 39–40.

114. *Izvestiia*, no. 207, October 26, 1917.

115. *Vtoroi Vserossiiskii s"ezd sovetov*, pp. 42–43.

116. Ibid. pp. 43–44.

117. Ibid.

118. Ibid., pp. 45–46.

119. *Men'sheviki v 1917*, vol. 3, pt. 2, p. 244.

120. *Izvestiia*, no. 208, October 27, 1917; no. 209, October 28, 1917; see also Leopold H. Haimson, "The Problem of Social Identities in Early Twentieth Century Russia," *Slavic Review*, vol. 47, no. 1 (Spring 1988): 1–20; and Haimson, "The Problem of Social Identities in Early Twentieth Century Russia: Observations on the Commentaries by Alfred Rieber and William Rosenberg," *Slavic Review*, vol. 47, no. 3 (Autumn, 1988): 512–17.

121. *Vtoroi Vserossiiskii s"ezd sovetov*, pp. 80–82.

122. *Vtoroi Vserossiiskii s"ezd sovetov* p. 82; *Men'sheviki v 1917*, vol. 3, pt. 2, p. 249.

123. The protocols have been preserved in TsGASPb, formerly the archives of the CPSU in St. Petersburg.

PART II. THE WORKER'S MOVEMENT AFTER LENA

1. See *Novoe Vremia*, no. 12954, April 6 (19), 1912; *Russkiia Vedomosti*, no. 80, April 6 (19), 1912. The number of casualties continued to grow in subsequent reports. The names of 170 dead and 196 wounded are listed in V. Vladimirova, ed., *Lenskie sobytiia 1912 goda (Dokumenty i materialy)* (Moscow, 1925), pp. 89–91.

2. *Golos Moskvy*, no. 81, April 7, 1912.

3. *Novoe Vremia*, no. 12954, April 6 (19), 1912, no. 12955, April 7 (20), 1912.

4. Ibid., no. 12955, April 7 (20), 1912.

5. Ibid, no. 12958, April 10 (23), 1912.

6. Ibid.

7. Ibid.

8. See "Sostav komissii Senatora Manukhina i vyderzhki iz doklada Manukhina," in *Lenskie sobytiia*, pp. 217–218. The full report is in *Vsenoddanneishii Otchet chlena Gosudarstvennogo Soveta Senatora Manukhina po ispolneniiu vysochaishe*

vozlozhennogo na nego 27 aprelia 1912 goda rassledovaniia o zabastovke na Lenskikh promyslakh (St. Petersburg, 1912). On the conditions of work at Lena in the subsequent sections of Manukhin's report, see also "Otchet chlenu gosudarstvennogo soveta Senatoru Manukhinu starshego fabrichnogo inspektora I.N. Gorbunova," in *Leninskie sobytiia*, pp. 7–18.

9. See A.M. Nikitin, *Pravda o Lenskikh sobytiakh* (Kharkov, 1924), pp. 119–20.

10. See "Perepiska irkutskogo gubernatora Bantysha," in *Lenskie sobytiia*, pp. 94–111.

11. Ibid., pp. 54–55.

12. *Vsenaddanneishii Otchet Manukhina*, pp. 46–53; *Lenskie sobytiia*, pp. 89–93.

13. *Lenskie sobytiia*, pp. v–lxxiv, 196–254.

14. See *Utro Rossii*, no. 83, April 12, 1912.

15. Ibid.; *Novoe Vremia*, no. 12960, April 12 (25), 1912; *Russkiia Vedomosti*, no. 85, April 12, 1912; *Golos Moskvy*, no. 85, April 12, 1912.

16. Gosudarstvennaia Duma, *Stenograficheskii otchet*, Tretyi sozvy, sessiia V, zasedanie 99, April 9, 1912, cols. 1666–74.

17. Ibid., cols. 1674–1675.

18. Ibid., cols. 1675–76.

19. Ibid., col. 1679.

20. Ibid., col. 1684.

21. Ibid., cols. 1685–87.

22. Ibid., cols. 1687–89.

23. Ibid., cols. 1689–90.

24. Ibid., cols. 1690–94.

25. Ibid., cols. 1698–1700.

26. Ibid., col. 1713.

27. Ibid., col. 1714.

28. Ibid., cols. 1826–30.

29. *Russkiia Vedomosti*, no. 85, April 12, 1912.

30. *Golos Moskvy*, no. 85, April 12, 1912.

31. *Stenograficheskii otchet*, cols. 1941–43.

32. Ibid., cols. 1944–45.

33. Ibid., cols. 1948–53.

34. Ibid., col. 1953.

35. Ibid., cols. 1952–53.

36. Ibid., cols. 1953–1963.

37. Ibid., col. 1963.

38. The text of this reprimand, whose existence was widely reported in the contemporary press, is reproduced *in extenso* in Nikitin, *Pravda o Lenskikh sobytiakh*, pp. 119–20.

39. *Stenograficheskii otchet*, cols. 1956–60. See also the demands listed in the Manukhin report in *Leninskie sobytiia*, pp. 205–07.

40. Ibid., col. 1963.

41. Ibid., cols. 1968–69.

42. Ibid., cols. 1969–1974.

43. *Novoe Vremia*, no. 12960, April 12 (25), 1912.

44. Ibid., *Russkiia Vedomosti*, no. 85, April 12, 1912.

45. *Russkiia Vedomosti*, no. 85, April 12, 1912.

46. Ibid., no. 86, April 13, 1912.

47. N. Lopatin, "U mogili," *Utro Rossii*, no. 83, April 10, 1912.

48. Ibid.

49. *Golos Moskvy*, no. 86, April 13 (26), 1912.

50. GARF, fond DP, OO 1912, del. 342, ll. 16–17. Report of St. Petersburg DP, O.O., no. 5, 408, April 12, 1912.

51. Ibid.

52. Report of St. Petersburg, O.O., no. 5537, in ibid., l. 39.

53. *Russkiia Vedomosti*, no. 87, April 14 (27), 1912; *Novoe Vremia*, no. 12962, April 14 (27), 1912.

54. The details of this description of the demonstration of April 15 are pieced together from the reports of the St. Petersburg O.O. of April 15, 1912 (f. DP, OO, 1912, del. 342, ll. 31–33; *Rech'*, no. 103, April 16 (29) 1912, and the dispatch of the St. Petersburg Telegraph Agency, printed in *Utro Rossii*, no. 89, April 17, 1912.

55. Reports of St. Petersburg O.O. of April 16, 17, and 18, in GARF, fond DP, OO, 1912, del. 342. See also official reports of St. Petersburg Telegraph Agency published in the St. Petersburg press of April 17, 18, and 19.

56. Report of St. Petersburg O.O. of April 11, 1912, in GARF, fond DP, OO, 1912, del. 342, l. 15.

57. A number of protest resolutions sent by provincial workers to the Social Democratic deputies in the Duma are cited in GARF, fond DP, OO, 1912, dela 307 and 342. 1912.

58. Report no. 589, 2 May 1912, in GARF, fond DP, OO, 1912, del. 342, l. 143.

59. GARF, Report of St. Petersburg O.O., 2 May 1912, no. 6559, fond D–4, no. 61, ch. 2, 1912, t.l (St. Petersburg Guberniia: Rabochee dvizhenie). Other details about the May Day demonstrations in Petersburg in 1912 are drawn from *Rech'*, no. 119, May 3 (16), and *Pravda*, no. 9, May 3 (16), 1912.

60. *Rech'*, no. 127, May 11 (24), 1912.

61. Ibid.

62. GARF, Report of Moscow O.O., April 17, 1912, in fond DP, OO 1912, del. 342, l. 98.

63. *Novoe Vremia*, no. 12981, May 3 (16), 1912.

64. Ibid.

65. Ibid.

66. *Rech'*, no. 106, April 19 (May 2), 1912.

67. See *Utro Rossii*, nos. 102 and 104, May 4 and 8, 1912; also *Pravda*, no. 12, May 6 (19), 1912.

68. GARF, Report of St. Petersburg O.O., May 8, 1912, no. 6945, in f. 102, D–4, no. 61, ch.2, 1912.

69. GARF, Report of St. Petersburg O.O., May 16, 1912, no. 7358, in fond DP, OO, 1912, del. 342, t. 2, l. 196.

70. GARF, fond 102, DP, D–4, no. 61, ch. 2, 1912, t. 1, ll. 115, 164–165.

71. *Pravda*, no. 25, May 29 (June 11), 1912. See also RGIA, f. 150, del. 352, *passim*.

72. GARF, fond 102, DP, D–4, no. 61 ch.2, 1912, t.1, l. 171.

73. *Pravda*, no. 22, May 25 (June 7), 1912.

74. Ibid., no. 42, June 17 (30), 1912.

75. *Pravda* no. 96, August 25 (September 7), 1912.

76. See N. Sibirskii (K.N. Samoilova), "Vezhlivoe obrashchenie," *Pravda*, no. 15, May 10 (23), 1912.

77. Unless otherwise cited, I am indebted for the quotations cited in this part of my discussion to the articles written during these months in the periodical *Sovremennyi Mir* by the remarkable contemporary observer of the labor scene, L.M. Kleinbort. See "Ocherki rabochei demokratii," no. 4 (April, 1913); no. 5 (May–June, 1913).

78. *Pravda*, no. 64, July 13 (26), 1912.

79. Kleinbort, *op. cit.*

80. *Russkiia Vedomosti*, quoted in *Rech'* no. 119, May 3 (16), 1912.

81. *Pravda*, no. 56, July 4 (17), 1912.

82. Ibid., no. 105, August 31 (September 13), 1912.

83. Quoted in L. M. Kleinbort, "Ocherki rabochei demokratii. Stat'ia pervaia." *Sovremennyi Mir*, no. 4 (April, 1913): 22–45.

84. *Pravda*, no. 58, July 8 (19), 1912.

85. Ibid., no. 62, July 11 (24), 1912.

86. Ibid., no. 55, July 3 (16), 1912.

87. The findings of these quantitative analyses are summarized in an appendix to this volume. See also L. Haimson, "Labor Unrest in Imperial Russia on the Eve of the First World War," in L. Haimson and C. Tilly, eds., *Strikes, Wars, and Revolutions in an International Perspective* (Cambridge, UK and Paris, 1989), pp. 500–11; L. Haimson and R. Petrusha, "Two Strike Waves in Imperial Russia, 1905–1907, 1912–1914," in ibid. pp. 101–66; and L. Haimson and E. Brian, "Labor Unrest in Imperial Russia during the First World War: A Quantitative Analysis and Interpretation," in L. Haimson and G. Sapelli, eds., *Strikes, Social Conflict and the First World War* (Milan, 1992), pp. 389-452.

88. On this point, see my article, "The Problem of Social Stability in Urban Russia, 1905–1917," *Slavic Review*, 23, no. 4 (December 1964), pp. 640–41, as well as the findings of the statistical analyses by Haimson, Ronald Petrusha, and Eric Brian, summarized in the appendix to this volume. See also my more recent article, "'The Problem of Political and Social Stability on the Eve of War and Revolution' Revisited," *Slavic Review* 59, no. 4 (Winter 2000), pp. 848–75.

89. A contemporary study of literacy among workers in Moscow *guberniia* by Kuzmin-Lanin indicates that among male *podrostki* (i.e., workers under the age of 18), 93% were literate, while the figure for the age group between 35 and 40 was 70%; among women, the comparable figure for *podrostki* was 75%, while only 10% of women between 35 and 40 were literate. In St. Petersburg the level of literacy among all these groups was notably higher, and we can surmise that literacy among workers under 21 was practically universal. See "Gramotnost' rabochikh," *Pravda*, no. 105, August 31 (September 13), 1912. See also data pre-

sented by Haimson and Petrusha, *op. cit.*, and especially in the analysis of the data on literacy of peasants in the St. Petersburg 1910 municipal census, discussed by Haimson and Brian.

90. L. M. Kleinbort, "Ocherki rabochei demokratii (Stat'ia vtoraia)," *Sovremennyi Mir*, no. 5, May–June, 1913, pp. 151–52, 154.

91. Kleinbort, "Ocherki, rabochei demokratii (Stat'ia pervaia)," pp. 40–45.

92. V. Sh-r' (Sher'), "Nashe professional'noe dvizhenie za posledniye dva goda," *Bor'ba*, nos. 3–4, 1914.

93. No detailed statistical data are available about the pattern of rural immigration for the years after 1910. But the pattern I have described is clearly established by the previous decade, and can be presumed to have been substantially accelerated during the years of rapid industrial expansion on the eve of the First World War. For the relevant statistical data on the immediately preceding years, see A. G. Rashin, *Formirovanie rabochego klassa Rossii* (Moscow, 1958), pp. 438–39.

94. As G.T. Robinson pointed out many years ago, the Stolypin land legislation enabled individual householders in the repartitional commune to obtain under certain conditions "a permanent and more-or-less unified holding against the unanimous opposition of the communal assembly. Similar conditions obtained for those repartitional communes which were converted to hereditary tenure under the Arbitrary Dissolution Law of 1910, and they were unquestionably put to full use by various zealous provincial officials responsible for the implementation of *zemleustroistvo*." See G. T. Robinson, *Rural Russia Under the Old Regime* (New York, 1932), p. 219; see also note 28, p. 305.

95. L. M. (Martov), "Narodniki i peterburgskoe rabochee dvizhenie," *Severnaia Rabochaia Gazeta*, March 28, 1914; and "Tak i est'," ibid. April 12, 1914.

96. *Russkaia Mysl'*, June 1913.

97. The seizure of control by the Bolsheviks of St. Petersburg's Union of Metal Workers (*Soiuz Metallistov*) in November 1913 was one of the most celebrated episodes in this struggle.

98. *Pravda*, no. 24, May 27 (June 9), 1912.

99. Ibid.

100. RGIA, f. 150, op. 1, del. 352, passim.

101. Ibid.

102. *Utro Rossii*, no. 102, May 4 (17), 1912; and *Pravda*, no. 12, May 6 (19), 1912.

103. RGIA, f. 150, op. 1, del. 352, ll. 83–99. The text of the convention was eventually published in *Metallist*, no. 21, 1912, and *Pravda*, no. 90, August 14 (27), 1912.

104. *Pravda*, no. 46, June 21 (July 4), 1912.

105. *Pravda*, no. 18, May 20 (June 2), 1912; and no. 20, May 23 (June 5), 1912.

106. The details about this part of my account of the strike are drawn from letters of worker correspondents from Simens i Gal'ske published in the following issues of *Pravda*, no. 24, May 27 (June 9), 1912; no. 27, May 31 (June 12), 1912; no. 34, June 8 (21); no. 37, June 10 (23); and no. 56, July 4 (17), 1912. Increasingly aware of the symbolic significance of the strike and of the agitational use to which it could be put, *Pravda*, by early June, began publishing reports on it in almost every issue.

107. *Pravda*, no. 54, July 1 (14), 1912.

108. *Pravda*, no. 62, July 11 (24), 1912.

109. *Nevskii Golos*, no. 6, July 8, 1912.

110. Ibid.; *Metallist*, no. 17, 1912.

111. RGIA, f. 150, op. 1, del. 352, ll. 117–118.

112. *Pravda*, no 87, August 10 (23), 1912; also, GARF, fond 102, D-4, no. 161, t. l, ll.108–110, Report of St. Petersburg, O.O., no. 12264, July 28, 1912.

113. *Pravda*, no. 68, July 18 (31), 1912.

114. *Pravda*, no. 70, July 20 (August 2), 1912, no. 71, July 21 (August 3), 1912; no. 74, July 25 (August 7), 1912.

115. The last such report, of a meeting attended on July 31 by 800 of the workers at Simens i Gal'ske, appeared in *Pravda*, no. 80, August 1(14), 1912.

116. GARF, fond D-4, no. 161, 1912 (St. Petersburg), t.l, ll. 108–119. Report of St. Petersburg O.O., no. 12264, July 28, 1912.

117. *Pravda*, no. 87, August 10 (23), 1912.

118. Ibid.

119. Ibid., no. 104, August 30 (September 12), 1912. The previous report is in *Pravda*, no. 92, August 16 (29), 1912.

120. Ibid., no. 104, August 30 (September 12), 1912.

121. The monthly figures published by the Factory Inspectorate of the Ministry of Trade and Industry for the period January-December 1912, for the enterprises under its jurisdiction are as follows. (Because of the limits on its jurisdiction, these figures are significantly lower than the incidence of strikes and strikers in Russian industry during this period, but they are suggestive because of the changes in proportions that they reflect, from month to month, of politically as against economic, strikes).

	Economic		*Political*	
	STRIKES	STRIKERS	STRIKES	STRIKERS
January 1912	20	3,932	1	1,622
February 1912	21	9,383	none	
March 1912	28	4,852	none	
April 1912	68	14,913	591	231,459
May 1912	132	46,089	492	170,897
June 1912	109	30,801	none	
July 1912	76	19,880	2	859
August 1912	115	10,501	none	
September 1912	226	10,784	30	8,734
October 1912	70	6,329	72	52,470
November 1912	46	9,796	99	65,853
December 1912	21	8,418	13	17,919
Total for year	732	175,678	1,300	549,813

The figures for mechanical and metal-processing enterprises alone—the heart of the phenomenon we are considering—are considerably more suggestive:

	Economic		Political	
	STRIKES	STRIKERS	STRIKES	STRIKERS
January 1912	9	1,8333	1	1,622
February 1912	8	6,412	none	
March 1912	10	2,046	none	
April 1912	16	2,341	287	132,058
May 1912	38	11,892	187	77,573
June 1912	44	13,238	none	
July 1912	15	2,313	2	859
August 1912	7	871	none	
September 1912	2	106	16	4,948
October 1912	6	1,790	44	33,533
November 1912	21	6,431	58	44,933
December 1912	5	911	8	15,097
Total for year	182	60,084	603	310,587

Source: Ministerstvo torgovli i promyshlennosti, Otdel promyshlennosti, *Svod otchetov fabrichnykh inspektorov za 1912 god* (St. Petersburg, 1913), LXXVII, LXXVIII, 303.

122. RGIA, f. 150, op. 1, del. 58 and 352, *passim*.
123. F. Dan, "Politicheskoe Obozrenie: Posle Leny," *Nasha Zaria*, no. 5, 1912.
124. *Luch'*, no. 41, 1912.
125. *Pravda*, no. 168, November 14 (27), 1912.
126. *Nevskii Golos*, October 1912.
127. *Pravda*, no. 168, November 14 (27), 1912.

The rendition of Lenin's April Theses was recorded as follows in his article, "O zadachikh proletariata v dannoi revoliutsii," published in *Pravda*, April 7 (O.S.) 1917:

1. In our attitude toward [the conduct of] the war on Russia's part, which unquestionably continues to constitute, under the new government of Lvov and co. a rapacious, imperialist war, given the capitalist character of the government, the slightest concessions to "Revolutionary Defensism" remains intolerable. The conscious proletariat can justifiably support "Revolutionary Defensism" only under the [following] conditions: a) the transfer of power into the hands of the proletariat and of the poorest strata of the peasantry, which are allied with it; b) the rejection of any annexations in deeds, and not merely in words; c) the complete break with all the interests of the capitalists.

In view of the indubitable good faith of the broad masses of the representatives of "Revolutionary Defensism," who accept the war only out of [a mistaken sense of] necessity and not for the sake of conquest, one must patiently explain to them their errors, in the light of the deception they've undergone on the part of the bourgeoisie, one [must] clarify the unbreakable tie between capital and the imperialist war, and demonstrate that one cannot end the war by the achievement of a truly democratic peace [rather than by force] without the overthrow of capital.

Organize the broadest propaganda in support of this view among the armed forces.

Fraternization.

2. The peculiarity of the moment in Russia lies in this *transition* from the first stage of the revolution, which gave power to the bourgeoisie, because of the inadequate consciousness and organization of the proletariat, to its *second stage* which must deliver power into the hands of the proletariat and the poorest strata of the peasantry.

This transition is characterized, on the one hand, by a maximal degree of legality, Russia *right now* is the *freest* of the belligerent countries, by the lack of any imposition of force on the masses, and finally, however, by a trusting attitude, devoid of consciousness [on the part of the workers] in the government of the capitalists, the worst enemy of peace and of socialism.

This peculiarity [of the present situation] demands of us a capacity to adapt to the *special* conditions for the conduct of party work among the masses of the proletariat, which have only just awakened to political life.

3. No support of the provisional government [a necessity] to clarify the complete falsehood of its promises, especially by the renunciation of annexations. To expose, rather than "demand," a formula which fosters illusions, since one cannot "demand" that this government of the capitalists *cease to be imperialistic.*

4. Recognize the fact that in the majority of Workers' Soviets, our party is in the minority in face of the *bloc of all* the petty bourgeois opportunistic elements under the influence of the bourgeoisie, with the help of elements ranging from the *Narodnye Sotsialisty* and the SRs to the O.K. [of the Menshevik Party] (Chkheidze, Tsereteli, Steklov etc. etc.).

To make clear to the masses that the Soviets of Workers' Deputies constitute the *only possible form* of revolutionary government, and that, therefore, as long as they remain under the influence of the bourgeoisie, our task can only be to seek to *enlighten* the masses through patient, systematic, clarification of their errors, in a way specifically adapted to their practical needs.

As long as we remain in the minority, we must conduct this task of criticizing and clarifying these errors to the masses, while preaching to them at the same time the imperative need of transferring all powers to the Soviets of Workers' Deputies, in order that the masses rid themselves of their errors through their own experience.

5. Not a parliamentary republic—a return to one from the Soviets of Workers' Deputies would constitute a step backward—but the republic of soviets of workers, poorest peasants, and peasants, deputies from top to bottom, in the country as a whole.

The elimination of all police, army, and bureaucracy. All bureaucrats have to be replaceable at any time, and to be paid no more than the wages of a good worker.

6. Shift the major emphasis in the agrarian program to the soviets of deputies of the *batraki.*

Confiscation of all gentry land-holding. Nationalization of all land in the country, distribution of the land to local soviets of *batraki* and peasants' deputies. In every large estate (of 100 des. to 300, depending on local and other conditions,) and on the basis of selection by local institutions, establish model economies under the control of deputies of *batraki*, and at public expense.

7. Immediate fusion of all banks in the country into a single national bank under the control of the Soviet of Workers' Deputies.

8. Our *immediate* task is not to introduce socialism, but only to transfer *control* over public production and distribution of goods to the Soviets of Workers' Deputies.

9. Party's task: a) immediate calling of party congress; b) changes in party program [which ought to include chiefly a treatment of the following issues]:

    1) imperialism and the imperialist wars

    2) relations with the government and our demand for "a commune-state."

    3) change the name of the party to *Communist Party*

10. Creation of [new] revolutionary international, an international opposed to social chauvinists as well as to the *center* (i.e., wavering between chauvinists and internationalists): such as Kautsky and co. in Germany, Longuet and co. in France, Chkheidze and co. in Russia, Turati and co. in Italy, MacDonald and co. in England, etc.

APPENDIX II
SUMMARY OF MAJOR FINDINGS OF QUANTITATIVE ANALYSES OF SOCIAL CHARACTERISTICS OF PARTICIPANTS IN POST-LENA STRIKE WAVES

Since many of the readers of this work are likely to be familiar with the major findings of the quantitative analyses of the social characteristics of the participants in the post-Lena strike wave, which I conducted in collaboration with Ronald Petrusha, and more recently with Eric Brian, I will confine myself to the presentation in this appendix of a summary of the major findings of the articles on the subject presented by Haimson and Petrusha in the volume entitled *Strike Waves in the Late Nineteenth and Early Twentieth Century*, L. Haimson and Charles Tilly, eds. (New York: Cambridge University Press, 1989), pp. 109–166, as well as in the conclusions contributed by Haimson to that volume, pp. 500–511. A more summary version of these findings, involving a comparison with those of our quantitative analyses of the 1905–7 and 1915–17, strike waves is to be found in the article by Haimson and Eric Brian in the volume entitled, *Strikes, Social Conflicts, and the First World War*, L. Haimson and Guilio Sapelli, eds. (Milan: Feltrinelli, 1992), pp. 389–452.

The first of these major findings, consistently confirmed by our bivariate correlations of the data presented in the *Svody Otchetov Fabrichnikh Inspektorov*, collected by the Labor Division of the Ministry of Trade and Industry of strikes conducted in enterprises under Factory Inspection, but also by our analyses of the statistics on labor unrest published in the Bulletins of the Moscow Society of Factory and Mill Owners (*Biulleteny* nos. 16, 17, and 18, 1912–1913), amply confirm that, notwithstanding the scope that the post-Lena strike wave assumed, it was disproportionately concentrated in large urban centers of over 200,000 inhabitants, and even more disproportionately so, when St. Petersburg *guberniia* was examined as a separate fact.

However, a far more important finding emerged when we examined the breakdowns of strikes in the data presented by the Factory Inspectorate for political and economic strikes. In these breakdowns, economic strikes, and in particular, the relative intensity of strikes over wages, the findings of our quantitative analyses were correlated with only one factor, the size of enterprises, and more specifically, the degree of concentration of the workforce in enterprises employing over 500, and especially over 1,000 workers.

Political strikes, on the other hand, were even more strikingly correlated with the degree of concentration of the workforce of these enterprises in urban centers, over 200,000 in population, and even more strikingly so when the concentration of these workforces in the capital was considered as a separate factor.

Just as significant was the fundamental distinction that emerged when one focused attention on the one category of economic strikes classified by the Factory Inspectorate as "strikes over order in the enterprise." In this category the findings of our analysis were comparable to those of our findings about political strikes.

We should also note that in our bivariate correlations, the relative intensity of political strikes was consistently correlated with the factors of high levels of pay and of literacy, and the lack of connections of the workers to the land and to the countryside, whether measured by the actual possession of land by these workers or their families in their villages of origin, or by the proportion of these workers who went to the village in the summertime to help in the collection of the crop.

I wish to comment briefly on two of the major conclusions that I drew from my quantitative analyses of labor unrest during these years. The first is to emphasize the exceptionally important role played by *young* workers, especially those employed in metal-processing enterprises, in the most militant and explosive forms of labor unrest in the immediate prewar period, whether those were classified as political strikes, or as strikes over order in the enterprise. One should also recognize the staccato character that "economic" strikes assumed by the eve of the war, which made them essentially indistinguishable from political strikes, as revolts against authority, rather than labor actions designed to obtain economic gains. This fact was even more clearly reflected in the inflated, totally unrealistic, character of the demands advanced by the eve of the war by the participants in these so-called "economic" strikes.

While subscribing in principle to the Mensheviks' growing complaints by the eve of the war that these strike actions constituted from their point of view, a *statechnyi azart*, I must emphasize, as I have in earlier studies, that this "revolt of the young" constituted a revolt against *all* forms of superordinate authority hovering over them: in the enterprise, on the street, in their encounters with members of "polite, census society," as well as in their conflicts with representatives of the state order.

In the original version of my article on the "The Problem of Social Stability in Urban Russia" (*Slavic Review*, no. 4, 1964, and no. 1, 1965), I was inclined to emphasize that the young workers who were recruited from the countryside in the course of the period of industrial expansion, beginning in 1910–1911, contributed an additional element of resentment to the explosive character that distinguished the behavior of the young workers in the immediate prewar period, because of the character of the Stolypin land legislation of 1911, which reassigned the title to the land in peasant families to the heads of households, thereby effectively dispossessing the younger members of these families from any claim to the land previously possessed by the family as a whole. However, as I indicated in my more recent discussion of this issue in the *Slavic Review* (no.4, 2000), I would no longer emphasize to the same degree that the dispossession of young workers as a result of the Stolypin legislation that reassigned the family title to the land to the exclusive benefit of the household actually added a very significant element of resentment to the explosiveness of the behavior of young St. Petersburg workers in the course of labor unrest during the prewar period.

The reason for my change of view on this issue can be summarized on the basis of two factors. The first is the rapidity of the processes of urbanization that these young immigrant workers underwent precisely as a result of the severance of their ties to the land. The second, and most important, is that because of the degree of literacy and skill required for employment in mechanical and other metal-processing enterprises of the capital—in which the most militant forms of labor unrest were observable in the pre-war period in the capital—the likelihood of the employment of recent immigrant workers in these enterprises (except in their "hot shops") was minimized by the degree of skill and literacy demanded for the work performed in them.

The data required for a statistical examination of this problem are generally unavailable for this period. In one specific case, I found these data for the workers employed in the gun sight shop at Novyi Aivaz in 1915, a mechanical enterprise located in the outskirts of the Vyborg District. (I do not believe that this evidence, even though it obtained for a period of several months after the outbreak of the war, significantly modified the character of these data, because the workers employed in this gun shop were engaged in the production of armaments, and so they were deferred from the draft calls which affected other workers after the out-break of the war.) The analysis of these data is presented exhaustively in the Haimson and Sapelli volume, *Strikes, Social Conflict and the First World War* (see partic-ularly pp. 428–33). The findings of this analysis suggest that the proportion of workers born in the capital, or who had settled in the capital during their early and most formative years, was generally high among the workers in this shop—and even more so among the young males than among female workers employed in it. To summarize this finding in a slightly more accessible language, it suggested that most of the young male as well as female workers in this shop, *including those who had been born outside the capital, were in fact shaped during their early and most formative years in St. Petersburg's urban environment.*

A NOTE ON SOURCES

Let me take the opportunity afforded by this Note to explain what some readers might regard as the paucity of references in these two essays to the fairly abundant secondary literature that has appeared in recent years in Western countries, especially the United States, as well as in Russia, on the topics that they address.

Although it may surprise some readers, I can trace the primary reason why I have put references to these works aside to the effects of the Cold War, during which I deliberately insulated myself in pursuing my archival research from exposure to secondary literature published in Western countries as well as in the Soviet Union, however valuable these works otherwise might have been, because the vital questions concerning the historical background and eventual unfolding of the Russian revolution were all so politically charged during these years. I grew accustomed then, and still prefer now, to let the "sources" speak for themselves, or more precisely, to seek to analyze them as much as possible without the impact of externally politicized frames of reference.

My inclination to focus exclusively on primary sources was reinforced during the period of Soviet rule by the fact that access to the most important historical archive in Moscow (TsGAOR, now renamed GARF), which holds the files of the Department of Police of the tsarist regime that have proved so crucial for an examination of the political behavior of Russia's industrial workers and their interactions with various underground revolutionary groups, was so carefully regulated. Access to the registers (*opisi*) that the Department of Police had used to organize and to categorize its reports on various topics, including the activities of various political parties in different provinces and major cities of the Empire, were not accessible to foreign scholars.

This handicap posed a special challenge to scholars like myself, who were otherwise given access, however reluctantly, to these archival materials. The challenge was to seek to reconstruct in the absence of any guidance the ways in which these reports were categorized and numbered. We sought to reconstruct the character of these *opisi* through the references to individual *fonds* that could be found in works by Soviet historians (and in some cases, with the generous help of the authors of these works).

It would be impossible for me to overstate the challenge that denial of access to these registers posed for me and other foreign scholars who conducted research in Moscow's main historical archives during these years. In my own case, this very challenge contributed to the almost veritable fixation of my attention on the sources themselves, and away from the many studies, however competent, that were then being produced, especially by younger Western scholars. During and after the fall of the Soviet regime, when the quality of both Western and Russian scholarship greatly improved both in the sophistication of its analysis as well as in its relative freedom from political bias, an additional factor further contributed to my concentration on primary materials *per se*. This was the increasingly close contact that I developed, already in the period of Soviet rule, with a number of scholars of my generation associated with the St. Petersburg filial of the Institute of History of Russia's Academy of Sciences.

These invaluable contacts, especially those with Rafail Sholomovich Ganelin, Boris Vasil'evich Anan'ich and Valentin Semenovich Diakin, reinforced the wisdom of the lesson to which I have already had occasion to refer, but which bears repeating here, of the St. Petersburg historical school: that the significance of any historical work ultimately depends on its author's original selection of the primary sources. As I have had the pleasure of acknowledging earlier, V. S. Diakin's own scholarly writings came to stand out in my eyes as veritable exemplars of the importance of this basic principle, as did the work of R. Sh. Ganelin and B. V. Anan'ich in subsequent years. Indeed, it was in good measure under their influence that I continued to concentrate my attention on primary materials even after the collapse of the Soviet regime in relative insulation from the estimable and substantial body of secondary works that were now being published in increasing numbers by younger historians in the West, as well as in Russia.

Under these circumstances, I have thought it unnecessary, and indeed, would even be somewhat hypocritical, to layer my texts at this late date with the customary references to recent secondary works, however worthy of praise, since they did not, in fact, influence my reading of the various documents on which these interpretative essays are based, or the conclusions that I have drawn from these labors. I very much hope, however, that readers will understand from my earlier acknowledgements that I have hardly lacked inspiration from many very able historians in my efforts to shape the themes addressed here, as well as in my other historical studies during the fifty-odd years of my scholarly career.

INDEX